# A LIFE IN THE 20ᵗʰ CENTURY

AUTOBIOGRAPHY OF
Nathalie Marguerite Grandjean

# A Life in the 20<sup>th</sup> Century

*Autobiography by*

# Nathalie Marguerite Grandjean

*FLP Media Group*
Georgetown, Kentucky

*Studebaker in Memphis when I was born*

# PERSONAL HISTORY OF
# Nathalie Marguerite Grandjean

*From 1922 to 1945 and a bit beyond*

Copyright © 2024 by Nathalie Marguerite Grandjean
ISBN 978-1-59924-829-5 Second Edition
All rights reserved under International and Pan-American Copyright Conventions. No part of this book may be reproduced in any manner whatsoever without written permission from the publisher, except in the case of brief quotations embodied in critical articles and reviews.

Publisher: Leah Huete de Maines

Editors: Leah Huete de Maines
       Christen Kincaid
       Jackie Steelman

Cover Art: Nathalie Marguerite Grandjean at 4 years old by wandering photographer

Author Photo: Nathalie Ward

Cover Design: Elizabeth Maines McCleavy

Author inquiries and mail orders:
FLP Media Group
P. O. Box 1626
Georgetown, Kentucky 40324
U. S. A.

# Table of Contents

PROLOGUE..................................................................................ix

THE FAMILIES:
GRANDJEAN FAMILY................................................................ xiii
DARCEY FAMILY ......................................................................xvii
NELSON FAMILY..................................................................... xxiii

One to five years old.......................................................................1
Beginning of My School Days......................................................27
So Began Our Many Years of Wandering....................................43
Good Bye French Camp ..............................................................71
High School and Beyond.............................................................77
So Now I was a Soldier .............................................................105
Back to Civilian Life..................................................................127
The Next Sixty Years or So........................................................131
First Year....................................................................................133
The Rest of the Years ................................................................138

FAMILY MEMBERS .................................................................167

*Pancho Villa,*
*arrow points at Louis Grandjean in front of a theatre in Matamoros, Mexico*

# PROLOGUE

My life covered three quarters of the Twentieth Century. Since I was born in 1922, four years after World War I ended in November of 1918, I suppose I could be considered a World War I baby boomer. I joined the world during the era of the "Lost Generation." That was during the last gasps of the "Victorian Era." The wildest thing about the "Lost Generation" was that women wore short skirts, smoked cigarettes, and drank whiskey. The men did pretty much as they had always done, chased women, and drank whiskey. They danced holding each other in close embrace. My, my! Then they married, went to work, had children and life settled down to pretty much what it had always been—the daily grind. A few women worked outside the home, cut their long hair, then got a permanent. The most wicked thing was that people who married the wrong person could get a divorce and did not have to live their life out in misery. Within all of this new freedom there were those who abused its privileges. That's a law of mankind. The pendulum always swings too far before it settles down to normalcy.

As I grew older, I heard much discussion of the events of World War I. There were movies made with World War I themes, so, though I had not been around since the beginning of the Twentieth Century, I was well informed about what went on before I was born. Not only did I hear about World War 1 but, because my grandmother Grandjean told me stories about the Civil War I learned a lot about that, at least from the Confederate side of the question. Her father was an officer in the Confederate Army. He was somewhat of an artist so in his letters home he often drew pictures of army life for his children that were included in the mailings. I saw all of those and I have copies of them. I also have a copy of his autobiography written after the war was over that covered a lot of his experiences in the army.

In my own lifetime I have lived under seventeen United States presidents from Warren G. Harding through Donald Trump. I remember the election of Herbert Hoover. My dad kept close track of the campaign speeches over the radio so, of course, I heard a lot about it. In his first year in office, he was faced with the Stock Market Crash of October, 1929 and the beginning of the Great Depression. When a job was advertised in the newspaper there were men lined up for blocks trying to get it. I heard all about the people who lost everything and jumped to their deaths from the skyscrapers in New York. I also remember all of the terrible twelve years of the depression that lasted from October 1929 until December 7, 1941, the day of the Japanese attack on Pearl Harbor and the cause of our entering the war that became known as World War II. Once war was declared the United States went into the frantic production of war materiel and everybody who wanted to go to work found jobs easily. Once the young men were called up to join the services even women who had never worked outside the home went to work to help the war effort. The men were gone and the women kept the home-front from collapsing to the astonishment of everyone, perhaps even themselves. The fact that women had brains and could use them was forced on the world's conscience and has fueled the feminist movement ever since.

My life has lapped over into the twenty-first century. It is now December 2020 and I just had my 98th birthday. In nine days, we will be headed into 2021. After my sickly childhood I am surprised I am still in the land of the living. Almost all of my contemporaries are dead. Out of my twenty-seven first cousins there are just two left, Alfredo Huete and Janet Darcey Haynes, both younger than I am but not by much.

The challenge of the present is the COVID-19 Pandemic. The virus is spreading rapidly and people are dying by the thousands. A vaccine has been rushed into production but cannot be produced fast enough to provide it for everyone. It is being given first to health care providers. I suppose next it should be given to teachers and school children. I just hope it is effective.

We have just elected another president, Joe Biden, number eighteen for me. It remains to be seen what will happen now.

*Grandma Grandjean*

*Grandjean Family*
*Sydney, Mrs Grandjean, Leon, Caroline, Melina, Louis*

# THE FAMILIES
## In This Autobiography

### GRANDJEAN FAMILY

My grandfather, Georges Henri Grandjean Perrenoud Comtess came to America from La Chaux de Fonds, Canton Neuchatel, Switzerland. He was a civil engineer who was recruited by the American government to come to America after the Civil War when America was building railroads to the western lands. He was made a United States Marshal to assist him in crossing private land so he could survey the railroad right of way. When he finished that job, he came to Louisiana. He dropped the names Perrenoud and Comtess for convenience. He established a business in New Orleans where he settled. In New Orleans he met Leon Joseph Frémaux, a civil engineer, and married his daughter.

Georges Henri Grandjean m. Francine Joséphine Frémaux. They had five children: Melina Flore, Leon Henri, Caroline Reine, Louis Emile and Sidney George.

Melina Flore m. Harry Gabriel died young. Her two children, Edmond and Harriet, grew up elsewhere so I never knew them.

Leon Henri m. Rose Todd—two children, George who died in infancy and Richard. Leon worked out of state and finally settled in Dallas, Texas. I met his son Richard after we were grown.

Caroline m. Albert Moreno—lived in New Orleans. Her three children; George, Albert and Louise.

Louis Emile m. Marie Blount—no children

Sidney George m. Gertrude Darcey—two children; Shelby George Henry who died in infancy and Nathalie Marguerite.

*Sidney and Gertrude Grandjean*

*Gertrude Darcey GrandJean*

*Pierre Darcey*

# DARCEY FAMILY

Pierre Joseph Darcey m. Marie Oceana Pierce—eight children; Helena Veronica, Peter Joseph, Jr., Jesse John, Gertrude Marguerite, Mabel Marie, Inez Julia, Cyrus Charles and Beatrice Ann.

Helena m. Emile Hidalgo—eight children, Dorothy, Everett, Stanley, Shirley, Soledad, Carmen, Sylvia and Peter.

Peter m. six or eight times—no children.

Jesse m. Judite Labat—five children; Jesse John, Jr., Allah Mae, Betty, Wilbur and Juliette.

Gertrude m. Sidney Grandjean—two children; Shelby George Henry and Nathalie Marguerite.

Mabel m. Matthew (Mac) Acosta—one child; Beverly Marguerite. M.2. Christopher Dickson (Dick) Wood—one child; Alma Mabel. Dick Wood adopted Beverly so she was known as Beverly Wood.

Inez m. Carter Ben Cook—no children.

Cyrus m. Margaret Hilma Rydell—four children; Cyrus Charles, Jr., Dolores, Warren and Janet.

Beatrice m. Alfredo Francisco Huete—two children; Alfredo Francisco, Jr. and Carlos Cyril.

*Inez, Gertrude, and Helena with grandma Darcey*

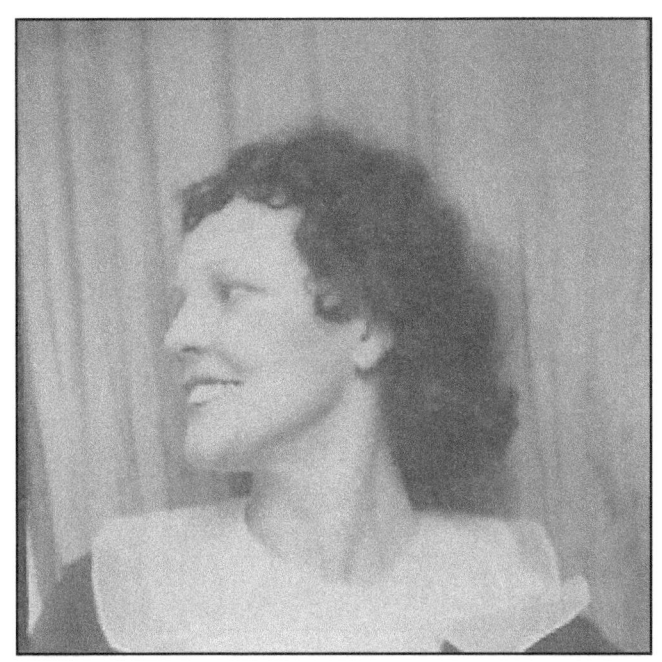

*Helena Darcey*

*Mabel Darcey*

*Beatrice Darcey Huete*

*Beatrice Darcey Huete*

*Alfredo and Carlos Huete*

*Bill Nelson in Istanbul*

## NELSON FAMILY

William Clark Nelson, Jr. known as Bill m. Nathalie M. Grandjean—five children; Barbara Marguerite, William Clark III known as Clark, Shelby George Henry, Christine Marie known as Tina and Nathalie Elisabeth.

Bill's father, William Clark Nelson of New Orleans m. Barbara Mary Schmitz who was born in Chicago.—two children William Clark, Jr. known as Bill, and Joseph Jacob known as Jack. W. C. Nelson, Sr. worked for the United Fruit Company. He was a diesel engineer who served aboard ship. On 2 June 1942 he was aboard the Tela when the ship was torpedoed and sunk by a German U-boat in the Caribbean Sea just off of the island of Santa Helena and sunk. He went down with the ship. Bill's mother, Barbara Schmitz Nelson died 3 Jan 1940 in New Orleans. Bill had himself emancipated but Jack was only seven years old when his father died. Barbara's sister Lucille, known as Lucy who was married to Gustave Lyncker, took Jack into their home to raise him to adulthood. These two people are referred to in this story as Uncle Gus and Aunt Lucy. They acted as grandparents to Bill and Jack's children.

*Lucielle Schmitz Lyncker, Aunt Lucy*

*Gustav Adolf Lyncker, Uncle-Gus*

*Joseph Jacob (Jack) Nelson*

*Gus and Lucy Lyncker, Barbara, Clark and Jack Nelson, Bill's brother*

*Nathalie at 2 and Beatrice drying her hair*

# *One to five years old*

Writing a personal history might seem to be the ultimate conceit but from my own experience with genealogical research, I know how much I have valued the few scraps of written personal history that I have found so I am hoping that those who come after me and are interested in family history will feel as I did and will be glad to find these words recorded.

My mother and I cooperated in trying to reconstruct the chronology of my life so between the two of us I think we have it nearly correct. There might be a few spots where our collective memories may have failed us.

I was born in Memphis, Shelby County, Tennessee, on 20th of December 1922, daughter of Sidney George Grandjean born 15th of October 1891 in New Orleans, Orleans Parish, Louisiana son of Georges Henri Grandjean and Francine Josephine Frémaux, and Gertrude Marguerite Darcey born 17th of July 1900 in Lockport, Lafourche Parish, Louisiana daughter of Peter Joseph Darcey and Marie Oceana Pierce,. Dad told me that he had taken Mother to St. Joseph Hospital earlier in the day but I seemed reluctant to arrive. The doctor told him that nothing was happening so he might as well go home and get some sleep. He had not been home long when he was called to hurry back to the hospital. The weather was miserably cold with icy wind blowing the snow that was freezing to the windshield making it impossible for him to see. He had to drive with his head out of the side window to be able to see where he was going, but he made it in time. So did I. The next day his brother, Louis, went to the hospital to see the new baby. He looked over the whole nursery and picked me out as his brother's child. I suppose he could do that so easily because I looked so much like my brother Shelby did as a newborn.

I have pictures in my mind of white bars against a passing white something that I feel is a memory from the hospital nursery. I asked my mother about it and found out from her that all of the cribs in the nursery were made of white iron. So that checks and in those days nurses wore starched white uniforms, so that could have been the moving white background I seem to remember so clearly. It is just a snapshot memory but I swear I do remember it. It is not something I had been told because who would think to tell a child such a small detail and from such an angle as the inside of a baby bed? I am convinced that it is my first memory.

My first home was at 971½ Saxon Avenue in Memphis.

Mother had been very ill during her pregnancy for me. She said no food would stay down except for spaghetti. We both still like spaghetti very much. Perhaps I was preconditioned to love spaghetti since she and I had survived on it.

My father and mother had gone through the terrible experience of losing a child in May 1922. My brother, Shelby George Henry Grandjean who was born on the 28th of April 1921 in New Orleans died four days after his first birthday in Memphis of pneumonia. He was christened Catholic, I know, but I have never hunted for his baptismal certificate. Since Dad and Mother were living in Braithwaite where Dad was working, I suppose Shelby was christened at the church in Violet, Louisiana, the closest Catholic Church to Braithwaite.

My father was an electrical contractor who had worked with his brother Louis in New Orleans. For some reason Louis had gone to Memphis where he found so much work for an electrician that he sent for my father to join him so the family relocated to Memphis.

Instead of an electrician Uncle Louis should have been a couturier. When he saw a dress in a store window that he thought would look good on his wife he would buy the material, take it home and cut it out without a pattern and sew it up on the sewing machine. He must have learned how to do that from his eldest sister Melina who could do the same thing. He always made his own silk shirts, too.

He must have been adventurous because in about 1916 he took a movie camera and went to Mexico to film Poncho Villa who was rebelling against the Mexican Government. I have a picture of him with Pancho Villa in front of a theater in Matamoros, Mexico. Perhaps it was during his sojourn along the Mexican border that he met his wife, Marie Blount of El Paso, Texas. I wonder whatever became of the film. Or of Marie for that matter. After Uncle Louis' death in Memphis we lost track of her.

Uncle Louis had become a Mason and had given up Catholicism. My father had made his confirmation to please his mother but refused to go to church after that. My mother had never been a very good Catholic though she still considered herself Catholic when she married but she was wavering. I believe that Uncle Louis' influence and the fact that she found no solace in her religion when my brother died were the forces that started her looking for consolation in some other religion. She went with her friends in Memphis to the Baptist Church for a while but she was never baptized in that faith. She and Dad finally settled on becoming Presbyterians in about 1928.

The family returned to New Orleans when I was about two years old and I was entered on the cradle roll at the Baptist Church on St. Charles Avenue but I never was Baptist. Much later when I was about six years old I was received into the Presbyterian Church by Reverend Edward A. Ford in Raceland, Louisiana. My parents switched to the Presbyterian Church sometime before that. Mother and Dad even taught Sunday school. From then on, the family remained Presbyterian until we finally decided to be connected with no formal religion at all. I think of myself as an agnostic. I am undecided about man's purpose on earth so I am waiting to find out the truth and holding an open mind.

When Shelby died in Memphis Mother and Dad brought his body to New Orleans to bury him in the Frémaux tomb in St. Louis Cemetery #3. When they arrived, they tried to get in touch with Grandma and Grandpa Darcey who were still living in Braithwaite. However, there had been a crevasse (the Mississippi River levee had broken and flooded the area) and everyone had been evacuated). They deduced that Grandma and Grandpa had gone to Aunt Helena's house in Raceland, so they went to the train station to buy tickets to go there, too. While they were standing in line at the ticket counter, they recognized Grandpa Darcy in line ahead of them. He had come to New Orleans to see about help being offered to flood victims by the Red Cross. The first thing he asked was, "Where is Shelby?" When they told him it was the first news any of Mother's family had heard of Shelby's death. The three of them traveled to Raceland together.

Meanwhile in Raceland Aunt Bea, who was fourteen years old then, told her mother she had a sad dream the night before. She had seen Gertrude and Sidney walking down the road to the house but Shelby was not with them. When she asked in the dream where he was, she had been told that Shelby was dead. Sure enough, just as in her dream, Gertrude and Sidney came walking down the road without Shelby.

My parents went back to Memphis after burying Shelby and visiting family. All the time they were in Memphis Dad went to work on public transit carrying his tools in a toolbox. Mother tried to convince him to borrow money to buy a truck but he was afraid to go into debt. He could have gone into contracting in a big way since there was plenty of work.

Then tragedy struck again! Uncle Louis took his own life on Christmas Eve 1923. It seems he had been unfaithful to his wife and she threatened to expose his transgression to the rest of the family. They had a big argument. He walked into the next room, put a gun in his mouth and pulled the trigger. He killed himself December 24, 1923 and was buried in the Masonic Cemetery in Memphis, Tennessee. Grandma Grandjean had been living with him. After he died, she went back to New Orleans to live with her daughter Caroline Grandjean Moreno.

While we were still in Memphis a man who lived across the street gave my parents a dog. They named him Bruno; I suppose because he was brown. He and I grew up together so he considered me his special charge. If I started to wander all Mother had to say was, "Bruno, she has gone far enough." He would come to me, take my arm gently in his mouth and guide me back to her. He would never let a stranger pick me up. If I was visiting a neighbor, he would wait for me on their porch. All Mother had to do to find me was to look down the street to see where Bruno was sitting. He was such a good nursemaid to me that he even pushed me with his nose while I was sitting in my canvas swing. Just the week before we were to move to New Orleans a neighbor poisoned Bruno because he said the dog barked too much.

Within a year of Uncle Louis' death Dad heard about the planned building of the alcohol plant in Poydras near Braithwaite so he went there and put in a bid on the electrical part of the job and got the contract. We joined him a few months later. The trip on the train must have been miserable for them because Mother told me that I cried from the moment we boarded the train until we arrived in New Orleans.

I have always had an eerie feeling about trains. As I grew older, I never minded riding in them but when standing on the platform watching a train approach I feel as though I am being drawn under the wheels. I think the eerie feeling I have about trains might be caused by the powerful sound of the steam engine and, more especially, by the lonesome call of the steam whistle. It reaches deep into my soul and stirs up something very sad.

The family was back in Louisiana where it belonged. I have always felt that I was a Louisiana native who just happened to be born away from home. After all, all of my early memories and all of my immediate family ties are centered in southeast Louisiana,

We lived at Grandpa Darcey's house in Braithwaite while the alcohol plant job continued. Mother became very ill and had to go to the hospital in New Orleans. When she left the hospital, she went to convalesce at Aunt Mable's house before she could come back to Braithwaite. In the meantime, Aunt Inez and Aunt Bea, who were still unmarried and living at home, were taking care of me. I can still remember when they were teaching me to use the enamel chamber pot. I have a clear mental picture of myself sitting on it. One day I saw Aunt Bea with a mop and bucket going outside to clean the steps. I must have thought, "Here's a good chance to play a trick on her." I pulled up a chair, climbed on it and hooked the screen door. Then I went to the back door and hooked that screen. I clearly remember doing it. I wouldn't unhook it. She had to call for Aunt Inez to come to open the door for her. They fussed at me but they laughed, too.

All of my story up to now comes from stories told to me by my parents with the exception of a few snapshot memories of my own but from now on it will be what I remember myself plus corroboration of some of the facts by my mother.

In mid-1926 when the alcohol plant job was finished and Mother was back on her feet Mother's uncle, Joe Darcey, invited them to go to his house in Texas City, Texas to stay for a while so Dad could look for work. We drove on Highway 90 west known then as "The Old Spanish Trail." Texas City is on the Gulf of Mexico a bit east of Galveston. Highway 90 was a two-way graveled road then and very dusty. We were traveling in an 'open touring car,' probably a model-T

Ford. There was no such thing as roll-up glass windows then. There were roll down curtains of water-proof material fastened to the top of the window frame to be rolled down and buttoned to the frame to protect riders from rain, but when I say 'OPEN' I mean really open everywhere but the roof and the back window. The roof was made of some sort of waterproof material as was the back where there was an isinglass window sewed into the material so you could see behind you with your rear-view mirror. Isinglass is a semi-transparent substance made from the stomach of sturgeons. in the event that you never heard of it before. There was no bridge over the Sabine River so at Lake Charles we crossed the river on a ferry. We stopped the first night at one of Dad's relatives in west Louisiana or Orange, Texas. I'm not sure which and I forgot to ask. We arrived in Texas City the next day. We made good time. It took us only two days to get there. In those days under those conditions that was good time. Remember, in mid-1926 I was only three and a half years old.

Besides Dad using time looking for work we had fun swimming in the Gulf. Dad took an inflated innertube and fashioned a cloth sling on it so I could enjoy the water. Then he set me afloat. I was carefully watched, of course. No one wanted to see me float off to sea. Mother was never a good swimmer but she floated really well. In fact, she couldn't sink. She had always wanted to be able to swim underwater so she could sneak up and startle someone the way the rest of us could but she could not stay under. We would push her down to the bottom to get her started swimming underwater and she would pop up like a cork. Her face was underwater but the rest of her was on the surface. She learned to enjoy floating on her back. That day she was floating on her back and did not realize that the tide was carrying her out deeper and deeper. Dad saw what was happening. He asked Uncle Joe to watch me while he took care of Mother. Dad was a good swimmer so he swam out to her and started talking to her and pushing her back toward shore. When they got back to where she could stand up, he told her what had happened. He was afraid that if he told her while she was so far out that she would panic and be harder to rescue. That was a story told to me after I was an adult.

This next story is one I remember. There was a terrible storm with loud thunder, lots of lightning and heavy rain. It must have been a lightning strike on one of the oil storage tanks nearby that started a tremendous fire. I stood at the bedroom window looking at it. The fire was soon burning so fiercely it was turning night into day. At night I could see the flickering shadows of the flames on the bedroom wall and ceiling. Uncle Joe was afraid we would have to evacuate but the firemen got it under control and we didn't have to leave.

Like all small children I was put to bed for a nap every afternoon. I always felt like a nap was a waste of daylight and all of that good playing time. Anyway,

I was supposed to be taking a nap at Uncle Joe's one afternoon while the adults were playing cards. I really didn't want to sleep. I slipped out of bed and looked for something quiet to do. I spied Dad's tobacco pouch and cigarette papers on the dresser. I had always wanted to try rolling a cigarette the way he did so here was my chance.

I sat on the bed to do my experiment. I folded the paper into a V and tried to shake some tobacco into the channel I had made. At first I poured too much tobacco in it. I put all I could back in the pouch. Try again. This time too small an amount. When I tried rolling it. it made a very skinny, straggly cigarette. I licked the gummed edge anyway. Now to try again. I was concentrating very hard on my endeavor and didn't hear my mother come in. The first I knew of her presence was when she called out, "Oh no!" The other players came to see what happened. That was when they found the results of all my efforts—all the tobacco shreds and soggy cigarette papers all around me. You can be sure after that Dad kept his cigarette makings well out of my reach.

After we returned from Texas City we moved from Braithwaite to New Orleans. We lived in the upstairs apartment at 2024 Coliseum Street in the home of Mrs. Despommier. I can remember playing on the upper front gallery in the sunshine while Grandma Grandjean sat out there with me when she came to visit. I had a flat cardboard cut-out of Sunbonnet Sue. She was attached to a stick and had a wheel with about eight shoes printed on it. When I held the stick and pushed the doll it looked like she was walking. I enjoyed walking her back and forth from one end of the gallery to the other.

I had an earlier memory of this house. Aunt Mabel was living in the upstairs apartment then. The house has fourteen-foot ceilings so therefore it has a very long stairway from the front hallway to the second floor. I was too small to stand up to climb the stairs. I couldn't reach the hand rail so I crawled up. Coming down I sat on the step and slid from one step to the other. Someone, seeing me slipping down each step said, "Well that's one way to do it." and made me aware of myself at that moment and so the memory stuck.

I have a dim memory of that Christmas. I remember waking up and finding a grey rattan doll buggy with a baby doll in it and a big doll, as big as I was, standing beside it with her arms leaning on the side of the buggy as though she was looking at the baby inside.

I clearly remember the day we were to move from Coliseum Street. I had a black tin covered foot locker that was my toy box. I kept my stuffed oilcloth Felix the Cat on top of it because he was too big to fit inside. I decided that I needed to play with Felix so I hurried to the room where my toy box was kept and was shocked to find both the box and Felix gone! Then I suddenly remembered, "This was moving day!" I was filled with anticipation to see the new house.

Dad had a new job with a man named B. A. Russ. Mr. Russ owned a lot of rental property in New Orleans so he had hired Dad to handle any electrical problems that affected any of them. Mr. Russ had a reputation as a very good landlord because as soon as the renter reported a problem on the property Mr. Russ had someone there to solve it. He owned the house we were now renting at 305 ½ Hennessey Street. The house was originally designed and built as a two-story double but was then divided into a fourplex, one apartment upstairs and one downstairs on each side. We had the apartment downstairs on the right as one faces the house. There was a living room separated from the next room, a dining room, by large double doors with glass panes. There was a window seat in the living room that intrigued me. It was like the ones I had seen in my story books but it didn't have a cushion, so it didn't look cozy as the pictures in my books. There was a storage compartment under it. To lift the lid there was a ring set in a shallow cup that one had to pull up on. Mother never did put anything in it so it was a great place to hide, but only for a very short while, too scary.

The next room after the dining room was a bedroom with a fireplace. Next was a hall with a door to the side alley. In the same hall were the stairs to the upstairs part of the house that were now cut off by having the opening floored over. I thought it was great that a person could climb the stairs and touch the ceiling. Mother used the stairs as a storage area. What was once a coat closet in the hall had coats in it but it also had my toy box in it. I remember having to sit on the toy box in the closet as punishment for some rule infraction or other. The door was not closed all the way. It was not a pleasant experience.

The next room after the stair hall was the kitchen and behind that was a narrow hall with the bathroom to the left and a door to a bricked patio on the right. The patio was roofed over by the floor of the upstairs apartments' back porch. I think there was a laundry room—the wash tub, washboard kind. Dad made a hammock from an old Army blanket and hung it back there. I took an occasional nap on it though I always resented it when I woke up. I still felt the same way; naps were a waste of daylight. Beyond the covered patio there was a big backyard.

When we moved to Hennessey Street Grandma Grandjean came to live with us. She found life difficult with Aunt Carrie and so she was glad to make the change. Since there was only one bedroom Grandma and I had to sleep in what was called a daybed in the dining room. It became a sofa in the daytime and opened as a double bed of sorts at night. As I think back on it now, I realize that was a poor arrangement for an elderly woman but I saw nothing wrong with it as a child. I enjoyed sleeping with her but I don't think she enjoyed sleeping with me. She once commented that sleeping with me was like sleeping with a Chinese football team. I have no idea what significance the designation 'Chinese' had to do with a football team. The Chinese didn't even play football.

During the day she wore her long hair in a single plait that she wound into a bun on the nape of her neck. The bun was secured in place by several tortoise shell hair pins. At night it was my special privilege to take out the pins for her so she could let her hair loose for sleeping. We would talk a bit before she said her rosary and I would drift off to sleep. I remember feeling the sensation of floating off in the dark. It seemed to me that the head of the bed always floated lower than the foot. It was not frightening but just a pleasant floating off to sleep. I asked Grandma if she felt what I felt but she said that she didn't. I found it very strange that here we were sleeping in the same bed and I was floating and she wasn't.

There was no such thing as central heating in those days, at least not in any of the houses we ever rented. Keeping the house warm in winter was a problem. We closed the big glassed doors into the living room and used a portable kerosene heater in the dining room. It barely kept the cold at bay. We had to keep a pot of water on top of the heater to keep moisture and oxygen in the air. At night the fire had to be turned off because of the danger of carbon monoxide poisoning. We spent most of the winter days in front of the fireplace in the bedroom. It had a coal grate that heated that room nicely. Dad would get up and light the gas oven to warm the kitchen. In the morning when it was very cold Dad would pick me up out of the bed and roll me in a blanket. He would sit me in a chair in front of the oven where I stayed nice and warm until I could get dressed.

Some of my happiest memories are centered on the hearth in the bedroom. It was a cozy feeling to sit there gazing at the burning coals while listening to the grown-ups talk. I would sit there at night, often on someone's lap, soaking up the heat while watching for the sudden flair of gas released from the burning coals and watching the fire shadows dancing on the opposite wall. During the day I sometimes deliberately slipped into the deep, quiet cold of the living room just to experience the cold loneliness of it and to intensify the satisfaction of going back into the lovely warmth, good smells and companionship of the rest of the house.

The hearth was the family social center where we gathered after supper. This was just before the popularity of radio entertainment. The only mechanical entertainment we had was a wind-up portable record player that we didn't use very much. It looked like a suitcase when it was closed. We had to make our own fun. Since Dad worked on construction sites he often brought home surplus bits of things he thought I would enjoy. I loved the crystal prisms from chandeliers. He would put a loop of string on them and I could put the string loop over my ears to let the prism dangle like earrings. Electricians had to use porcelain tubes to insulate where wires had to pass through wood. He would keep a few of those for me. My favorites were the loose tiles left over from a job of tile setting, Dad and I would sit on the floor in front of the fireplace and Dad would build palaces with the tiles and use the porcelain tubes as columns in the front of the palace door. In those days tiles were sold in loose batches and each tile was set separately by a tile setter. Now, tile patterns are set on a woven background, the grout is poured over the whole thing and the excess is wiped off. No more loose tiles for palaces.

Another hearth related memory is sugar cane. In the fall Uncle Emile always gave me a few stalks of the big fat purple sugar cane used at the mill to make sugar. Grandma would peel a joint or two of the stalk and cut it into bite-sized pieces for me so I could chew the juice out of it. In later years some sort of blight attacked the purple cane so it is no longer grown. Now the cane farmers grow a hard-skinny green cane that is disease resistant. It makes good sugar but it is so hard it is impossible to chew.

The Christmas of 1926 was a big disappointment because Santa misunderstood my letter. What I wanted was a pedal car I could ride in. What he left for me was a foot-long tin roadster with a wind-up spring motor. How can things get so screwed up? I did get a tricycle, two dolls, a table and chair set, china dishes and other odds and ends but I didn't get a car I could ride in—not then or ever. That was the year that we each hung up our stockings, Mother, Dad and I. The next morning I found candies, some small toys, a peppermint stick, an apple, an orange, some nuts and a dime in the toe of my stocking. Dad had several packages of firecrackers in his stocking while in Mother's long silk hose Santa had put firecrackers, roman candles and skyrockets. Dad saved his and Mother's fireworks until New Year's Eve when he shot it all off. He always did love fireworks.

My life was filled with a safe predictable routine. In the morning I got up and dressed, ate breakfast and then went outside to find my playmates and played until lunch. After lunch I stayed inside and napped or at least rested or played quietly until about three o'clock when I took my bath and dressed for the afternoon. It felt good to be clean, dressed and waiting for my father to come home.

Children dressed differently from the way they do now because our homes were colder in the winter and warmer in the summer. Air conditioning had not been invented yet and as I said before, we did not have central heating. In the winter next to my skin I wore a Union Suit. Think long johns with the arms and legs cut short. It was a knitted cotton all-in-one underwear that buttoned up the front and had a drop seat in the back. There were buttons attached by cotton tape sewed at the waist front and back to which we attached supporters that held up my thigh high lisle cotton stockings. Over this arrangement I wore bloomers that often matched my dress, plus a dress and a sweater for wearing inside the house. To go outside I had to add a coat, hat, muffler and mittens. I wore white kid buttoned high top shoes with black patent leather heels and toes. There were about five buttons and each button hole was set in a scallop. The only way to button leather was to use a buttonhook to catch the shank of the button and pull it through the buttonhole. In winter I slept in Dr. Denton's. It was a footed pajama that covered every part of me but my head and hands. They kept you toasty warm.

 I was wearing my Dr. Dentons on my fourth birthday 20th December 1926. I was so excited. I jumped out of bed and ran into my parent's room shouting HAPPY BIRTHDAY. I was embarrassed when Mother told me that they were supposed to say Happy Birthday to me. I was not supposed to say it to them on my birthday. I guess it was better to learn that early on. My birthday present that year was a silver plated junior sized knife, fork and spoon set.

 Air conditioning had not been invented yet, or if it had it was used in commercial buildings but not yet in homes. All we had was an electric oscillating fan that stirred up the hot damp air but didn't do a lot of cooling. We tried to stay cool by wearing light clothing. My summer wear was a pair of panty briefs and a light dress. Girls did not wear pants at all. The first time I ever wore pants I was about twelve years old I was visiting in Raceland. I must have messed up my dress so they loaned me a pair of overalls to wear until my dress could be cleaned.

 I had some very pretty clothes because my grandmother sewed and did beautiful handwork; embroidery, smocking, Mexican pull work and tatting by the mile. She never just sat in a chair doing nothing. When she sat down, she was either repairing clothing, darning socks or doing fancy work. I remember a blue silk dress she made for me. It had smocking at the yoke and there were satin picot ribbons that were blue on one side and peach color on the other. They hung from the shoulder to the hem. I thought that dress was really elegant. I have fond memories of a simple summer dress made of thin cotton print with no sleeves and a V neck. The sleeve holes and the V neck were edged in lace. The body of the dress was gathered on a yoke so it was very full. I used to stand outside and let the wind fill the dress while I tried to keep it from touching me nowhere but on the shoulders. That made the dress seem like a bell with me as the clapper. Anyway, it was a way to stay as cool as possible. In winter I wore long stockings or knee socks with oxfords for every day and ankle sox with black patent Mary Janes for dress wear. In summer I wore ankle sox and T-strap sandals for every day and the same short socks and Mary Janes for dress. One-time Mother bought me some oxfords with snake skin toes. I absolutely refused to wear them. I cried and carried on so much about it she finally gave up and returned them. I always hated snakes. I even hate to turn a page in a magazine and find pictures of snakes.

 In the summer of 1927 my cousins Everett and Stanley visited us in the city. I found it strange to have boys visiting. Besides, they were both older than I was. I wanted one of their sisters to visit. However, it was only fair for them to have a turn at experiencing city life. Dad enjoyed having them because they could do male things together.

Across from the entrance to City Park where Dumain Street meets City Park Avenue there used to be an amusement park. Among all of the usual rides and attractions found on a boardwalk there was a wooden roller coaster called the Scenic Railway. I had never desired to go on it myself but I was jealous when Dad took the boys to ride it and would not let me go with them. He said I was too young to ride it. I'm sure he was right but being left behind hurt just the same. I was jealous of the boys. After all—he was my Dad. Dad was a roller coaster aficionado. Since he loved to ride roller coasters so much, he was glad to have someone to share his pleasure.

That was the year that Dad finally broke down and bought a truck. It was a Model T Ford pick-up truck. I don't think that the body style was known as a 'pick-up' at that time. I don't know what it would have been called. Automobiles were still new to everyone then. The truck bed was open so Dad built a cover for it. He had curtains that rolled down on both sides and the back to protect his tools and equipment from the weather. The cab could hold only two people so Dad put a bench he had built into the truck bed so he could seat two more people. It was not a comfortable way to ride so we didn't ride that way often.

Now we had a way to visit Grandma and Grandpa Darcey. Braithwaite was only about sixteen miles from New Orleans but the only way to get there was by bus if you didn't have a car. Braithwaite was a small but bustling town then. The E-Z Opener paper mill was the main employer of the people who lived there. So, it was a mill town. The mill provided housing, electric power and running water and a powerful stinky SMELL. We would start to smell the paper mill just as we left Poydras. The strange thing was that after we had been there a while we didn't notice the smell any more. There were about thirty houses and a hotel to house the mill workers. There was a two-story school house and a large brick building in the center of town near the levee that housed a commissary that sold groceries, dry goods and hardware. The building also housed a post office, a saloon and a gas station. On weekends the large entry space was turned into a theater. Many backless benches were set out, a screen was unrolled, a hand cranked projector was set up and voila! A theater. Comedies and cartoons were shown, I don't think they ever showed any feature length films. I was used to the big city movie houses in New Orleans so this arrangement looked primitive to me. However, the arrangement was appreciated as a welcome diversion in this backwater mill town.

I enjoyed going to Braithwaite because Uncle Jesse worked at the mill so he and his wife and children lived about a block from Grandma's house. He had five children, J. C. (Jesse junior), Allah Mae, Betty, Wilbur and Juliette. Allah Mae was a bit older than I was and Betty was a bit younger so I had someone to play with. Juliette was just a baby then. Around the late 20s or early 30s the mill moved to Tuscaloosa, Alabama and took their machinery, their smell and all of the workers who wanted to transfer with them. Grandpa said he was too old to start over in a new situation so the mill kept him on salary to be caretaker of the property left behind. Uncle Jesse and Uncle Cyrus transferred to Tuscaloosa. Later on, Uncle Jesse took a job with the St. Joe paper mill in Port St. Joe, Florida but Uncle Cyrus stayed in Tuscaloosa even through his retirement. So, my playmates were gone. Now Aunt Bea, Alfredo and Carlos were living with Grandma and Grandpa Darcey. I'm five years older than Alfredo and eight years older than Carlos.

One day Dad came home from work with a beautiful full-grown collie dog in the truck. He had found it wandering around on the construction site. I fell in love at first sight and asked if we could keep him. Dad said he would have to try to find the owner first. We started calling him Bob. Either Dad put an ad in the paper or they did. The owners said his name was Prince and that they were traveling. The dog kept getting out and running off. Since they were going to be traveling quite a bit it would be best if we kept him. We were still living on Hennessey Street and had a big backyard so Dad brought home a big wooden piano shipping box and put it in the yard. It became my playhouse and a shelter for Bob. I tore up cardboard for make-believe food to serve to my dolls so I tried sharing some with Bob. He chewed and chewed and chewed it and finally spit it out. At least he tried. He made a good companion and a great pillow. He had his aberrations like everybody else. He tolerated cats. He even let them eat from his food dish but he absolutely detested yellow cats. He killed every one of them he could catch. Another aberration of his was that he was afraid of thunder. When we had a thunderstorm, he begged to be let into the house where he promptly took shelter under the bed as far back as he could get, the big coward.

Dad had started a game with me when I was very small. He would bring home some small gift, a candy bar, a box of cookies, a small toy, then he hid it somewhere in the house. He would then say, "I think the fillilou bird has been here." That was my signal to start hunting for the hidden gift not knowing what I was looking for or where to start. He would say as I hunted, "You're cold." "You're getting warm, warmer, hot." Then I would find whatever it was. I loved these surprises. When he bought the truck, he fashioned a tin pocket to hang on the dashboard. He would sometimes say the magic words, "I think the fillilou bird came today." I would go out to the truck and look in the pocket. That lasted until one day the fillilou bird put a Hershey's chocolate bar in the pocket on a very hot day. When I took it out it was almost liquid. It made a big mess so that finished the use of the pocket.

Up until then it had not occurred to me to get in the truck while it was parked. But one day I decided to sit in the driver's seat and make believe I was driving. I had seen Dad reach over and turn a gadget on the dashboard so I reached over and turned it. To my horror it caused the engine to turn over and move the truck forward a fraction. I didn't know what I had done but I knew it was bad. I got out as quickly as I could on my very shaky legs and went inside the house. I hoped no one had noticed anything. I never told anyone about it but the experience scared me so much I never played in a parked car again.

It was while we lived in this same house that I learned a lot about courage. There was a little boy named Kenneth who lived down the block from us who took delight in running after me and chasing me home crying. I complained to my parents about him hoping they would go and do something dreadful to him to make him stop. Instead, Dad cut a short length off of an old broomstick, placed it under the front steps and said, "The next time he comes after you take this and chase him home. He'll leave you alone after that." Well, I could hardly wait to try out Dad's theory. I hung around outside waiting for Kenneth to chase me but he didn't show up. I got tired of waiting so I took out my tricycle and rode past his house. Sure enough, he came roaring out of his house, across the porch and down the steps. I pedaled madly home, got out my broomstick and chased him home. I didn't catch him but he was a changed boy after that. He even came over to my house and played with the other little girls and me when we played house. All was peace between us ever afterwards. That was how I learned that if you faced a problem squarely you could find a solution. Also, I learned that bullies aren't brave.

Mardi Gras 1927 is the first Mardi Gras I remember. Grandma made me a clown costume. She even made a skullcap to cover all of my hair. Dad did my make-up. My face was first made white with water and cornstarch, then he used water colors to paint a clown face on me. I knew it was a good disguise because when I went outside none of the children recognized me. I went inside to hurry the family to go to the parade and found that mother was preparing some food to take along. She was eating something so I asked her if I could have some. She said she was eating an olive and that it had an odd taste that I might not like. She gave me one and I liked it so I have been a fan of olives ever since. We went to see the parade on Canal Street. Dad held me on his shoulders as long as he could then he found a post to set me on. He held me so I wouldn't fall off. It was all very new and exciting but very tiring. I have no memory at all of the parade itself.

There was a lady who lived in one of the apartments next door to us on the corner of Hennessey and Palmyra who went about most of the day in her negligee.

I had heard the family refer to her as 'Miss Few Clothes.' One day when I saw her in her yard I called out, "Hello Miss Few Clothes" proud that I had remembered her name. I heard gasps of surprise from my family and suddenly knew I had made a faux pas but I had no idea what it was. Mother explained what had happened. That is when I learned that things said in the privacy of the home are not to be repeated in public.

On the morning of Good Friday, 15 April 1927 I woke up on my daybed in the dining room with an extraordinary amount of light streaming over my face. I rolled over on my stomach, lifted my body on my elbows and looked toward the front door. Strangely, the door was wide open, even the screen door that should never be left open was pulled back! I had to get up and see what was causing this unusual behavior. When I got to the front door and looked out all I could see was water and my Dad out in the middle of the street in hip boots. The water covered the porch and lapped just under the door sill. My tiled porch was a wading pool! I wanted to jump right in but Mother said I had to wear my bathing suit and eat breakfast first. I never ate breakfast so fast before. I stepped down off of the board Dad had placed from our door to the steps going upstairs and started playing in the water. When I sat down the water came up to my waist. Dad was out in the water having so much fun I think he was enjoying it as much as I was. I asked him if I could go down the porch steps to the banquette (sidewalk) and he said, "Come on." I can still remember the delightful apprehension I felt as the water came up higher and higher on my body. Once I was down on the banquette I had to stand on my tip-toes to keep my chin out of the water. Every time anyone went by and caused waves the water lapped over my face so I gave up on the banquette in favor of the steps where I could watch all of the people going by in rowboats and frolicking about without my getting my face wet. We have talked about that day for years. Every heavy rain since then has been compared to the Good Friday Flood of 1927.

On Easter morning I found four Easter baskets, three regular sized and one tall one like the ones used by florists to hold flower arrangements. I thought when I looked at it, "What a waste of space." because the surface was big enough for only four chocolate eggs. When Dad saw my expression he said, "Take the eggs off then take the grass up and see what's under it." That tall basket was filled with Easter goodies! Dad loved thinking up things like that to surprise me.

My world then was very small. I was not allowed to go any further than the sidewalk that ran in front of our house from one corner to the other unless I was with an adult. Thankfully, Grandma would take me for a walk around the neighborhood every afternoon in nice weather. On our walks we explored the whole area. Our favorite walk was the one that took us to Carrollton Avenue where we could observe the progress of the building of Jesuit High School. I began to think of as *my* school. It is only fitting that when I grew up, I married one of its graduates. On the corner of Hennessey and Canal Streets there was a drugstore where I bought my infrequent ice-cream cones. On Hennessey and Banks Streets there was a neighborhood grocery where I was allowed to go alone to buy a loaf of bread, a marvelously grown-up thing to be able to do.

That reminds me of another but not so pleasant story. One day Mother asked me to go to the corner grocery for a pint of milk so she could have milk for her second cup of coffee. I didn't want to go but she kept insisting. I kept resisting and crying and carrying on for what seemed like hours. I was getting tired of the whole thing but I didn't know how to end it. Aunt Helena arrived in the middle of all of this commotion and wanted to know what was going on. When Mother told her, she turned to me and said, "Don't be silly Nathalie. Go get you mother some milk." I was so glad it was finally over that I went without another word. Besides, it embarrassed me that she had found me acting so badly.

There was a small restaurant near our house though I can't remember exactly where it was located. I think it was on Canal Street. It must be gone now since that was ninety-three years ago. Anyway, they made the best oyster loaves I have ever tasted even to this day. They were made from a fresh baked whole pan loaf of bread that was cut so it opened like a trunk. The soft part of the inside of the bread was partially scooped out then the inside was liberally painted with melted butter. The cavity thus prepared was then filled with large delicious fried oysters and topped with slices of dill pickle. It makes my mouth water just to think about the wonderful taste of it.

All children are leery of new tastes. I was especially suspicious about a vegetable my parents were trying to get me to taste. It was called cauliflower and I thought it was *collie flower* and therefore had something to do with our dog, Bob. I finally got up enough nerve to taste it and found it very good. Strangely enough, though I was persnickety about food, I liked pickled pigs' feet and hogshead cheese.

Not long after we adopted Bob, Mr. Hillman Labat, Uncle Jesse's brother-in-law from Raceland, came to visit us. He brought us a turtle. Grandma promptly made turtle soup out of it. It was a female turtle and was full of eggs. The eggs were soft shelled and it was fun playing with them. I don't think I ate any of the soup then but since I've grown I have enjoyed it in restaurants that really know how to prepare it. The shell made a fine food dish for Bob.

Mr. Hillman visited us often and stayed for dinner sometimes. I was intrigued to watch him eat because he ate peas with a knife. I kept close watch to see if he would cut himself but he never did. I wanted to see if I could eat peas with a knife. I couldn't get enough to stay on the knife on my first try and was discouraged in my endeavor by my Mother, Father and Grandmother so I never got to practice.

There was always plenty of activity in our neighborhood. Venders of every sort came by. In the morning the Italian vegetable man came by selling fresh fruit and vegetables, either from a truck or a mule drawn wagon. He called out, "I gotta da peach, I gotta da eggplant, I gotta da." whatever was in season. Then there was the banana vendor who called, "I got ba-a-a-na-a-nas lady," or the watermelon man who called, "Wha-a-a-tah mel-lon ripe to de rine." The first part of the call was drawn out but the last four words were delivered quickly with a staccato beat. In strawberry season a black woman came around with a large basket on her head calling, "Stra-a-aw berries. Ripe stra-a-awberries." My grandmother would make the woman dump out the pints of strawberries she had chosen to be sure that the berries were ripe all the way to the bottom and not a few ripe ones on top and not very ripe ones underneath. There were scissors sharpeners, umbrella repairmen, tinkers, icemen, milk men and in the winter, the man selling coal by the bushel. There was always someone coming by. I especially remember the waffle man. He had a pretty white, glass enclosed wagon with a roof. The glass windows all around went from about the waist up to the roof. On the sides the word "Waffles" was lettered in red with gold edges. He announced his coming with a bugle. He cooked the waffles right there in the wagon. The rectangular waffles were four for a nickel, all hot and covered with powdered sugar and they smelled divine and were delicious. In the afternoons the hurdy-gurdy man would come and all the children would scatter to get a nickel to pay him to play a tune for us. Often the organ grinder and his monkey would show up. We would get pennies to give to the monkey so we could watch him take the penny and tip his hat. I wish there had been a way to record the street sounds, I am finding verbal descriptions inadequate to convey the ambiance.

It must have been 1926 when we spent Christmas in Braithwaite where I received my first pair of steel roller skates. I could hardly wait to try them so Dad fitted them to my shoes and showed me how to tighten the clamps with the key that came with the skates. There was not an inch of concrete in all of Braithwaite except in the basement of the school so I had to try skating on the wood floor of the front porch. I stood up and skated a few feet. This skating was a cinch. As soon as we got back to the city I put on my skates and launched myself on the sidewalk. Well, I soon found out that skating on wood and skating on concrete were two entirely different things. I made a wild dash for the neighbor's steps then went shakily back to my steps until, after many falls, I became adept enough to stay up more than down. I heard an adult say, "It's best to learn to skate while you're still small because you haven't so far to fall." If so, I'm glad I learned when I did but falling hurt just as much no matter the distance between the sidewalk and me.

I've always considered myself a tomboy but when I was very small, I loved playing ladies, dressing up in one of Mother's old dresses and flopping around in an old pair of her shoes and playing with dolls. I had been given a beautiful jointed doll when I was three. She was as big as I was. She had a porcelain head with sleep eyes and a wig of real hair. Her curls reached her shoulders. The only way I could move her was to put my back to her back, slip my arms under her arms then lean forward enough to get her feet off of the floor. I admired her but she was unwieldy to play with. Grandma made her many pretty dresses and Mother bought ribbons to match each outfit. I think they had more fun with her than I did. I loved the Bye-lo babies that Mother brought me when she went shopping on Canal Street. They had soft bodies with porcelain heads modeled to look like a newborn baby. I was forever breaking them and though she replaced them several times none of them survived very long.

Mother and Dad had a group of friends who gathered every week to play cards. There were Vic Tournier, Bob Soniat, Everett Villarubia and Eugene Lundsgaard. I loved standing around watching them play and listening to them talk. To keep me from being a pest my grandmother took me into another room and taught me to play 'Battle.' By doing this I learned my numbers and number values early on. One time, when Grandma was visiting Aunt Carrie for the weekend, the group finished their game and decided they would all go to the French Market for coffee and doughnuts. I had fallen asleep. They woke me up and took me with them. I thought it was great that I got to go out with them in the middle of the night. Eating beignets wasn't bad either.

When we had been living in Memphis my mother met Irene Hunter, a French World War I war bride. Her husband was in the Coast Guard and they were living right across the street from us. Irene was delighted to find someone who could talk French so she and Mother became good friends. Once we moved back to New Orleans they must have written back and forth over the intervening years because when I was four years old Irene invited us to visit her while they were stationed in Mobile. We went, Mother and I. Mr. Hunter must have been on sea duty because I never did meet him. I loved listening to Irene speak English. She had a parrot who could imitate her perfectly. She also had a poodle dog named Bebe (pronounced B B). The parrot, who stayed on the sun porch, would call, "Bebe, Bebe, Come here." Bebe would run to answer the call only to find that it was just the parrot again. Poor Bebe! That parrot led him a merry chase. Bebe was very friendly. He was also an early riser. Once Bebe was up, everybody had to get up. He would come to the bed and lick our faces until everyone was awake. Irene kept ginger ale for mixing highballs. She let me try some and I loved it, still do. It's my favorite carbonated beverage.

It seemed that one of the fun things to do in her crowd was to go flying. Irene knew Mr. Pickup, a former Army pilot, who had his own plane. She and Mother flew with him often. They usually left me with one of the ground crew who would sit me on the hood of Irene's car and give me a Baby Ruth candy bar to keep me happy while they were gone. One memorable day they took me flying with them. That was a red-letter day for me. Mr. Pickup flew an open cockpit biplane. It was what the service called a 'Jenny.' The front cockpit was about three people wide (maybe only two and a half) and was upholstered in black leather. The back cockpit where the pilot sat was big enough for only one person. I seem to remember that the body of the plane was painted gray. There was a small windscreen in front of each cockpit that kept the slipstream from blowing directly in our faces. There wasn't much sensation once we were airborne. I stood up by the side of the cockpit and looked down at one point and saw a house, a pond and some trees set among endless green fields. It all looked doll sized. I was not afraid. I enjoyed the whole trip though it got a bit boring after a while and I believe I nodded off to sleep listening to the engine noise.

A memorable thing I did there was eat in a cafeteria (Morrison's) for the first time. I thought it was a wonderful idea to have all that food on display so a person could pick out just what he liked and didn't have to eat stuff he didn't like just because everyone else was eating it. I was sold on cafeterias from then on.

I suppose that everything that happens when you are four years old is a first. Either it really is a first or it is the first time you can remember. Watching a child's mind develop is a fascinating thing, If you have an introspective turn of mind, watching your own mind develop is quite fascinating, too. I remember becoming aware of myself in relation to the universe. Now, that sounds quite grand when said by an adult and it is too profound to have been said by a child. I did not try to verbalize it because I didn't know the words then. I do remember a feeling I could trigger just by sitting quietly and gazing up at the sky. I felt the vastness of the universe and a oneness with it. It was a comfortable sense of belonging that I was unable to sustain as I supposedly became older and wiser. I kept that lovely secret to myself and enjoyed it alone. Somehow, I knew that to talk about it would diminish it and I also knew that I didn't have the right words to explain it clearly. I also enjoyed looking down into a rain puddle because it gave me the giddy feeling of the possibility of falling up into the deepness of the sky reflected there.

Other mundane firsts came to me at this time. I did my first job of dishwashing while standing on a chair with Mother's apron tied around me. I was watching my mother clean the ashes from the fireplace and then mop the hearth leaving it shining. That looked like fun to me until the day she let me try it. Once was enough. I had never before realized how heavy a wet mop could be. I was quite willing to leave that job to her. There must have been many other such firsts.

Oh yes, there was another one, the first time I got drunk. That sounds terrible because I was only four but it happened innocently enough. My parents knew the Gomez family who had a fishing camp in Littlewoods. Littlewoods is on the southeast shore of Lake Pontchartrain along Hayne Boulevard in Gentilly. They gave a seafood party and invited us. The back screened porch was the width of the whole building so it made a nice spot for such a big lot of people. They put up saw horses, set boards on them, covered the tables with paper and dumped boiled seafood in the middle. The long table took up the whole width of the porch. Everyone took a chair, had their beer mug filled and started peeling shrimp and crabs. They were eating and talking and having a good time. I had eaten all the boiled shrimp I wanted so I slipped out of my chair and went to Mother and Dad for a taste of beer. They each gave me a sip. Then I started going around the table asking each person I felt might share a sip of beer. They were all so busy eating and talking that quite a few gave me a taste and pretty soon I had too much. One of the older children asked me if I wanted a ride on the swing. She gave the swing a few pushes and in no time I fell asleep. I was a very quiet drunk. When I woke up, I realized what had happened. I had the grace to be embarrassed.

Memories of all sorts come crowding in when once a person starts digging back in his mind. One memory leaves me with mixed feelings. On Banks Street near our house on Hennessey Street there was a barbershop. The red and white barber pole that went around and around outside was very attractive. So was the large sunny shop with all of the clean smells and the big white chairs that could go up and down and could turn all the way around. I even looked forward to sitting on the booster seat that fit over the arms of the chair to lift a child high enough so the barber could work on him. I didn't mind too much the actual cutting of my hair. I didn't quite enjoy having my bangs cut because the hair fell all over my face. But then the barber took his long-bristled brush with a bit of powder and brushed all the hair off. I wasn't crazy about my hairstyle either. Since I had straight hair it was cut with bangs and the sides cut just to the ear lobes and shingled up the back. It was called a Buster Brown style haircut. It was that *'shingled up the back'* part I hated. It was not so much because of how it looked; every child who had straight hair had his hair cut the same way. I hated it because of the electric clippers that made buzzing sounds in my head and shivers down my back. If we happened to be downtown shopping on Canal Street when I needed a haircut Mother took me to the barbershop in Maison Blanche. Instead of a barber chair they had prancing horses like the ones on the merry-go-round in the parks. The delight of sitting on those wonderful horses made up for the clippers I had to endure.

Talking about Canal Street reminds me of occasional shopping trips I went on. At first it was a fairyland experience but somewhat terrifying. One time while Mother made a purchase, I got busy looking at something. I failed to notice when she was finished. When I looked for her, she was gone! I turned to look for her but all I saw was a forest of legs. The mounting panic I felt was cut short when I heard her voice and saw her coming back for me. I never forgot that feeling of terror so I never allowed myself to get separated from her again.

Shopping was dull for me but the reward for patience was a promised trip through Kress, the big dime store next to Maison Blanche. Now there was a store to delight any child! In the front just after you entered the door were the cookie counters with bin after bin of cookies on tempting display. Then we came to the candy counter. It took me a trip around the whole display before I could decide which candy I wanted today. Next, we went to the back of the store where there were several counters of toys. Some were mostly for boys and some were mostly for girls. I went slowly around all the counters, even the ones for boys. I was allowed to choose one thing. Usually I picked out girls' toys but I did occasionally choose from the boys' counter. Once I picked out a popgun that had a cork on a string. When I cocked it and pulled the trigger it made a lot of nice noise. A bonus for shopping at Kress was the beautiful organ music. At the back of the store on the mezzanine behind a lattice screen was a pipe organ. The music filled the store and was a very pleasant background to shopping. When I was older, I would go to the soda fountain in the middle of the store, order a coke and sit there sipping it slowly while I enjoyed the music.

On rare occasions a movie was part of the day in town. I must have gone to other movie houses but the one that stands out in my memory is the Saenger. It was like a palace inside! The mood of quiet elegance started in the lobby with the thick red carpet and sparkling crystal chandeliers. Red velvet ropes on polished brass stanchions guided the customers to the ticket taker. The wide marble stairways on each side led up to the second level where there were beautiful sofas and chairs where one was welcome to sit to wait to meet someone or just sit to rest. There were marble statues, alabaster lamps, oil paintings, gold lace, brocades, gilt mirrors. It was magnificent!

The seating in the auditorium of the theater was in what would have been the courtyard of an Italian villa. The boxes on each side and the loge were like the balconies. Overhead was the evening sky complete with stars and moving clouds. The stage was vast. In front of the stage was the orchestra pit on an elevator. It sank into the floor with all the musicians in place but out of sight. When the movie ended the pit would rise. The musicians would have on white gloves. Their hands were raised and moving with a blue spotlight picking out their gloved hands. That happened when there was a vaudeville show for the musicians to play for.

At different times there were acrobats, contortionists, magicians, comedians, singers, dancers, trained animal acts—everything. All of that was offered along with a movie, short subjects, a cartoon and later on, newsreels. We really received our money's worth of entertainment. When there was no vaudeville following the movie, a huge pipe organ would rise up on the left side and the theater would be filled with music. The pipes were installed in the walls all around the theater. I suppose you could say it was an early version of 'surround sound.'

Sunday afternoon was reserved for going to the park. That usually meant City Park for us because we always lived in the section of the city called 'down town' somewhere near City Park. I had never gone 'up town' to Audubon Park until I went there on a picnic with Aunt Helena and her family when I was twelve. My parents would take me to play on the playground equipment, feed bread to the swans and ducks, and to ride on the 'Swan boat' or the 'flying horses' (carousel). The swan boat was fitted out with several seats like the seats on a streetcar. It was painted white and had a swan head and neck on the front. For a fee you got a nice long ride on the lagoons. The 'Flying Horses' were glorious with all those beautifully painted horses with jewels in their harness. They were in rows of three. The outside and the inside horses went up and down. The center ones did not. There was a section made like a sled or carriage with seats facing each other for people with little babies. In the center was the place where the music came from. After all that activity we were glad at dusk to find a seat in front of the bandstand after having gone to the Casino refreshment stand for a treat. There were many different bands in the city, Firemen, Police, etc. They each had splendid uniforms. They took turns playing on Sunday evening. At full dark the silver screen would drop down and cartoons, slapstick comedies or melodramas would be shown. In late spring and early summer the local dance schools would have their end-of-the-year recitals on the stage in front of the bandstand. To me the dancers were as glamorous as movie stars. Most of the time on these Sunday outings I was given a balloon. If it survived (didn't pop in the park or escape and fly away, I would tie it to the foot of my bed where it would grow smaller and smaller each day until it was just a wrinkled thing on a string lying desolately on the floor. It was time to throw it away. I supposed that was how I learned that nothing lasts forever.

We soon made the fourth of about thirty-two moves that we were to make together. We moved to a nice house at 1428 Verna Street just off of Esplanade Avenue near St. Louis Cemetery#3. I don't remember very much about the inside of this house because we didn't stay there very long but it was a pretty place in a nice neighborhood and I was proud of it. Young children are aware of their surroundings and are affected by them. The house had what is now called 'curb appeal.' It was a bungalow style and had a deep porch with a swing. The swing on the porch was a lovely place to be on hot summer days. There were large oak trees for shade and cicadas and mocking birds for music. On Leda Street, the next street over towards the cemetery, was the abandoned clubhouse of the old Jockey Club. From our house I could see the top of it through the trees with its blank windows staring back at me. It gave me a morbid thrill to think of it as haunted. I never wanted to pass by it on my walks with Grandma.

I enjoyed the other places that we walked. We went to the different cemeteries and I did not find that a bit frightening. My brother is buried in St. Louis #3 and so are many other members of my family. Grandma and I visited the tomb often. At one time there was an iron settee in front of the Frémaux family tomb. When the cemetery was restored the bench was removed because it suffered from neglect. It had become rusty and no one had done anything about it. Anyway, when she and I went to the cemetery she would sit on the bench and say a rosary while I ran in the aisles chasing butterflies. I never caught one. Later on, when we lived in Passera Court Grandma and I used to walk down to Greenwood Cemetery where Grandpa Grandjean is buried in the Swiss Society Tomb, then we would walk back by Odd Fellows Rest where I liked to go up and down the steps of the tomb near the entrance. We don't have anyone buried there. I thought that it was a cemetery for peculiar people because of the word odd in the name. I found out much later that "Odd Fellows" is the name of a lodge.

My Hidalgo cousins in Raceland and I loved visiting each other. We often stayed at each other's house for a short visit, overnight, for a week-end, a week, a month whatever we could wangle. One of my earliest memories of Raceland was when the Hidalgo family lived in the Yellow House. It was about the third house in the row just past the dummy railroad track on the east bank of Bayou Lafourche as one turns right off of highway 90 before crossing the bayou. It backed onto the sugar cane fields as do all of the houses on the east bank that face the bayou. There was a pond back there whose banks were covered in wild violets. I picked a big bouquet of them for my mother while thinking of myself as a child in a picture in my story books. You must know the sort; the sweet-faced English child in a sunny meadow full of flowers with the wind blowing its hair and clothes.

I guess I was about four when I first became acquainted with the pond. Mother and I had gone to Raceland for an afternoon visit. We children were all under strict orders not to go out of the yard. Once our mothers were busy talking, Everett and Stanley enticed all the little girls out to the pond to witness the launching of a boat they built. Who could resist such an invitation? So out of the back gate we all trouped. We stood on the edge of the pond and watched as the boys dragged a cumbersome looking construction of planks through the grass and launched it into the pond. It promptly sank. Momentarily I felt sorry for them but then we all started to laugh including the boys and that was that. Now we had to get back into the yard without being seen if we could. I heard my mother calling me so I knew the jig was up. What to do? Hurriedly we all started picking violets to give bouquets to our mothers to placate them and hopefully to avoid punishment. It worked! Mothers cannot resist children bearing flowers.

One special time Soledad, always known as 'Deda' in the family, was visiting at our house on Verna Street. Dad came home from work with a wooden mailbox someone had made for him. I was intrigued with it because it had a window in a wooden door that opened. It looked more like a doll house than a mailbox. Dad let us play with it and, subsequently, when set sideways on a chair it reminded us of the booster seat in the barbershop. The logical next step was for me to go into the house and get the scissors to play barber. First Deda sat on the mailbox and I cut a good amount of her hair in the back. Then I sat on the mailbox and Deda returned the favor by making a crooked job of trimming my bangs. Mother took one horrified look at us and marched us right off to the barber to get the damage repaired. The barber's solution was to give us both a "boyish bob." Dad took one look at us when we returned and promptly christened us "Sammy full of Hammy" and "Tony full of Baloney." I was glad when my hair grew out.

Not long after this episode we moved again. I asked Mother why we moved from such a lovely place? She said the rent was too high. We moved to a house in Passera Court. I don't remember the number of the house but it was on the left side as you entered the street from Orleans Avenue. I went back recently to look at Passera Court and it still looks the same, sort of tired and bedraggled but I couldn't be sure of the number. It might have been 518. It doesn't matter a lot because all of the houses there look exactly alike. They're shotgun doubles with divided porches. I know the houses on the left side had garages behind them but the ones on the right did not. I kept my tricycle in ours. The street dead ends on the railroad track. I felt it was quite a comedown from the house on Verna. I was ashamed of it. The following stories took place in this house.

Mother's brother, Uncle Cyrus, was always one of my favorite people. He was just barely grown-up and he always took time to play with me. He would fling me around, or hoist me up on his shoulder so I could reach the chandelier in the living room. Often, he became my horse. When I was two and a half or three, I used to call him my big 'pocifer' (policeman) because he had been a deputy sheriff in Plaquemine Parish under his older brother Jesse. One day when he was visiting us Mother said she had some errands to run so would he stay with Nathalie for a while. He agreed. When he went to have a smoke, he found he was out of cigarettes. He said he would run over to the local grocery and buy a pack. I was to sit in the chair by the front door and not move until he returned. I was not to talk to anyone either, or touch anything that might hurt me, or let anyone who might come to the door know that I was alone. Our front door had two sidelights—two half doors. They were always open to get air circulation through the house. The chair I was to sit in was right next to an open sidelight. I was afraid to move. I had never been alone before. Soon after Uncle Cyrus left, a door-to-door salesman knocked. He saw me sitting there but I wouldn't talk to him. After several attempts to get a response from me he must have realized I was alone and frightened so he left. It seemed a long time since Uncle Cyrus had left, then I heard the back door close. Uncle Cyrus found me exactly where he had left me. I told him about the salesman. Soon after, Mother returned and life became normal again.

Grandma Grandjean and I were together a lot. She was living with us again. She did things to amuse me. She told me stories and sang songs. She would sing me to sleep with arias from operas she had attended. In the afternoon we would sit on the porch swing where she used the advertising flyers to make different things by folding the papers in intricate ways. I know now that the skill she used is called 'origami' but I never heard that term until I was much older. She made chickens, picture frames, purses, boats and other things I can't remember. I learned how to make chickens but I never learned how to make the other things. They were much more difficult.

She spoiled me about food. I was a picky eater so after pushing my food around my plate I would leave the table without eating much. Later in the night I would wake up hungry. She would get up and make me pancakes or blanc-menge, a cornstarch pudding. I can still see myself sitting in the kitchen half asleep and really not all that hungry but gratified by the extra coddling.

She also used some strange remedies on me, some she had learned from the Indians who lived around her house when she was young. I often picked up ringworm from kneeling in the dirt. She would mix powdered sulphur with gunpowder applied on a bandage that she would then tie around my knee. It worked. For a boil she would wait until it was ripe (had a core and pus in it) She would sterilize a sewing needle to pop the boil, then she would drain the pus out of it but it wouldn't cure until the core was removed so she would get a length of silk thread and roll it over the top of the boil. The thread would catch the core and pull it out. Then she put medicine and a bandage on it. Her remedy for an earache was very comforting. In those days salt came in a cloth bag. She would dump the salt into an iron frying pan, set it on a lit burner on the stove on low heat stirring it constantly. When the salt reached the right temperature, she would pour it back into the cloth bag, sew it shut and then put the heated salt bag on my pillow. The salt held the heat for a long time and eased the pain so I could go to sleep. And she could go to sleep, too.

One night I became very sleepy while sitting on Dad's lap listening to the adults talk. I heard Mother say, "Oh look. She's sound asleep." I wasn't sound asleep but I pretended I was and went limp as she lifted me, undressed me and put my pajamas on. It was fun to be babied.

Mother's younger sister, Beatrice had married Alfredo Francisco Huete (pronounced Wetty) about a year ago and now she had a baby, Alfredo, Jr. She brought him with her when she visited us one day. It was the first close-up look I had ever had of a real baby. I was so interested. He looked like a big sweet blue-eyed doll to me. He was so soft and smooth to touch. She let me watch him nurse. She even let me hug him and kiss his plump cheek. It was a wonderful experience.

A not so wonderful experience that stands out sharply in my memory from this time in my life was a visit from Aunt Mabel, another of Mother's sisters and her daughter Alma. Alma is younger than I am by about two and a half years. I was sitting close to her on the sofa trying to get acquainted when all of a sudden, she slipped off of the sofa and bit me on the toe through my Ked sandals. I was so surprised at this sudden attack that I yelled and started crying both because of the surprise and because it hurt. For a long time after that I did not care much for Alma.

Soon I became aware of my personal appearance. I learned to comb my own hair and, from looking in the mirror to do that I became aware that straight hair is not as attractive as curly hair. All of Aunt Helena's children except Soledad had curly hair. Allah Mae and Betty had curly hair, even J.C. had curly hair. He hated it. Boys were supposed to have straight hair—curls were for girls. I would gladly have traded with him. It wasn't fair that Soledad and I were the only girl cousins to suffer straight hair. Then too, my hair was dark brown with copper highlights and I wanted to have black hair like my mother's. Every night I prayed that when I woke up in the morning, I would have curly black hair. Every morning I would jump out of bed to check in the mirror and every morning I was disappointed—still straight, still brown. My hair did get a bit darker but it never got any curlier.

*Sammy full of hammy
Nathalie with her boyish bob*

## *Beginning of My School Days*

I learned in August 1927 that I was going to start school in September. I was going to be in kindergarten. I could hardly wait. Every day I asked if this was the day I would be going. Every day I was told, "Not today." Until I was told to quit asking. I would be informed in good time. So, I held my questions and waited to be told when it would happen. School in New Orleans didn't start until the second week in September so I had about six weeks of anxious waiting. Finally, the big day arrived. We walked past "my" school, Jesuit, down a block or so until we arrived at Crossman School on Carrollton Avenue. When we were registered the principal showed us to the kindergarten room. It was grand. I had never had many children to play with, now I had a whole room full. I sailed right in and made friends, joined a building project with the brick sized wooden blocks, argued about who was going to get to use the dishes next, took my turn going down the big sliding board that was in the room. It was a whole new world. We had a sweet teacher who read us stories in the afternoon. I was in heaven. For two weeks I went to this lovely place until I caught the "grippe."

The grippe is an old-fashioned name for influenza. Dad and I had it at the same time and both of us were quite sick. When we were able to be up a bit we put on our robes and went into the dining room. Mother draped each dining room arm chair with a blanket. The chairs were in front of the fire. She folded the bottom point over our feet and the two side points over our bodies but under our arms to leave them free so we could amuse ourselves. She took the leaves of the table and set them across the chair arms thus making a table where we could play cards, hold a book or, for me, color in my coloring book. I had an A B C coloring book that started with A is for aeroplane. Charles Lindberg had just made the first nonstop solo crossing of the Atlantic Ocean so the picture to color was his plane, The Spirit of St. Louis.

I was beginning to learn to read just by picking it up from my books. Dad sat me on his lap to read me the funny papers so I could see the pictures. I would follow the words he read from the balloon above each character. Soon I was hunting for words I recognized from the newspapers and magazines. I would read the word then show it to Mother, Dad or Grandma so they could check if I had read it right.

By the time I was well enough to go back to school Mother said I had missed so much she thought it best that I not go back, especially since we were going to be moving after Christmas to Lockport where Dad was going to be working. I was very disappointed until I realized that Lockport was not far from Raceland so I would be seeing my Hidalgo cousins more often.

We spent Christmas in Raceland that year. We got up very early the day before Christmas and traveled in the touring car. It was a cold day so we each wore warm clothes plus coats, hats, mufflers, and gloves. Grandma and I sitting in the back seat had a lap robe over our legs. The side curtains were rolled down. They protected us somewhat from the wind. The most that can be said for them was that they kept rain out of the car but they did little to keep out the cold. Cars did not have heaters in them.

To get to Raceland by car we had to use one of the numerous ferries to cross the Mississippi River. There was one at Canal Street, Jackson Avenue, Napoleon Avenue and Kenner so you could cross to the west bank and ride the river road on that side to Luling or cross at Kenner and land in Luling. The roads were better on the east bank so we usually crossed at Kenner. The road the rest of the way to Raceland was gravel so there was no way to drive fast. Cars couldn't go fast anyway. Between Luling and Paradise (pronounced Pare-ah-dee) there was a bad stretch of road through a swampy area. The surface was always rough and was called a washboard road. We considered ourselves fortunate if we made the whole trip without any flat tires or car trouble. We had risen at six and arrived in Raceland at noon just in time for dinner, which is served at noon on the plantation, and so we considered we had made good time.

Mr. Godchaux who owned the refinery where Uncle Emile worked was Jewish but every year at Christmas he provided gifts for all the worker's children. Everyone would gather in a big room, probably the dining room of the men's dormitory. There were large tables of toys that were arranged by age and sex groups. When the child's name was called, he went up and chose a gift from the appropriate table. Since I was visiting, I went with my cousins to get their gifts but I did not expect a gift myself since my father didn't work there. However, my parents provided a gift of a big rubber ball for me to receive. When we returned with our gifts Dad lined us all up around the room and gave each of us a nickel. We were holding hands and dancing around the room. Since I had no pocket in my clothes, I put my nickel in my mouth for safekeeping so I could hold hands. In all of the commotion I swallowed it! I shed copious tears not so much in fear or discomfort as in sorrow for thus being without my money.

On Christmas morning when we went to the tree, I found that Santa had left an electric train for me. Unfortunately, he had forgotten to leave a transformer. Dad and Uncle Emile went out and found two huge dry cell batteries. I never knew that batteries came that big. They were about eight inches tall and two to two and a half inches in diameter. They hooked them up and made the train run. I had never in my life dreamed of wanting an electric train. Santa should have given it to Dad. He had a lot of fun with it. We children had a big noisy, wonderful time as we always did when the families got together. Aunt Helena was a really good cook so the dinner was very good.

After Christmas we moved to Lockport where Dad went into the electrical contracting business with Mr. Sidney Naquin. Louisiana Power and Light had just recently extended its electric distribution up and down Bayou Lafourche and everyone was anxious to get connected. Dad also had an appliance shop where he sold everything from toasters, lamps and irons to refrigerators and electric stoves. There were no electric washing machines yet. He also did maintenance work at the movie theater Mr. Naquin owned. He even filled in for the projectionist when needed.

The house we rented at 520 Barataria Street in Lockport was an unfurnished two-bedroom single house with a porch wrapped around the living room. The house was painted barn red and the trim and wooden picket fence were painted a cream color. Dad put up a porch swing. For the first time we had our own furniture. I loved this place. We had a big side yard with a garage, a peach tree, grape arbor and pomegranate tree. There was a privet hedge along part of the front fence that stopped at the edge of the vehicle gate. The front yard was L shaped with a Japanese plum three on the side of the side porch. When the plums were ripe, we could reach over the banister to pick them. The backyard was large. Of course, it had clothes lines. There was a gate in the backyard fence that led to the side street that we used when we went to Lusko's grocery on the street behind us. There was also an outside toilet back there behind the garage that was convenient when we were playing outside. I had seen outside toilets before in Braithwaite so that was nothing new. One thing I had never seen was the lightning rod that was attached to the chimney. The chimney served the back to back fireplaces in the dining room and my room. The room I shared with Grandma had once been two rooms but at some former time the wall was removed making one big room. It was great to have all of that space. There was a bay window in the side toward the garage yard. There was a separate entrance to our room from the porch. I had a lot of room for my toy box and table and chair set and Grandma had room for a rocking chair. We still shared a double bed.

We were very modern because we had a Frigidaire refrigerator and an electric stove. Dad brought home a twelve-tube radio phonograph. I was never sure of the significance of the twelve tubes but I guess it was the latest thing on the market and was superior to anything coming before it. We had an odd collection of records because Mother liked the popular music of the day including what we now call Country Western while Dad bought Victor Masterworks renditions of operatic arias and semi-classics. I never will forget the pounding rhythm of the Anvil Chorus from Il Trovatore.

Radio entertainment was beginning to flourish. There were programs we listened to regularly. I particularly remember 'Amos and Andy,' a comedy program. There was a drama program that started out with the sound of a steam engine approaching, thundering down the track while whistling mournfully. I have always had a thing about trains. The sounds give me the willy-wams. I shivered whenever this program came on. I drew up my legs and hugged my knees to my chest. The program was good and I enjoyed it once it got past the introduction.

Directly across the street from us was an abandoned house falling in on itself. Next to it was a big syrup kettle that had been used as a cistern. It was still catching rainwater and had all sorts of interesting things growing in it. I was strictly forbidden to go over there but, of course, that just made it that much more interesting and I went anyway.

Lockport was a very small town. Barataria Street ran from the main street along the bayou to the side street that ran along the side of our house. Beyond that were empty fields as far as one could see. The street behind us was the last street in that direction. Lusko's grocery backed onto the Intercoastal Waterway.

For all I know Lusko's grocery was the only grocery in town. They had a strange arrangement for purchasing goods. At least it was strange to me. Mr. Lusko kept a small notebook for each customer. Whenever anyone in the family bought anything Mr. Lusko wrote it in the book. At the end of the month you went in and paid the bill. It was a good idea for a child to go with it's mother at this time because Mr. Lusko gave the child lagniappe. Lagniappe means something extra; a 'thanks for doing business with me' gift. Usually I got an all-day sucker. I don't know why they were called that because I never had one last more than an hour or so.

Our dog Bob enjoyed all of the space but mostly he stayed in the house. He was getting old. I loved all of the yard space, too and the plants. I particularly enjoyed the room Grandma and I shared. Since it had its own door to the porch I didn't have to go through the rest of the house to go in or out. That way I stayed out of Mother's sight and avoided being sent on some errand or another. Grandma had all the space she needed and I still had room for my sixteen dolls. She would sit and tat and tell me stories. The ones I remember best are stories of when she was a little girl during the Civil War. As I said before she would sing opera arias for me. When Grandpa Grandjean was alive they kept a box at the French Opera House so she had been to quite a few opera seasons. When the opera house burned in 1919 she was one of the ladies who helped the cast by making new costumes to replace the ones lost in the fire, so they could continue their tour.

Dad's mother was a tiny lady. She may have been only five feet tall but she was brave. When there was a thunderstorm and both Mother and Bob were hiding in the house, Grandma and I sat on the porch and watched the lightning flickering across the sky. I don't like being startled by a big boom of thunder but I have never been afraid of a thunderstorm.

Mother and Dad's card playing group of friends used to spend the weekend in the country with us to play the game they loved called 'Five Hundred.' It is something like Bridge I think because you have to bid your hand. I never learned to play the game myself. Mr. Lundsgaard nearly always brought me a pound box of Hershey's kisses. We called them silverbells. Has any child ever been so lucky? Imagine my having so many silverbells that I could play with them. I made believe I was serving them to my dolls. I would set my table and put them in my dishes for my dolls to eat. Since they couldn't really eat, I would have to eat for them. Clever for a five year old wasn't it?

During Prohibition a person was not legally able to go out and buy alcoholic beverages at a bar or restaurant but legally they could make beer or wine for their own use. All the law did was make more people want alcohol than ever before just because it was prohibited. It encouraged the gangsters to buy and distribute it in places called 'speak-easies.' It was served in a teacup to fool observers into thinking a person was having tea or coffee. Actually, it fooled no one. The gangsters doing this were called 'boot-leggers.' A strange term. I don't know what 'boot' had to do with it, or 'leggers' either for that matter. My Dad had always said, "The government cannot legislate morality." A person will choose to be a moral citizen or not. It has to be the choice of the individual. Look at all the laws against illegal drugs and look at all the people who are hooked on them anyway. Dad always contended that the government should legalize all the sinful stuff and collect taxes on it.

Since it was legal to make beer for your own use Dad made homebrew for himself and the friends who came to play cards. He used a big earthenware crock that was kept in the pantry into which he put malt (bought at the local grocery), yeast, rice and water. I'm not sure of the proportions of the receipe but I think the rice was to settle out impurities. I loved to eat the yeast cakes. I liked the smell and the taste and biting a yeast cake is somewhat like biting an art gum eraser, something I always liked to do though I did not eat the erasers. Dad always bought an extra cake of yeast for me. During the brewing that takes a week or two or three, the liquid had to be skimmed to remove stuff that rose to the top. Dad let me do that sometimes. When the brew was ready to bottle Dad used a siphon from the crock to the bottles. The siphon had a clip to shut it off when the bottle was full. Dad had a hand operated bottle-capping machine. Capping was my job. First, I put a new cap on top of the bottle then I pulled down the handle that crimped the cap around the lip of the bottle thus sealing the brew. I thought of that as fun. Helping was a side issue. When all the bottles were capped, they were put in wooden twenty-four bottle cases and set on the back porch until needed.

When the card game group was due to come Dad bought a block of ice, put it in a wash tub and, using a hand held icepick he chopped it into chunks and buried the beer bottles in the ice. He set the tub under the edge of the dining room table where they played cards so the beer would be cold by the time the card game got started.

One big plus about living in Lockport was being able to go to the movies so often. Since Dad was in business with Mr. Naquin who owned the theater, we went several times a week. I saw the original Our Gang comedies, Harold Lloyd comedies, melodramas, westerns, love stories, serials, Tarzan, everything. I even went, at Dad's invitation, on the precarious trip to the projection booth. Just getting to the projection room was an adventure. There were about five or six wooden steps to a landing but neither the steps nor the landing had a banister. From the landing was a catwalk with no banister that led from one corner of the big room all the way across to the projection room in the opposite corner. There were two big carbon-arc-lamp projection machines in there. Carbon-arc lamps are too bright to look right at. A light that bright was needed to light up the screen. There was a small square window cut through the wall so the projectionist could watch that everything was working properly on the screen. Dad said I could look through it if I wanted to. I tried but I had to stand on my tip-toes to be able to see through that little window. After having seen what went on in the projection room, I was satisfied to watch the movie from the auditorium. When something scary was showing on the screen, I would slide down in my seat so that the back of the seat in front of me blocked out my view. I would peek around the side of the seat-back to see if the scary scene was over so I could sit up straight again.

The really best part of going to the movies was that I could get a bar of candy without having to pay for it. All I had to do was to go to Mr. Naquin's daughter, Mildred, who sold the tickets and ran the concession stand, and ask for it. I did not abuse the privilege. I realized that if I made a nuisance of myself that privilege could be revoked. I surely wanted to avoid that. Sometimes, after the show, we would go across the street from the theater to Mr. Sidney Delaune's Ace High Café where I invariably ordered a Mavis pop. Mavis was a chocolate drink in a pop bottle that might have had some milk in it. Sidney must have been a popular name in the days when these three Sidneys, Grandjean, Naquin and Delaune were born.

There were some disadvantages to living in Lockport. For one there were only wooden sidewalks so there was no place to skate. For another the children talked strangely. They were different, sometimes hostile. There was one girl, Laura, who was especially obnoxious. Every day when she came home from school she would curse at me. That went on for a few days until one day I beat her to it. I was hanging on the front gate waiting for her to come by. As soon as I saw her I said, "Go to shit." That was what she had been saying to me. I had no idea what it meant but I was getting my own back and that was all that mattered. Mother overheard me. She knew what had been going on so she understood why I had done it. She told me that it was not a good idea to lower one's standards to the same level as the person who was wronging you. That may be true when you get older, but for children, getting even works wonders. Laura never did curse at me again. In fact, we played together in my yard after that but we never did become good friends.

I had always had a lot of colds and croup so Dr. Deverges, my pediatrician in New Orleans, said that I needed my tonsils removed. When I had been clear of a cold long enough Mother took me to New Orleans to the Eye, Ear. Nose and Throat Hospital in the spring of 1928. There Dr.Irwin took out my tonsils and adenoids. We went in the morning and I was released late that same afternoon. Aunt Mabel had come to the hospital to be with Mother. She visited with me after it was over and gave me a blue silk drawstring purse with a mirror on the bottom and money inside. Since we lived too far away to return home Aunt Inez had us stay at her house during my convalescence. All I could eat was Coca-Cola and ice cream, my favorite foods! I didn't develop any complications so I was soon home.

Once during that summer Mother and I were at odds over something. I threatened to run away. Instead of her pleading with me not to leave as I was expecting her to do she offered to pack my suitcase and started naming off items of clothing I would need. I had all I could do to keep her from packing the suitcase and leaving it on the porch and still be able to save some face. Intimidation does not work well on some people, especially my mother. That's another one of life's valuable lessons. Do not threaten what you are not prepared to carry out.

During the weeks before Christmas 1928 I was looking at all of the advertisements in the newspaper to make up my Christmas list to send to Santa. When I came across an ad for a baby doll whose mouth was slightly open so she could seem to be sucking the pacifier that hung around her neck. I thought I could read fairly well by then so I said, "Oh look Mother, I want this new doll that sucks its apostrophe." The adults all had a big laugh at my expense and I was kidded about my gaffe for years afterwards.

That year Mother suggested that I go through my toy box and select some toys to give to the poor children. I had seen that the children around us had very few playthings, or even clothes or shoes. It was hard giving up some of my toys but finally we had a box full. I don't know who ever received them but I hope they enjoyed them.

We had a huge Christmas that year. Dad brought the largest tree he could find that would fit in the living room. As it was, he had to cut a good bit off of the bottom and some off of the top to be able to fit the spire on it. We had quite a few strings of lights. One string had glass Japanese lanterns with a little silk tassel hanging from each of them. One string had silk lampshades over the bulbs. We had a huge collection of ornaments. Some had belonged to Grandma. I was allowed to put ornaments around the bottom where I could reach. Dad had bought paper cornucopias. They came flat so we had to fold them into shape. Then he filled them with candies. When all of the ornaments were on the tree, Dad strung the bead garlands and the tinsel garlands. Grandma asked him to clip on the small candle holders that used to light the trees before electricity. Into each holder a little twisted candle was set. The candles weren't much bigger than the birthday candles we now use on our birthday cakes. They weren't lit but they added a nostalgic note to the decorations.

On Christmas morning the first thing to do was to dump out the stocking that hung on the mantelpiece in my room. As usual there was a peppermint stick, other wrapped candies, apple, orange, nuts and a dime in the toe. Next we went to the tree to see what Santa had left. Well, he had outdone himself! The toys spilled out from under the tree into the middle of the room. There was an electric stove, aluminum pots and pans, a small desk and chair, books, new crayons, a big doll dressed in a snow costume. The baby doll that sucked its 'apostrophe' was sitting in a high chair. There were other things but those were the most memorable. The neighborhood children had never seen a lighted Christmas tree before. Dad invited them in and gave each child a cornucopia of candy. The rest of the day is just a blur in my memory. I'm sure we ate a big dinner, visited with friends and relatives etc. as usual.

Whenever I heard keys rattle, I asked if I could go no matter where. Often, it meant going to Raceland. I certainly never wanted to miss out on a trip there. I enjoyed the ride because almost every farm had a pond in front of the house where the cattle drank and on every pond and the bayou the surface was covered with beautiful lavender water hyacinth. Every time we went To Aunt Helena's house I would try to stay for a visit or get one of the girls, preferably Deda, to come home for a visit with me. Deda and I spent as much of our time together as possible and had a lot of adventures.

Since there was no kindergarten in Lockport I had to wait until September 1928 to start school when I was almost six years old. Mother had talked Aunt Helena into letting Soledad come to Lockport to live with us and go to school. She was entering second grade that year. That summer we spent a lot of time getting clothes made, choosing lunch boxes and getting book bags ready with pencils, tablets, library paste; all the paraphernalia. needed for the coming year. Deda and

I had several outfits made alike. The one I remember particularly was the one with the navy-blue serge box-pleated skirt with the pongee blouse. (pongee is a creamy colored cloth woven from raw undyed silk). The blouse had four big pearl buttons at the waist, two in front and two at the back. The skirt was buttoned onto the blouse. That's how we kept the skirt from falling around our ankles. Otherwise we would have had to have straps over our shoulders to hold it up because at six and seven years old we didn't yet have a waist., Since we dressed alike so often, both had straight hair cut in the same style and freckles the other children thought we were twins. We had fun with that. When they asked Deda if we were twins, she said, "Yes, except that her teeth are missing at the top and mine are missing at the bottom."

    I was so anxious to experience real school, as opposed to kindergarten, that it seemed to me that September took forever to come. When the big day arrived, we dressed carefully, ate breakfast as fast as possible, took our school bags and lunch boxes and left for school. Country schools did not have cafeterias so everyone had to carry their lunch, even the teachers. The school faced the bayou and was about eight or ten blocks from our house. Deda, being older, was in the lead. It seemed to me we walked and walked and still didn't arrive. Finally, there it was! We made it. First-graders were told to line up at a certain line in the sidewalk. There was a girl at the line already. She was bigger than the rest of us. She put me in front of her so I could be first. It turned out that she had failed first grade and was somewhat retarded but somehow she took a liking to me and always let me be first in line until the teacher saw what was happening and made us all take turns being first. The first-grade teacher came and led us to the first-grade cloak room. As we passed through, we put our lunches on the shelf and went on into the class room. We always entered through the cloak room. If it had been raining, we hung our raincoats on the hook and placed our galoshes under it. In winter our coat and muffler went on the hook, hats, gloves and lunches went on the shelf. That first day we took desks as we filed in. The teacher went to her desk and introduced herself as Miss Reed. We told her good morning. She taught us the 'Pledge of Allegiance' to the United States. After that we sat down at our desks and sang songs the teacher taught us. Miss Reed is the one who taught me the song I sang to my children to get them up in the morning:

                    Good morning to you
                    Good morning to you
                    We're all in our places
                    With sunshiny faces
              This is the way to start a new day.

    The first day in school Miss Reed passed out primers. She passed them out by rows. Since I was in the second seat in the second row I received mine early. While she passed them out to the rest of the class, I opened mine to the first page. There was a picture of a lady wearing an apron standing in a kitchen. Underneath the picture was the phrase "This is the" *(words I already knew)* "mother." Which I guessed from the picture and besides it started with the 'm' sound. On the next page there was a picture of a man in a business suit reading a newspaper so I read, "This is the father." Once I understood the pattern it was a cinch to figure out the words in the rest of the book so I read page after page until I finished the whole thing before she was finished passing out the books.

She then went to the blackboard and wrote a cursive capital 'A.' We had to get out our tablets and pencils and write a whole page of capital A's. When that was done, she showed us how to write small 'a's and we wrote a whole page of them. Since I loved to draw and had been drawing for years, cursive writing was easy. Every few days we learned a new letter.

That first day she asked if anyone knew a story they could tell the class. I raised my hand. She asked me to stand in front of the class. (I guess that shows the 'ham' in me coming out at a very early age). I could have told any of the standards like *The Three Little Pigs* or *Little Red Riding Hood* but I chose the story about the little old lady who couldn't get her pig to go over the stile. It is essential to keep that story straight in its progression or the whole point of the story is ruined. I was proud of myself when I did it right. When you succeed at an endeavor it is rewarding so I loved school from the first day.

Deda and I tried to find a short cut to school so one day we decided to take a diagonal path across a big empty looking field. It wasn't empty. A big bull lived there and he objected to our use of his space. So, back we went to the long way to school.

The lovely arrangement of having Deda live with us lasted through the first months of school until I came down with pneumonia. I was so sick I felt as though I would die. It was so hard to keep breathing it seemed it would have been easier to just give up. Dad would read to me but I couldn't keep the thread of the story, yet it was comforting to hear his voice and to have him sit there nearby.

My mother and grandmother took good care of me. They spoon fed me. They put warm flannel cloths on my chest. They also put wet mustard plasters on my chest. I had to tell them when it started to prickle because that was the signal to take it off before the plaster burned the skin. I remember the smell of the tincture of Benzoin in the humidifier to help me breathe.

I was sick for six weeks so I was not surprised when Mother told me Deda was going home. It certainly wasn't fun for her with me so ill. I hated to see her go because I knew she would never come back to stay.

One night when I was getting better, I was sitting up in bed eating my supper while the family was in the dining room. I noticed the fire was dying down so I got up to poke the fire up a bit and was astonished to find my legs were rubbery and the bottoms of my feet felt as though pins were sticking in them. I was glad to get back in bed. I was able to get up a little more each day until I finally got my strength back. By then it was time for the Christmas holidays. I had missed the Christmas party at school but the teacher sent me my gift.

When school started again in January, I was well enough to return but was soon sick again. In my weakened condition I had caught the measles. Grandma Darcey heard I had measles so she came to Lockport and brought a roll of the paper they made in Braithwaite. She used it to cover up all my windows leaving me in twilight darkness. That was to save my eyesight. Sometimes measles left a person with impaired vision. The lowered light must have worked because I didn't have to start wearing glasses until I was forty-seven years old.

It was a good thing I had started learning to read before I started school. I missed so much by being sick. But I made it. I caught up and passed to second grade.

By then I was an old hand at going to school. In second grade I had Miss Toups for my teacher. She was the daughter of the baker who lived down the street and had his bakery shop right behind his house. We could smell the fresh bread as it was baking. Grandma would send me to the bakery to buy a loaf of French bread just out of the oven. She would cut off the 'nose,' scoop out the soft inside, butter it all around inside then pour in some syrup. It made a nice but somewhat messy treat.

Mother had a tubercular spot on her lungs so the doctor made her stay in bed for several months. We had to hire someone to help. Dad hired a Miss Adams, a white lady, to do the cooking. We had always had a servant to do the washing and ironing so now we had two servants. Miss Adams came early in the morning to cook breakfast so she made the coffee and brought everyone coffee in bed. Even I got my café au lait or really, my lait au café, in bed. I enjoyed that. Just like I was a grown-up. However, it is Lena I remember best. Patient Lena. While she was ironing, I would sit on the floor nearby and ask question after question. She answered the ones she could but when we came to one she couldn't answer she would say, "I doan know, honey chile, it jes bees dat way." Those words became bywords in the family when we come up against a question we can't answer.

During the summer of 1929 Mother and I went to visit Uncle Pete, her brother, who had just remarried and was living in Port Isabel, Texas. He had married Felicity Valdez of Brownsville, Texas. We went by train, probably on the Southern Pacific line and it was a long trip. We left New Orleans late in the day. We were in a Pullman car since we had to travel several days and we had to have a place to sleep. There was no bridge across the Mississippi River then. It had never occurred to me to wonder how we would cross. When I realized what was happening, I stood at the window and watched. I could see we were crossing on a barge probably at Kenner. The cars were shunted onto rails on the floor of the barge. The engine remained on the east bank. When we landed on the west bank an engine on that side reassembled the train and took us to Texas. We ate dinner in the dining car and later had the porter make up our bed. Mother and I shared the lower bunk. There was no one in the upper bunk. Somehow, we passed the weary days either looking out of the window or reading books and magazines. I think it took three days to get to Brownsville where Uncle Pete met us and took us to Port Isabel. He was living in an apartment on what had been an Army post from World War 1.

Port Isabel was not much to look at. I remember sand, heat and the Gulf of Mexico right outside the window. Oh, and my first experience with red ants. I stepped into a nest of them when I went exploring outside. There were no screens on the windows or doors so we had to sleep under mosquito bars that were tucked under the mattress to anchor them at night. If you rolled up against the mosquito bar the mosquitos could bite you anyway so while you were asleep you had to be mindful to stay away from the edges.

Both my mother and I liked Uncle Pete's wife. I was soon comfortable calling her Aunt Felie. She had heard from Uncle Pete that I liked tamales so she made some for me. They were delicious. That was the only time in my life that I ever had homemade tamales.

Some of Aunt Felie's relatives lived in an apartment in the same building and they had children. We played together even though we couldn't speak each other's language. By the time we left I began to learn a little Spanish and they began to learn a little English.

Aunt Felie took us swimming at Padre Island, a barrier island off of the coast near Port Isabel. The only way to get there then was by boat. It must have been a regular passenger run between the mainland and the island because the motor launch we rode in had woven straw seats just like the seats in the streetcars at home. On the island there was a large white bath house where we changed into our bathing suits. I was staying on the beach playing in the sand because the waves knocked me down when I tried to go out in the water. Mother and Aunt Felie came to get me. They held my hands and when the big waves came, they lifted me up. I still got wet but I at least kept my face out of the water and I wasn't knocked off my feet and pummeled into the ground. They made it fun. They got tired of fighting the waves and so they joined me making sand castles until it was time to leave.

Uncle Pete was a good baseball player so he was coaching the local team. He wanted us to see where they played so he took us out to the field. It was hard packed sand. We were in his car so I asked him if he could run the bases in the car while we were in it. He drove right out on the field and did it.

Another outing he took us on was a visit to Aunt Felie's parents in Brownsville. I don't remember much about them except that they were very pleasant and welcoming. While we were there, we crossed the border into Mexico to visit Matamoros that is right across the border from Brownsville. Uncle Pete bought Mother some filigree earrings made of gold wire and seed pearls from one of the shops we passed. They were very pretty and suited her well. I spent a long time admiring a doll sized woven rattan porch set made up of a settee, a table and a chair. I really wanted it but no one took the hint and bought it for me. Shopping is hot business especially in the summer in Mexico so we went into a café where the adults ordered beer and I had a coke. Mother let me taste her beer. I found it strong and somewhat bitter. I said, rather too loud, "My Dad makes better beer than this." They laughed as they promptly shushed me. After we left the café we passed an outdoor meat stand. I watched a while and noticed that the seller had to shoo the flies off of the meat to discover the cut of meat ordered by his customer. I was glad I didn't have to eat any of it.

On the way home we found that it had rained while we were gone. The roads were all just smoothed sand so when they were saturated with water they became very treacherous. We were slipping and sliding. There was a deep ditch on the side of the road. When we came near it, I saw that a bus had fallen in but we couldn't even see the top of it until we slid in that direction. Uncle Pete was laughing at my screeches as we slipped and slid home.

We stayed in Texas about two weeks before it was time to go home. The trip back was so uneventful I don't have any memory of it.

Sometime after we arrived home, I received a package. In it was the rattan porch set I had so admired in Matamoros.

One time when I was out with Dad in Lockport, he went into a store to buy a pack of cigarettes. Behind the counter there was a beautiful big doll. It seemed odd to me that there should be a doll in this place. After all, it was not a toy store. Dad told me it was a prize for a punch board. Then I wanted to know what a punchboard was. He showed me. It was made up of several layers of thick paper stuck together. There were rows and rows of holes pierced through the layers with numbered pieces of paper folded into each hole. You had to pay the shop person, a nickel in this instance, to let you use a small key (actually a straight piece of wire with a handle) to push through the punch board. When you unfolded the paper that fell out there was a number printed on it. If you were lucky enough to get the right number you won the doll. Dad gave me a nickel to pay the man so I took the key and pushed out a number but it was not the right one so no doll. I thus learned early in life that gambling was a good way to waste money.

When I went with Mother to the local doctor I met Dr. Gough (pronounced go). His office was in his drugstore. He had a good thing going. He prescribed the medicine and then filled the prescription. Dr. Gough always gave me a quarter when I went with Mother. I promptly spent it in his drugstore to buy candy or ice-cream or I put money in the big music machine. It was as big as a chest of drawers. The spindle on which the record turned was parallel to the floor. The record was made of steel and was about three feet or more wide with holes in it that caused the music. What made the music was a mystery to me. I never tired of playing *Springtime in the Rockies* and watching the machine operate.

I have always been interested in music. Hearing certain pieces can take me back to some time or event so strongly that I feel that I am back there again. There was a piece of music used as mood music in the theater when they showed silent pictures that I loved very much. I learned the name of it years later. It was "Serenade" by Toscelli. Whenever I hear it, I am transported back to that time and place. The piece "To A Waterlily" by McDowell always brings back the sight of water hyacinth floating in every pond and stream when I was young. I think the plant had been brought here either from China or Japan. They clogged the bayous and made it hard for boats to get through. They were considered a nuisance until LSU found a way to eradicate them. Just about that same time someone found a use for them but by then they were gone.

Dad was doing a lot of electrical wiring of houses up and down the bayou. Everyone wanted to be hooked up. He would go in with his crew and wire a house installing drop-lights with just a bare bulb in the center of each room. It was not pretty but it was better light than they ever had before and a lot safer to use than the kerosene lamps it replaced.

One fisherman asked Dad if he could put electricity on a boat. Dad said he could so they made arrangements to meet at the boat dock. The man's boat was named "Eleven Sons." Dad asked him if he had eleven sons. The man said, "Yes, and I have eleven daughters too." The fisherman was so pleased with having electricity aboard his boat that every Friday after that there was either a sack of select oysters or a huge redfish on the dock for Dad to take home. The oysters were always large and salty. Dad would take the sack to Raceland where he and Uncle Emile opened them eating a few raw ones while they worked. I never learned to eat oysters raw. Dad would then fry the oysters and put them in the middle of the dining room table piled high in Aunt Helena's big turkey platter. All of us would sit around eating those delicious fried oysters until they were all gone.

One day when I came home from school, I could tell by the way Grandma and Mother looked that something was wrong. I soon found out that Bob had died of old age during the day while I was in school. I cried a lot because I really loved Bob and knew I would miss him. I realized it was the way of things and I accepted it. Dad and some of his crew were digging a grave under the privet hedge to bury our dear dog friend. When I drove by there recently, I saw that the privet hedge was gone. I wonder if Bob's skeleton is still there ninety years later?

Dad and Mother liked to go target shooting with a twenty-two-caliber rifle. Dad saved burnt out light globes until he had a boxful. He would toss them into the water one by one and they would take turns shooting at them. When they ran out of globes they would shoot at snakes if they saw any.

One time Dad turned over an old washtub in our backyard and leaned it against the fence. I was astounded when he then offered me the rifle to try out. I was only six years old! He showed me how to hold the gun and how to aim it. He let me shoot several times. I was apprehensive but willing to try. He told me the idea was to aim at the center circle that was about one to one and a half inches wide. Well, that may have been the idea but I certainly didn't shoot any bull's eyes that day. I considered myself lucky to have hit the tub! Actually, I hit about halfway from the edge to the center which I considered was quite good for a first time try. Since I have grown up, I have been a good shot as long as the target is inanimate. I cannot make myself shoot live animals.

Life for us seemed idyllic and I expected it to go on that way. It was quite a shock when on the 29th of October 1929 the Stock Market crashed and the banks closed. Very few people had any cash on hand and as long as the banks stayed closed, they couldn't get any. Construction jobs were the first to go because no one could start a project with no money. Dad had a hard time collecting for jobs he had already completed so he couldn't pay for supplies he had already bought and used. There was less and less work available. So began the long dreary years of the Great Depression.

We managed to hang on for a while. I don't know how. The Christmas of 1929 was vastly different from the one in 1928. We had a small tree on the table beside my bed, thanks, I think, to Mr. Lundsgaard. Mother had saved Luzianne coffee coupons that she exchanged for a Lucy Anne doll for me. The doll had a dollar bill fastened to her arm with a rubber band, Thanks also to Mr. Lundsgaard. I understood that my parents and Mr. Lundsgaard were trying hard to make Christmas as merry as possible so I never said a word that would have made them feel worse than they did.

Finally, we could hold on no longer. Since we had little money coming in we had to give up the furniture. All we had left was the radio phonograph. Grandma had to go back to New Orleans to live with Aunt Carrie. We couldn't pay the rent in Lockport so the Presbyterian minister, Reverend E. A. Ford of Thibodaux, made arrangements for us to stay in the back part of the house they were using for a church in Raceland. The house had double parlors. The church used the front parlor and we slept in the second parlor and had use of the kitchen to cook our meals. We often ate at Aunt Helena's house. At least we had a roof over our heads.

## *So Began Our Many Years of Wandering*

For me, being in Raceland was no hardship. It was great. I could visit my cousins every day. We had moved from Lockport during the Christmas holiday. I still had some holidays left before school started again. Finally, I got tired of walking the half-mile from where we lived to my cousin's house so I opted to just stay at Aunt Helena's house. The adults agreed that it was a good idea. I would stay at the Hidalgo home and go to school in Raceland while my parents went to New Orleans to try to find work.

I was still in second grade. I don't remember much about my time in the school in Raceland since it lasted only about six weeks. My parents took me to the city to live with them at 526 North Olympia Street, another double house. It was in the middle of the block between Toulouse Street and the railroad tracks and was very noisy. Dad said that he thought that the trains held a convention in the middle of every night on purpose just to annoy us. He always made jokes to try to make bad things easier to bear. The closest school to us was John Dibert so that was three schools I attended in second grade.

There was a grocery store across Toulouse on the corner of N. Olympia that made and sold for a penny a treat they called an iceberg. It was made from water flavored with snowball syrup and was frozen into a three-inch square ice cube served on a small square paper plate. I was allowed to buy one when I ran an errand to the store about three times a week. My favorite flavor has always been grape.

While we were living there, I played with all of the kids in the neighborhood. One boy who lived in the block behind the store had a two-wheel sidewalk bike. He came over in our block and played with us and taught all of us to ride who didn't already know, how to ride a two-wheel bike. For all who don't know, a sidewalk two-wheeler has wheels a bit smaller than the front wheel on a tricycle and it is against the law to ride them in the street. I don't remember the boy's name but I do remember that caramel colored bike with yellow stripes on the frame and fenders. It also had coaster brakes; a feature usually found only on street bikes. I fell in love with it. I wanted one so much I broke my rule of not asking for the impossible and begged my parents for one.

About this time when the doctor examined me, he found that I was anemic. Since I had to have special things to eat it was hard for my parents to provide them. Also, since they both had to work there was no one at home to take care of me so I was sent to Braithwaite to live with my grandparents. Aunt Bea was living there with her two boys so she could do most of the work of taking care of me. I went to the rest of second grade in Braithwaite. That was four schools I had attended since the beginning of second grade in September and all in the first semester. All of this being shifted around from school to school meant that I was always the 'new kid' having to make new friends and trying to fit in. It undermined my confidence and I became socially unsure of myself. I always kept my grades up. I wouldn't dare come home with a bad report and shame my parents and myself. I knew the teachers liked me, even when I was not so sure of my acceptance by the children. In Braithwaite my teacher would leave me in charge of the class if she had to leave the room for some reason. She would tell me to write the name on the board of anyone who misbehaved while she was gone. What a spot to put a kid in! I think the kids realized the situation and no one misbehaved. I had to write the name of the one boy who talked but when I heard her coming down the hall, I erased it and told the teacher that everyone had been very good. She was pleased, the kids were pleased and I was off the hook.

Some of my most vivid memories of Braithwaite at that time were smells. Since the paper mill had moved its operations to Tuscaloosa and had taken its stink with it other scents had a chance to come to the fore. One was the sweet smell of the honeysuckle vine Grandma had growing over the front porch. We learned to sit very quietly on the swing when the ruby throated hummingbirds came to sip nectar from the honeysuckle flowers so as not disturb them and so we could watch their incredible performance. Grandma still grew the wonderfully scented cabbage roses along the front walkway to the street. Another smell that came to the fore was the fresh cut wood smell of the bark that had fallen from the monorail that carried pulpwood from the ship in the river to the mill. It had accumulated over the years and was so thick that weeds couldn't grow where it had fallen. It made a nice smelling path I used every day to walk to and from school.

Not every memory was that idyllic. One thing the doctor insisted on was that every day I should have an egg boiled for only one minute. Now an egg boiled for only one minute is just a warm raw egg. I was supposed to drink it down right out of the shell. I hated it. It is worse than trying to eat a raw oyster. I hemmed and hawed every time I was faced with that odious task before I could be persuaded or could persuade myself to go ahead and get it over with. Poor Aunt Bea. She was not known for her patience. I must have caused her a lot of trouble. Once in a while she beat the egg into a glass of milk with vanilla and sugar. That was good and much easier to swallow. I don't remember giving them any trouble about any other foods I had to eat so long as it wasn't liver. No one in my whole family ever ate liver anyway so it was never a problem. Unfortunately, science found out too late to do me any good that the protein in eggs is more digestible when it is thoroughly cooked. Too bad they didn't find that out in time to save me all of that struggle.

With Alfredo and Carlos at Grandma's I at least had some children to associate with. Carlos was walking and trying to talk. I loved it when I came home from school that Carlos was standing at the door excited to see me and calling out, "Packalie, Packalie!" That was the best he could do with my name. He was such a sweet baby. Those two boys are the closest I ever came to having siblings because we lived together many different times over the years.

In the evening Grandpa Darcey went to bed early because he had to get up during the night to go check the property where the mill had been and punch a time clock to prove he had been there. The time between supper and bedtime was known as quiet time. All games that might generate noise were forbidden. Grandma, Aunt Bea, the boys and I went to sit on the front screened porch while Grandpa slept in the back bedroom. Grandma sat on the swing with one leg across the seat of the swing and one foot on the floor to control the motion. Carlos sat behind her leg to keep him from falling. He was soon asleep. Aunt Bea sat in a rocking chair. Alfredo and I sat on the floor. Grandma and Aunt Bea would talk in low voices or Grandma would tell us about when she was young. I enjoyed these quiet evenings. We could hear the frogs and the crickets, the boats in the river, even the bobcats in the woods. It was comforting to know that you were safe on a screened porch with adults to protect you even from bobcats.

One-night Grandpa met some bootleggers crossing the mill property. When they saw him, they asked him if they could pay him to let them take the short cut across the property regularly. Grandpa, who was not in sympathy with the prohibition law, said, "I don't want your money. You can cross. Just don't let me see you or I will have to report you to the sheriff." He never saw them again but I'm sure that the bootleggers always used the short cut but took care to remain out of sight.

Aunt Bea took good care of me while my grandparents provided the security I needed. Aunt Bea saw to it that I ate what I should. She kept my clothes and me clean and made me rest in the afternoon when I was not in school. I very well remember the vigor with which she attacked any speck of dirt that tried to hide in my ears. In the late afternoon she would sit on the floor of the front porch with Alfredo under one arm and me under the other and read us stories. The attention we were getting was as important to us as were the stories and pictures. My parents came to visit as often as they could. I think my mother was doing home nursing to earn some money and Dad was driving a taxi for the Bell Cab Company.

After school closed for the summer, my parents took me to New Orleans where they were living at 2826 LePage Street. We were finally together again. Mother was home during the day while Dad was working. She worked at night so things worked out. I met the children in the neighborhood so when school started, I had someone to play with at recess and someone to eat lunch with. We did a lot of roller skating that summer. In the fall of 1931, I started third grade at McDonough 28. The school is on Esplanade Avenue and was about a half block from our front door. The school had a cafeteria and lunch was only ten cents. It was usually pretty good. Dad would come home in the evening and would tell us funny stories about his cab customers. I was enjoying life.

Finances were thin but we had enough to eat and a roof over our heads and we were together.

All I remember about Christmas 1931 was that I received a side-walk bike at last. It was green with a white stripe on the frame, no fenders, no brakes but it was as fine as a golden chariot to me. I loved it. Now I was the big hearted friend who taught others to ride a two wheeler. We incorporated the bike into our perambulations with our skates and had a great time. The year had been a more settled one for me but it had been hard on my parents because they needed better jobs but they had to work it out that one worked in the day and the other worked at night so someone would be home for me at all times.

Around late February or early March of 1932 Reverend and Mrs. Ford suggested to my parents that I should be sent to boarding school for my own sake as well as theirs. They offered to sponsor me at the Presbyterian boarding school, French Camp Academy. It is in north Mississippi near Kosciusko. They were already sponsoring Dorothy Hidalgo, my cousin, and sending their own son, Nathan Ford to that school. Dorothy and Nathan were both in high school. I think that Mrs. Ford thought that my mother babied me too much and that was why I was sick so much. They thought that the piney woods, the stability of the school routine and, I'm sure, the discipline was just what I needed. It sounded like an adventure from a book to me and I was all for it, especially since I had to have a whole new wardrobe. My only regret was having to leave my new bike behind but I did take my skates.

Mrs. Ford was from New York and had received an inheritance from one of her relatives. She and Mr. Ford used some of the money to buy property in Thibodaux for themselves but they used a lot of it to do missionary work up and down the bayou. In one instance they bought a cow and gave it to a family that had a new baby and several other children who needed milk and would not have had any otherwise. They always carried cases of evaporated milk on the back seat of the car in the event that they heard of a family with a baby who needed formula. They also carried various sorts of canned goods in the trunk. The people on the bayous of Louisiana are mostly Catholic but they never asked people their religion. They just helped wherever they could. Rev. Ford decided that he and Mrs. Ford would drive us up to the school. Aunt Helena came along so she would have a chance to visit with Dorothy. We started out very early in the morning. Once we left the city, we were traveling on two lane gravel roads. I had never even so much as seen a hill before so I was anxious to see one. When I pictured one in my mind, I thought it was pointed at the top like a pyramid and I wondered how a car could go over the top without getting hooked up on the point. I soon learned what a hill looked like. We spent the whole day going over, around and between them. We had a lot of thrills because Mr. Ford was not a good driver. The only reason he survived his own driving was because God watched over him closely and kept him from harm. No road anywhere was wider than two lanes but no bridge in Mississippi was wider than one lane. We would go around a curve then downhill with one of those skinny bridges at the bottom. There would be another car coming down to the bridge from the other lane. Mr. Ford never slowed down. It was up to the other driver to give way. We were all holding our breath waiting for the worst. I whispered to Aunt Helena that it might be a good idea if she shared with Mother and me some of the new nerve medicine her doctor had just prescribed for her. She and Mother burst out laughing. Mrs. Ford wanted to know what was so funny. They couldn't possibly tell her. I don't remember how they got out of that one.

We made a break in the trip by stopping in Canton, Mississippi to visit some of Uncle Emiles' relatives. The two things I remember about that visit was that one of their boys gave me a ride sitting on the crossbar of a big two-wheel bike and the other was that the family owned a player piano. It was the first one I had ever seen. After watching it operate for a while, they let me sit on the piano bench to make believe I was playing the piano.

We arrived in French Camp in time for the evening meal that was served about six o'clock. The dining room was on the ground floor of the girl's dormitory. Since we were guests we sat at the main table with Dean Stewart's family. After dinner I was put in Dorothy's charge. There was no Little Girl's Dormitory because I was the first little girl who ever was admitted as a boarding student. An extra cot was placed in Dot's room. Mother came up and unpacked my suitcase arranging my clothes in the space in the dresser that was assigned to me. She helped me get ready for bed. I was so tired from the trip I went right off to sleep. I felt as though the bed was going up and down the same hills we had been traveling all day.

Mother, Aunt Helena and the Fords left the next morning. After breakfast I was escorted to the grammar school and introduced to the third and fourth grade classes who shared the same teacher and the same room. The class made me welcome and the teacher asked Annie Lou Downing to see that I learned where everything was. I was so pleased by the teacher's choice. Annie Lou was a pretty child with big brown eyes, long sausage curls and a sweet smile. We became best friends.

In the big schoolroom the teacher's desk was in the front of the room. In front of her desk was a large pew facing her desk. The way the teacher handled two classes was she called a class to come up front and sit in the pew. They were to be reading their lesson and reciting out loud while the other class was given a writing assignment. When they were finished they were given a writing assignment while the other class was reciting their lesson. Sometimes I could pick up on some of the fourth grade work but not often.

The grammar school was on the side of the hill next to the Big Boy's Dorm.

There was a little boy's dormitory in a cottage right next to the girl's dorm. There were about eight to ten grammar school students in it. The rest of the grammar school student body came from the town of French Camp and the surrounding farms. Some children came to school on a rickety old school bus and others came in a couple of covered wagons pulled by mules. The students had to bring their lunches because there was no cafeteria. All of the boarding students, both boys and girls, ate their lunch in the dining room in the girl's dorm.

To get more playing time Annie Lou would share her lunch with me so I wouldn't have to go to the dining room. Her mother packed biscuit and sausage sandwiches with a fried pie for dessert. We would rearrange the wood stack to make seats for ourselves to sit in while we ate. When her mother found out that we were sharing Annie Lou's lunch she started sending enough for both of us. The fried pies were made with a big round crust as big as the frying pan. On one side Mrs. Downing would put the filling then fold over the half crust and crimp the edges. She used whatever fruit was in season or if there was no fruit she made sugar pies as a filling. That lunch was much better than the one in the dining room.

I didn't pay much attention to the décor(?) in the dorm at first, but, looking back, I realize it was stark. The room was large with a clothes closet, an alcove with a washstand, enameled washbasin, pitcher, soap dish and toothbrush holder plus a chamber pot. There was a dresser with a mirror, a chair and link-spring cots with cotton mattresses. All the furniture was painted apple-green. That color has lived on in my mind as *institution green* because I have been in so many institutions that seem to favor that color. The ceiling was made of embossed tin painted a cream color as were the walls. Each room had two large windows with window shades but no curtains. There were no locks on the doors. We were on the honor system and it worked. We would never think of entering anyone's room unless we were invited in and they were present. Mostly we did our socializing in the parlor on the second floor or outside. The parlor was a large room with wicker chairs and a settee around a pot-bellied wood stove. There was an upright piano against one wall. Otherwise there were no decorations, not even a picture.

I was proud to be associated with Dorothy. She was pretty and very popular. Just being related to her made me feel special. I soon became a pet of the whole school and I did things no one else could get away with.

Most of the time the things I did that broke the rules were because I did not know what the rules were. On Saturday everyone who wanted to go to town had to line up on the sidewalk outside of the dorm. I thought it was going to be a big deal since I was a city child and going to town was quite an experience. I soon found out that downtown in French Camp was just over the hill and about three blocks away. The whole commercial part of town was on the Natchez Trace and consisted of a grocery, a drugstore, dry goods store, gas station and a café where they served the new (at least to me) hamburger sandwiches. There were about two churches and ten houses that made up the rest of the town. The school and its grounds made up at least half of the whole place. Once I found out where town was, I decided that I could go there by myself because it was no further to go than I had gone in the city to run errands. One day I went back to the café and ordered one of those delicious ten-cent hamburgers. I sat there enjoying it never realizing that I was breaking a rule.

When I returned to the campus, I found out that everyone was frantically looking for me. I was fussed at so much for going to town unchaperoned that I never did it again. I did go to play with some of the local children. That seemed to me to be all right because their mothers were home and they made good chaperones. Wrong again! I finally learned to ask permission to go to play with my friends from school who lived in town. The Dean of Women was good about letting me go as long as she knew where I was. I often asked my friends to come to visit me after school and sometimes they did come. Of course, none of the children who lived out in the surrounding country could come because they would have had no way to get home. When one of the local children did visit me, we played hop scotch or climbed around in the hayloft of the barn or just racketed around as children do. They were never allowed to come inside the dorm.

Another no no I enjoyed was jumping on a wagon when the big boys were going out to work on the school's farm. Many of the students worked for the school to help pay their tuition. I rode out to the farm with the boys who, on this particular day, were going out to pick green beans. I was happily helping them pick beans when somebody in authority came along and said I wasn't supposed to be there. I had to walk back to the campus, in trouble again.

That first stay at French Camp was all new and fun. The one child I could play with without going off campus was Billy McBride. He was the grandson of the housemother of the big boy's dorm up on the hill. He and his mother lived there with her. He was a cute little redheaded boy a year or so younger than I was. He and I tossed a football to each other and shagged balls for the tennis players. We also enjoyed jumping into the middle of dust devils when they came near. The second time I returned to French Camp Billy had a horse that he let me ride up and down in front of the Girl's Dorm and past the high school to the top of the hill as far as Dean Stewart's house. When I was on the horse, I felt I owned the world. What a joyous thing to get to ride. It must be wonderful to own a horse and be able to ride whenever you want to.

Grammar school ended two weeks before the high school did so I had to stay at French Camp until Dorothy was finished so we could go home together on the train.

Dad was waiting for me at the station. He took me home to another new place, 137 Sherwood Forest Drive. That was a great summer except for the time I suffered with chicken pox. I had it so bad that there was not a pinhead of space on my skin that was not covered with sores. I was so miserable mother took me on her lap while in a rocking chair to try to comfort me. I was so big by then that more of me was hanging off of her than was sitting on her. It was pretty ridiculous but it was sweet of her to try. Once I got past all of that I had a great time. There were mostly boys in the neighborhood. There was one girl next door named Sheila and she was younger than I was. There was a fellow across the street named Snooky who had a big two-wheel bike and Forrest Villarubia who had a beautiful green race style pedal car he let me ride in on rare occasions. Snooky became my boyfriend. He took me for rides on his bike around the neighborhood and on the rare occasions when he had some money, he bought me ice cream cones. Sheila and I played with paper dolls and her Patsy doll complete with a trunk full of clothes. The doll also had roller skates that clipped to her shoes. I loved that doll and wished I had one. I liked Sheila even though she was younger and a Christian Scientist. Strange. Sheila and I played together either on her porch or mine but she never was allowed to play with the boys. We all had a high old-time skating, playing ball games in the street, spinning tops or waiting for the iceman to come so we could beg a chunk of ice.

But all good things come to an end and soon it was time to go back to French Camp. I don't remember the trip at all. I suppose it was because Dorothy was in charge so I just did whatever she told me to do. The rickety school bus was waiting at the station for us in Kosciusko and soon we were back in French Camp.

I was surprised to find that I would no longer room with Dorothy. Another female grammar school boarding student had been admitted to the school so we were to be roommates. Her name was Gwendolyn Brock. She was so blonde I could almost see through her. Unfortunately, she was the quintessential female. She certainly was not a tomboy like me. We got along ok but I found her rather a drag. She thought she was super special because her mother had a civil service job with the state of Mississippi. I had arrived in the room before she did so I took the top drawer of the dresser for my folding clothes. One day when I came back to the room, she was removing all of my stuff and taking over the top drawer. I don't think she was expecting me. She looked up startled and said, "I didn't think you would mind." Well, I did mind. I didn't say a word. I just pulled the drawer out of the dresser, walked to her bed and dumped her stuff on it and returned the drawer to the dresser. I put all my stuff back in the drawer. Not mind? If she really thought that why did she try to switch without even asking me? I think once she found out who she was dealing with—not a wimp for sure—we got along much better than we would have otherwise. I'm sure she was the kind who if she once found she could take advantage of you, she would have kept on doing it. However, we never became good buddies. Whenever I talk about *we* in this story Gwendolyn is not included. I played with some of the local children and some of the boys from the little boy's dorm. I couldn't totally ignore the person I had to share a room with but I avoided her as much as possible. One of the few things we did do together was to buy crackers, cheese, cookies—things like that when we went to town then at night after bed check and lights out we would sit in our beds with the covers over our heads and a flashlight to see what we were doing and have a picnic or read a book. Since the halls were not carpeted and since there was an open transom above the door we could hear if anyone was coming in time to slip under the covers and look innocently asleep. We never did get caught at it.

Another girl moved in with us later on. Her name was Lavinia Oswald. She is the one who told us where babies come from. It had never crossed my mind to wonder about that subject and I could have lived a few more years in innocence. I suppose since she had this juicy bit of information, she just had to pass it on. She was ok I suppose. We all managed to get along.

Now that I was in fourth grade, I was on the right hand side of the double schoolroom. Annie Lou Downing was glad to see me and so was Eunice Branning. I was glad to see them, too. But I was disappointed to see that Annie Lou had cut off her long curls that I had admired so much. I liked both of them better than either of my roommates. School was easy, lunch was fun. Who could ask for more?

The classrooms were heated with wood stoves. It was the responsibility of the boys to keep the wood box filled and the stove stoked. They also had to clean out the ashes and build the fire in the morning. The girls cleaned the blackboard at the end of the school day, clapped the chalk dust out of the erasers, emptied the shavings from the pencil sharpener and swept the floor at the end of the day. There was no janitor.

After school I was free to play until dinner. After dinner we had to go to the auditorium in the high school building next door to the girl's dorm to attend study hall. Grammar school students attended for one hour and high school students for two. Every other seat in the auditorium had a fold down desk on the right arm.

We had to pick a seat with a fold down desk and distribute ourselves so we were isolated and unable to communicate with each other. If we didn't do it right the teacher-keeper of study hall would come along and redistribute us. Teachers took turns keeping study hall. If we needed help with our home work, we had to raise our hand and the teacher would come over to help. Sometimes students would write notes to each other especially those in love. They would fold them in four lengthwise. Then in half then over and over each other until they had a triangle. They then tucked the last piece into itself. The idea was to wait until the teacher's attention was elsewhere so they could sail it to the intended receiver. Sometimes they succeeded but often the teacher caught the movement out of the corner of his eye and intercepted it. Then the note would be opened and read out loud in front of everybody to the utter dismay of the note writer and the addressee.

One night I was leaving study hall by myself. As I came out of the door a boy jumped out from behind the hedge and kissed me. It was Billy Rogers, one of the boys from the little boy's dorm. I was so surprised and so thrilled I ran to my room, flung myself on my cot and went over and over the experience in my mind. My delight was unbounded. What a boost to the ego it is to be picked out as special by a member of the opposite sex!

Billy started buying me things with his allowance. He would meet me on the school yard and give me a candy bar or a new pencil. It must have been love. He was a grade ahead of me in school so he was *an older man!* When any sort of traveling show came to the school, he bought tickets and escorted me to these events where we were allowed to sit together and hold hands. On Sunday nights our meal was sandwiches in a paper bag. We took our bags outside to sit and eat them. After a while and for no apparent reason, we were out of love. I started eating my sandwiches and going to the shows with a boy named Alvin, a nice fellow, but Billy Rogers was the first love of my life.

Every evening in the parlor we had to attend a prayer meeting. When that was over it was time to get ready for bed. Then came 'lights out' and bed check. Bells regulated all of the day's activities. There was a bell to get up, a warning bell five minutes before breakfast, the breakfast bell. After breakfast we made our beds and cleaned up our room. There was even a bell to tell us when to go to empty the chamber pot. Then came the school bell, recess bell, lunch bell, end of lunch period bell and end of school day bell. In the evening there was a five-minute warning bell for supper, supper bell five minutes later. After supper the study hall bell and back around to lights out. On Saturday there were less bells ringing. Only bells for meals and the one for lining up to go to town. We had to go to church on Wednesday evening, chapel in the auditorium on Thursday morning, Sunday School at ten o'clock and church at eleven, vespers at seven Sunday evening so there were bells for each of those. When I first went to French Camp and Dorothy was there, I often fell asleep during vespers with my head in her lap.

The tight rules were somewhat relaxed at the Sunday night four-sandwiches-in-a-paper-bag suppers. We could eat outside in nice weather with anyone we chose, we could trade sandwiches if we wanted to. On nights when the weather was not nice, we stayed in the dining room and played parlor games or sang around the piano. That was the only time boys and girls were allowed to socialize except at the dinner table on regular nights.

The whole school from first grade through high school went to chapel on Thursday. We had a bit of preaching and prayer but the time was mostly given over to announcements and performances given each week by one class at a time in turn from high school seniors all the way down to first grade. I dearly loved being on stage so I volunteered every chance I could get. I even went on between acts of the high school performances. They would set me to reciting a poem (with gestures sometimes) in front of the closed curtains to give the players time to change the scenery. After all of that church and all of that stage experience I was torn between future careers as either a missionary or an actress.

At Thanksgiving that year, 1932, Eunice Branning's aunt invited me to spend the holiday at their home. Eunice lived on the Natchez Trace but her aunt lived three of four blocks from the school where town and country started to meld. The house was a typical 'dog-trot' style so popular in the south. There were porches front and back as wide as the house. One entered a large central hall that went straight through from porch to porch. There were two rooms on each side of the hall. One side had a formal parlor and the parent's bedroom. On the other side was the dining room and the kitchen. Upstairs there were four bedrooms, two on each side of the hall. There were no inside bathroom facilities. I was to sleep with the two sisters that I knew from school. What I found strange when we went to bed was that the mattress was stuffed with dried corn shucks. Every time we stirred during the night the mattress crackled. In winter the family lived mostly in the dining room and kitchen because it was warm there. There was absolutely no heat in the rest of the house.

The family was very welcoming, even the boys. The dinner was surely better than anything served in the school dining room. They used cornbread stuffing in the turkey while I was used to rice and oyster stuffing but I ate it and found it good. I especially enjoyed the beautiful and delicious pies. I was glad I had the chance to experience a home cooked meal with a family. They were different from the people I was familiar with but they were genuinely welcoming and pleasant.

In north Mississippi there are four definite seasons and late fall can be quite cold. Steam radiators heated the three-story dorm but the heat we received was dependent on the diligence of the student whose duty it was to keep the boiler stoked. Some of the boiler stokers were better than others. We did have a wood stove in the parlor where we went when the room got too cold. There were two bathtubs in the whole dorm; one on each floor, and four flush toilets, two on each floor and neither one was enclosed in a stall so there was no bathroom privacy. The boys were supposed to keep the boiler stoked but the tank size must have been inadequate to handle the kitchen and the bathrooms. I never heard of anyone having a hot bath the whole time I was there. Even a tepid bath was hard to come by. If the water was anywhere near bath temperature the girls went hollering the news in the halls so anyone who had been waiting for a bath could grab the opportunity to take one. I didn't much care whether I was clean or not so the lack of bathing facilities didn't matter much to me then.

We were expected to keep our rooms clean. No clothes could be left dragging and beds had to be made. On Saturday floors had to be swept and furniture dusted. Inspections were made every day and anyone falling short was given a demerit. Demerits were given for other shortcomings too. If we accumulated too many of them we were assigned extra work on Saturday and we were not allowed to go to town. At home my family may have been poor but we were very clean. Grandma Darcey's motto was, "Soap and water are cheap so there is no reason for any body to be dirty." She hadn't met a boiler stoker like ours. I kept up my end of the job of keeping our room clean and was fortunate enough to have neat roommates. Several times we won the prize for the week for consistently having the cleanest room.

That year we had a heavy snow. It was the very first snow I had ever seen. I was so excited I didn't know what to do first. In the evening when it first started to snow the older girls took a big dishpan from the kitchen and went out to gather the fresh snow. They added evaporated milk, sugar and vanilla to make snow cream. That was a nice treat but I could hardly wait until morning to get out in it.

The school bus and the wagons could not get through the snow so only the local children and boarders were present to go to school. There were so few of us that all of us were gathered in Miss Grave's second grade room. We were too excited to do much work. One boy opened a window, sat on the sill and reached up to break off an icicle from the eves. (I forgot to mention that the grammar school building was only one story tall.) Soon we all did it. Monkey see, monkey do, I guess. The icicle certainly had no taste yet there we all sat sucking on those tasteless icicles.

During the day the sun came out soon melting the icicles and the surface of the snow. During the night the melted snow froze leaving a glaze of ice everywhere. We could barely stay upright on the glazed ice much less try to climb the hill to school. School was closed so I asked permission to visit the Branning family where I had spent Thanksgiving. I was given permission to go. When I arrived, the children were gathered outside trying to figure out how we were going to take advantage of the hill behind their house to slide down since they had no sled. They had some folding chairs that might do. We put the folded chair down on the snow and sat on it. Someone gave the person on the folded chair a push to encourage it to move. All they succeeded in doing was to push the person off the chair into the snow. Nobody could think of anything that would work. Then Mrs. Branning came out with an old enameled dishpan. It was big enough for a child to sit in comfortably and slid on the snow very well. Yeah! We took turns and spent the whole day sliding down the hill. Of course, we couldn't control the direction and we often went round and round on our way down but that was all part of the fun. We wore ourselves out.

On Saturday the dean of women decided to take a group on a hike in the snow. Everyone who wanted to go gathered at the bottom of the steps on the outside of the dorm. We were hiking across a large pasture when we came to a small pond that was frozen solid. We each tried our luck at walking across but everyone who tried ended up falling down. We hiked a good way into the woods beyond the campus. At one point on the way back we had to jump the partially frozen creek. Unfortunately for me I missed the jump by a little bit and ended up in cold water up to my thigh. By the time we got back to the dorm my clothes were frozen. It took a long time sitting by the pot-bellied stove to thaw me out. I surprised myself by not even catching a cold from such a cold wet experience. French Camp must have been good for my health

When I went home for Christmas 1932, I found we were living in Thibodaux in the garage apartment on the Ford's property. Dad was building chicken houses and running a hatchery that the Fords had established to give Albert a job and let him learn something about building and chicken husbandry from Dad. One year when he was a teenager Dad had worked for his uncle in Georgia who raised prize chickens for showing. That is a bit different from raising chickens for profit but care and raising of chickens is the same whether for show or for profit. You have to get them to live and be healthy.

Aunt Bea, Alfredo and Carlos spent Christmas with us. Aunt Bea's husband had died in a sanitarium in Costa Rica and she had received some insurance money so she had a bit to spend on presents that year. I received a new pair of roller skates and Alfredo received a fine big red wagon. We ate breakfast, dressed and were about to go outside to test our new wheels when it started raining. It rained the whole miserable day. The next day dawned bright and sunny so we finally had a chance to enjoy our gifts.

Back at French Camp after the holidays life fell back into the old groove. As soon as the weather was warm enough, we were back to playing in the hayloft, climbing the sycamore trees in the pig yard and swimming in the creek that ran beyond the pasture behind the school, the same creek I had fallen into on the hike in the snow last winter. There was a low spot in the creek floor where the water was a bit deeper than the rest of it. We built a dam to make it even deeper so we could swim a few strokes.

There was a shelter for the pigs under the sycamore tree that had a lean-to roof. It was perfect for us. We could easily get on the lowest part of the roof and walk up to the highest part where we could grab a limb and climb into the sycamore tree. Otherwise the lowest branches would still have been out of our reach. I loved to climb to the very top where the new growth was still limber and sit there and sway in the wind while gazing far over the countryside

We had scrounged two empty cans from the kitchen and punched a hole in the bottom of each with a nail. Then we took a long piece of string and waxed it with an old candle stub. We threaded the string through the hole in the can and tied it to a nail. Two of us each took a can and climbed up the sycamore trees to try out our 'telephones.' They sorta worked. Actually, we could hear each other better when we hollered than we could with the so-called phones. So much for that experiment.

Another good use for tin cans was to boil the eggs we had swiped from the hen house. We went behind the high school where there were a few left-over bricks and borrowed four of them to make a square to set the can on, got some water from the well, built a small fire within the bricks and set our eggs to boiling. It wasn't that we were hungry it was just something to do that we could get away with. I never heard of any specific rule against doing it, probably because no one ever thought about it or they surely would have made a rule against it.

It might have been in the fall of 1933 or the spring of 1934 when the high school boys started digging what later became Lake Ann. They used a mule to drag what looked like half a clam shell digger to scrape up the earth. It was in the woods in a place where there were several springs. I loved watching them work. They must have used the earth they were digging out to make a dam between the hills to hold the water in place. The work went forward slowly but finally they were finished digging. It took several weeks for the hollow they made to fill up. While the lake was filling the boys made a raft and a diving tower. Near the end of the spring semester when the lake was finally filled Dean Stewart proposed a picnic and a cookout to celebrate. Food and faculty were loaded on wagons and taken to the site. The rest of us had to walk the three miles to get there. Boys and girls were not allowed to go swimming at the same time. The girls were allowed to go in first and stay until a whistle was blown. When I put my bathing suit on and rushed into the water. I found it shockingly cold. I don't know why I should have been surprised by the cold. I had walked the woods many times and had stopped to drink in these same springs and the water was always cold. I stayed in the water as long as I could. When I started turning blue, I knew it was time to give up. I was glad to spend the rest of the time sitting by the nice big cooking fire. I roasted my hot dog and myself. Though the swimming was something of a disappointment I enjoyed the day.

My friends and I often went walking in the woods. They helped me to learn to identify many plants and pointed out edible fruits. There were wild persimmons. They are small, two or three bites at the most. They have to be soft or else they will draw up your mouth like a styptic pencil. Then there were plums, mayhaws, hickory nuts and black walnuts. A mayhaw grows on a large bush and is about half an inch across. It looks like a very small apple and really hasn't much taste but we ate them anyway. We took the nuts back to the campus where we could borrow a hammer to break them. They both have very hard shells so you have to be careful not to smash them to pieces and ruin the nutmeat. The hickory nuts were not much but the black walnuts were delicious. And I mustn't forget the wild grapes, the muscadines and scuppernongs. I've heard of muscadine wine but I have never tasted any.

The farmers around French Camp grew peanuts so I have had peanuts every way they can be prepared; I've had peanuts boiled in salt water, raw, roasted, whatever. I've also had peanuts that were large, about three inches long and in proportion to ordinary peanuts, they tasted much the same.

One day we were walking in the woods and there were a lot of sticks on the ground. I was walking along kicking sticks when one wiggled quickly away. I was up in a small dogwood tree so fast. I didn't realize that I had kicked a snake until it was all over.

When I went home for the summer of 1934, I found out that Mother, Aunt Bea, Alfredo, Carlos and I were going to be staying in a house in Gretna on Amelia Street. The house belonged to a minister who was taking a long vacation with his family and the Fords had made the arrangement for us and for them. Dad was still working in Thibodaux building more chicken houses and setting up the hatchery. We didn't have to pay any rent at the house in Gretna but we did have to pay for utilities. I think Mother was the one who had a job in New Orleans because I remember that Aunt Bea was home taking care of us and the house.

Dad would come to visit on an occasional week end. One time he had brought us a big bag of okra from Aunt Helena's garden. Mother boiled them, dredged them in olive oil, vinegar, salt and pepper the way we liked them. That was all we had for supper that night. Dad had always called okra prepared that way 'slippery Sams.' Dad said, "Come to supper; be sure you sit down before eating." I asked him, "Why?" He answered, "Because if you don't the slippery Sams might go straight through." So we laughed instead of feeling sorry for ourselves. He made jokes to make the hard times easier.

One day Alfredo and I were giving Carlos a ride in the wagon, Alfredo pushing and me pulling. He was looking down at the sidewalk while pushing and saw a piece of paper all folded up. He picked it up and when he unfolded it, it was a dollar bill! That was a lot of money when you realize that a round steak big enough to feed the whole family cost only thirty-five cents. We went home and showed it to Aunt Bea. She took us to the drugstore and let Alfredo treat us all to an ice cream cone. A three scoops cone cost only a nickel. I suppose she kept the rest to buy food.

The place we lived in had only two bedrooms so I was sleeping on the couch in the living room. One night I was awakened by noises and an unusual amount of light coming through the pulled down shade. I sat up, lifted the corner of the shade and saw the house across the street was on fire and firemen were trying to put it out. I heard it said afterwards that people who lived on the west bank often settled grudges by setting a person's house on fire.

When summer was over Mother and I went to live with Dad in Thibodaux. That school year 1934-35 I was going into fifth grade and did not go back to French Camp. I went to school right across the street from the Fords' house on the corner of Seventh and Goode streets. I was surprised when I reported to my homeroom to find that my teacher was Miss Mildred Naquin, my old acquaintance from the Lockport Theater, Mr. Sidney's daughter. She taught Arithmetic and Penmanship. She had a beautiful handwriting that looked just like the examples in the Palmer Method Penmanship book. We had to change classes as they do in high school. I had Miss Catherine Tabor for English. I don't remember the names of the history or geography teachers. I suffered over Arithmetic. With all my moving around I had somehow missed learning my times tables. Dad wrote them out for me and drilled me relentlessly until I finally learned them but it was a struggle. I never did feel confident in plain old arithmetic. I wish we had had hand held calculators then. I wasn't very good in penmanship either. I never could make my writing look like the examples in the book. My *ovals* and *pushpulls* were a mess. The ovals never overlaid each other neatly and the pushpulls hung messily below the lines. I could clean up the pushpulls with my eraser but the ovals were hopeless. I did very well in English, History and Geography. I admired Miss Tabor's handwriting. She wrote backhand and it was very neat and legible so I decided to copy her writing since I knew that I would never be proficient in Palmer Method.

Miss Tabor was a small, sweet and gentle lady. She was a good teacher and she was also the town librarian. Every Friday I went to the library and checked out three books in my grade level. By Monday afternoon I had read them all and returned them. When I had read everything on the shelf in my grade level, I started on the next higher grade level. I read everything I could find. I was hoping to impress her with my brilliance. When I met her thirty-five years later in Baton Rouge at a genealogical meeting, I asked her if she had noticed what I was doing. She was sorry to say that she hadn't. No matter. I had developed the habit of reading everything in sight and managed to educate myself even though I never had the chance to go to college. I am still reading some of everything. I won't live long enough to cover all of the knowledge there is. I am not very interested in science though I know enough about natural science to understand about weather, plant growth, the logic of the periodic tables, a bit about plate tectonics. Science just is not my thing. I love history, literature, geography and since I have a phenomenal memory, I can call up most of what I have read when the occasion arises. People think I have a PhD in the humanities. That's very flattering but I always tell them that I had only one semester of college.

My sidewalk bike and I were reunited at last. I was almost too big for it but I rode it anyway. I used it to go to the post office for the mail and on my trips to the library.

Mother, Dad and I enjoyed being together again even in a garage apartment over a room-sized incubator. There was a small area downstairs in front of the incubator that had been walled off. We established our kitchen there. We had a table and four chairs and a kerosene stove in it. Dad built a screened cabinet where we kept our dishes and groceries. He put the feet of the cabinet in mayonnaise jar caps filled with ant poison to protect the groceries, especially the sugar. We had no refrigerator, not even an ice-box. We had to keep our perishables in Mrs. Ford's refrigerator. There was no plumbing so we had to go to the big house for that, too.

A flight of stairs led from the kitchen to the huge room over the incubator. It was not divided into rooms so Mother made a partition with curtain rings sewn onto an old blanket strung on the wire that Dad had strung from wall to wall. The back part of the room was theirs. Dad put up a shelf and a bar for hanging clothes in their part of the room. I had no hanging space and I put my folding clothes in an orange shipping crate stood on end. In the middle of the room we placed our radio-phonograph that we, miraculously, still had, into the middle of the room plus a table Dad made. I sat there to do my homework and we played cards or games there. We also played jacks on it. It was fun to watch Dad with his thick fingers being able to play jacks so skillfully. Mother could lag a whole set of jacks and not drop one. She never had to do onesies. Do girls these days play jacks? To play jacks you throw the jacks on the floor, or table in our case. Then you throw a small solid rubber ball about 1½ inches wide up and pick up the required number of jacks, catching the ball after one bounce. It has been so long since I played jacks I wonder if I still can.

We had a regular schedule of radio programs we listened to. At that time, we listened to, Bob Hope, Fibber McGee and Mollie, Edgar Bergen and Charlie McCarthy. Many others I can't recall. So, with work, games, reading and our programs life went on pleasantly and evenly.

Dad made a big trapdoor to cover the stairway. He rigged a pulley with a counterweight to handle it because it was too heavy to move otherwise. We closed it after supper when we went back upstairs. We had a Coleman radiant heater fueled with white gas. It had to be pumped up to put air pressure on the gas so it would continuously feed the flame. It kept us warm but it was dangerous.

I learned to candle eggs so I could do my bit to help with the work of running a hatchery. To candle eggs, you pass them over a powerful light that shows through the shell. If the egg is fertile a dark spot will appear. That spot is the embryo. It is no use to waste space in an incubator with infertile eggs.

Between cleaning out chicken pens, doling out food, filling water trays and all the rest of the work Dad and Albert started digging a gas well. A pocket of natural gas had been discovered under Thibodaux so Dad thought it would be great if we could tap into it. He made a piledriver out of a section of tree trunk, rigged a rope on a pulley so the tree trunk could be pulled up and then dropped on the top of the pipe driving it into the ground. He made a pressure storage tank out of an oil drum in the event that they managed to strike gas. I watched them work day after day. One day they struck water but that was not what they wanted to find. Small seashells came up with the gushing water. I found that interesting because in school we had been told that this part of Louisiana was once under water and here in my hand was the proof. They finally did hit the gas pocket and connected it to the house.

Aunt Bea, Alfredo and Carlos joined us for Christmas 1934. Mother had gone shopping in Thibodaux and somehow lost ten dollars. That may not seem like much money but it put a crimp in our Christmas that year. I had saved money from my allowance and had bought or made a gift for everyone. Mrs. Ford had been teaching me how to make patchwork for quilts. I made a big enough piece to make my Mother a throw pillow. I made a stuffed Rastus doll for Carlos. Rastus was the name of the black man on the Cream of Wheat box. I don't like cream of wheat but I ate it until I had enough box tops. I sent the box tops and ten cents for the stamped Rastus pattern the company offered. When it came, I cut it out, sewed it together and stuffed it. I was so proud of myself.

The work was getting to be too much for the two men so the Fords hired someone to clean the chicken pens. Dad was able to use the extra time to work in the woodshop for pleasure so he started building a model sailboat. It was large, somewhat over three feet long. It had a cockpit with seats on three sides in front of the cabin. The cabin had windows and a door with a window. The door opened and shut so he made a cleat that turned on a brad to lock it shut. He carved two lifeboats and hung them on davits one on each side. He also carved cleats and fastened them to the deck to wrap the sail ropes around. The rudder arm cane over the transom and could be placed between brads that were nailed on the deck in an arc. That way the boat could be set to sail in a circle so it would come back to you. The boat was gaff rigged on a single mast. Dad drew the patterns for the mainsail and the jib that were cut from flour sacking. Mother sewed them for him. Dad had built a form and pored melted lead into it. He fitted the lead piece onto the bottom of the keel to balance the boat. Dad then built a cradle to set it on for display. I loved it and wanted to keep it forever but it was unwieldy to transport. It was not practical to keep it since we lived such a nomadic life. When we left Thibodaux, he donated it to the American Legion to raffle off to raise funds.

He built a doll sized rocking chair for me. Later, when we were studying about Japan in school, he built a rickshaw. There was a pattern in our reader for a paper rickshaw. He traced the pattern, cut it out and glued it together but the wheels being made of paper collapsed when he tried to stand it up. He decided to make one from a tin can. First, he cut the ends off of two same sized tin cans for wheels. Then he used the rest of the can to make the body soldering it together. He even made a top to raise over the seat. He used heavy wire for the handles with a loop in them where the axel could pass. I brought it to school to show the children. The teacher just gave it a passing glance. I thought that she was very offhand about it and I resented her attitude. It was a very good example of a rickshaw. She should have shown more appreciation. I gave my small porcelain doll rides and had a lot of fun with it. Phooey on the unappreciative teacher.

The hatchery wasn't doing too well. Dad was still working with the chickens. He had trap nested hens he was feeding with good chicken feed and they were laying well but eggs were selling for only twenty-five cents a dozen. He had separated the roosters from the hens and grew them for broilers and fryers. He knew how to operate on a rooster, called caponizing. It made the rooster grow bigger than an ordinary rooster and it was tender. The only one who could afford a capon was the local Catholic priest. Mother decided to go to New Orleans to look for work.

Not long before Mother left, I caused an uproar. I should have known better but I had a friend who lived in the country and I decided to walk home with her after school one day without telling anybody what I was doing. It turned out that she lived three miles from the school. When we arrived at her house it was milking time and her father was in the barn doing the milking. He offered me a glass of it so I said ok I had never had milk straight from the cow so I tried it. It was warm! And foamy! I didn't care much for it but I drank it down. I didn't want to make him feel bad. Her mother was nice and had an after-school-snack ready in the kitchen. She told me I was welcome to stay but if I wanted to get home before dark I had better leave right after we finished the snack. I had to walk back by myself and arrived just as the sun was setting. Everyone had been looking for me and I was in big trouble. I should have known better than to do such a thing without asking permission.

Dad and I were living happily together. He would cook for us. When I asked him what he was cooking he would say, "It's a mystery dish." I never could figure exactly what was in it but it was always good. Soon Mrs. Ford came and said it was unseemly for me to be living alone in the house with a man. Some Victorian left overs! He was my father after all. Still I had to move into her house and Albert moved in with Dad. I was now effectively separated from both parents. It seems to me we spent more time apart than together. Most men living together never keep house right and these two were no exception. I'd go over now and then and do some straightening up and cleaning otherwise it would never get done. She may have been right but I hated being separated from him. I could visit with him whenever I wanted to but it was not the same.

One nice thing about the arrangement was that I had a room of my own for the first time in my life. Mrs. Ford was good to me but very strict. She taught me how to make ice-cream in the refrigerator tray and cream cheese out of sour milk. She taught me to darn socks and iron my own clothes. My assigned chores were to set the table and dry the dishes and generally help around the house. I also had to iron napkins, pillow cases and handkerchiefs. At night I had to kneel beside my bed to say my prayers, something I hadn't done since I was five or six years old. She also taught me a lot about gardening. She grew chrysanthemums for All Saints Day. She showed me how to disbud the plant of all but one flower so it would grow big and showy. She turned that whole bed of flowers over to me. I could have all of the profit from my work when we sold the flowers. I enjoyed learning about the cultivation of the vegetables she grew, especially about asparagus and artichokes.

When my birthday came, she gave me a party and let me invite my cousins and some of my school friends. It was the first official birthday party I had ever had. She served cocoa and cake because ice-cream was not sold in the winter months and the amount we could have made in the refrigerator would not have been enough (It wasn't all that good either). I always resented the fact that I couldn't have ice-cream on my birthday. Now with a freezer in almost every home and adequate heating I can enjoy ice-cream in December.

Mr. and Mrs. Ford had been missionaries in Africa and had worked with Albert Schweitzer. In fact, both their sons, Albert and Nathan, were born on the station. Albert was named for Dr. Schweitzer. There were boxes of interesting pictures of the natives and the station and many interesting artifacts that the natives had made for them. There were about eight ivory napkin rings no two alike. My favorite artifact was a drum made from a hollowed-out section of a tree. I drummed on it but only when the Fords were not there

In the living room there was a large glass fronted book case that drew me but I had to sneak in there to do any reading because reading to them was a waste of time better spent doing some sort of work.

Mealtimes were dreadful because Mr. Ford read from the Presbyterian lecture for the day that had a section to be read at each meal. It was always long and he added to it with endless comments. After that he prayed for every living soul in the universe. This repetition occurred so often I quit listening. Right now, I cannot recall one thought advanced in all of that religious stuff. It just built up resentment in me. Sometimes Mrs. Ford would whisper, "Hurry along Edward. The food is getting cold." Too bad she didn't hurry him more often. Like most preachers, once he got started on a thought he couldn't stop until he had completely exhausted the subject and the subjects.

The food was good (not great, just good) and well served. We ate on nice china and silver set on an immaculate white linen tablecloth. We each had our own napkin rolled into an ivory napkin ring. Dad and Albert ate with us.

All of that was nice but I missed my Mother. She would come to visit as often as she could. Though I was always delighted to have her there it was never long enough. It was just not the same as living together all the time.

In September 1934 I went back to French Camp along with Alfredo. After our parents put us on the train he was in my charge. I was told to be very careful of my purse and not to talk to strangers. The way I took care of my purse was to sit on it. That way if I fell asleep and someone tried to take it I would surely wake up. I had to see to the transferring of our luggage at Durant where we changed trains. Now I was the big girl taking care of the little cousin.

Things were much different for me at French Camp this time. Beside Dorothy not being there anymore there was another big difference. There were other younger girls boarding so I was no longer unique and surely at twelve years old much too big to be the campus pet. I was in sixth grade and my classes were in the Junior High building.

I'm trying to remember the names of some of the faculty. Miss Graves was still there still teaching first and second grade. Then there was Mrs. Cook, the music teacher and house mother of the little boy's dorm, she of the blue hair. She really had white hair but she used bluing to make it whiter. Bluing was designed to make white clothes whiter, not hair. When she used too much, she turned her hair blue. There was Professor Cain who lived up on the hill in the big boy's dorm and taught in high school, Mrs. McBride was still housemother in the big boy's dorm, Mrs. Ingram, still head of the dining room, Miss McNair who was new and had red hair and lots of freckles, was my home room teacher that year, and Mrs. Ellis who taught math in junior high. She was tall and slender and nice looking and very strict. She had the coldest blue eyes I have ever seen.

That year my bedroom was on the second floor on the side of the building overlooking the little boy's cottage. It was a good arrangement for me because I could sit on my windowsill and talk to Alfredo who would be standing outside. There weren't many chances for us to communicate since the school was so adamant about keeping the sexes apart. Every now and then I would make up an excuse to see him saying that I had news from home to share with him or I needed to discuss with him the use of the money deposited in the office for his needs.

I had always been given an allowance that was kept on deposit for me in the school office. I used it to buy school supplies. Once in a while I allowed myself a treat. I tithed ten percent for the church and saved enough to buy myself a Bible that I still have. I also saved for Christmas gifts for the family. I had handled my own money since I was in fourth grade.

Somebody had a great idea. I don't know who suggested it but the school decided to have parties in the library each month under the supervision of a teacher. It was for the younger boarding students and probably some of the local children. We played games and had refreshments. It was co-ed so it helped boys and girls to get used to each other and learn civilized behavior in a social situation.

Mrs. McBride gave a great Hallowe'en party up on the hill in the big boy's dorm that year. We played fun games and had cookies and hot chocolate. Dean Stewart then took us on a hike that ended at a bonfire where we roasted marshmallows.

That fall Dean Stewart took all who wanted to go with him on a possum hunt. Since I had never been on any kind of hunt I decided to go along. He took his hound dogs to track a possum down. We went crashing through the woods behind the dogs. We couldn't keep up with them but we could hear them barking in the distance. When we caught up with them, we found that all the dogs were below a tree barking their heads off and the poor possum was hanging on a branch scared to death. I felt so sorry for the possum! Hunting is just not my thing. If anyone killed it, I never knew because I turned back and went to the bonfire.

I have been writing this story by remembering in which house each event took place and how old I was when it happened. I'm finding it hard to keep the dates straight even though my mother and I got together and wrote down the address of every place we lived and when. I lived in twenty-four different places not counting the years I was in French Camp as one of them. I used my parent's address during those years. I have lived in nine different places in the sixty-eight years I was married, and two since Bill died.

When Alfredo and I went home for Christmas 1934 I was feeling quite the seasoned traveler. When the porter came around, I ordered slices of pie for each of us. I had read about minced meat pie but never tasted it so I ordered that for me. Alfredo didn't want to risk it so he ordered pumpkin pie. I expected an eighth of a nine-inch pie but what I received was a fourth of an eight-inch pie. It looked enormous! I had never had so much pie in one serving in my life. We dutifully ate it all. During the depression it was drummed into our heads that we mustn't waste food so we didn't let any of that big piece of pie go to waste. I gave Alfredo a bit of my pie to see if he liked it and he did but not more than the pumpkin pie he had. So both of us were satisfied. I have enjoyed minced meat pie ever since and have always had it for the Christmas holidays at my home.

It was back to French Camp after Christmas. Same old same old. Because French Camp was set in an agricultural area one of the required subjects was agriculture. I don't know if it was a state requirement or a local school board requirement. It was a strange subject for a city girl but I enjoyed learning about contour plowing, lime to sweeten acid soil, fertilizer, planting leguminous plants then plowing them under to put nitrogen back into the soil, etc. We also had to know how to recognize the different breeds of farm animals and the strengths and weakness of the different breeds. It was all a revelation to me. I didn't realize how much a person had to know to be a farmer. After having studied all of that I can better understand the political questions that come up concerning farmers.

No knowledge is ever wasted (except maybe algebra?). Knowledge is disseminated in pieces that the mind can assimilate. It is like eating dinner. You take a bite at a time. So, subjects are divided into assimilable portions of reading, history, geography, science, math etc. But each part is but a portion of the whole bank of human knowledge. No one can take in all of it at once. The more one knows the more one understands that everything is a part of everything else.

One of the things I'm grateful for is that English grammar was taught so thoroughly at French Camp. We had to know all the parts of speech and what job each word was doing in a sentence. We had to take sentences apart and we learned that by diagraming them. It is an old-fashioned method but when you do that it gives you an understanding of language that you can't easily get any other way. Grammar is so embedded in my brain I don't even have to think about it to use it correctly. At least I hope that is the case, especially in this story now that I have bragged about it.

In French Camp we used Elson Readers through all of the grades. The content was a good mixture of historical stories, mythology, poetry, fantasy, short story fiction, and biography so a person not only learned new words but received a store of general information in the process.

When we returned to New Orleans for the summer of 1935, Mother told me the news that Grandpa Darcey had died in February just past. He had died as the result of an automobile accident; not a wreck but a mishap. He had turned to talk to the man who was driving and his arm accidently pressed on the door handle. The wind caught the door and pulled it open. He must have been trying to catch it when he fell out of the car and hit his head on the pavement. The man wanted to take Grandpa to the hospital but he refused to go. He just wanted to go home. That night he wanted to get a drink of water. He always kept water on the bed table. He couldn't manage to sit up by himself so Grandma lifted him up and gave him a drink. He died in Grandma's arms. Mother said she did not want to tell me about it in a letter since I could not come to the funeral or do anything about it. I felt belittled. She should have told me. I could at least have written a condolence letter to Grandma. I don't believe in keeping the sad things that happen in families from the children. Instead of shielding them It just makes them feel left out and unimportant to the family unit.

That summer Mother and Aunt Bea had rented a house at 1540 Leda Street. Dad was still in Thibodaux. It was a two-or-three bedroom cottage with a front porch and a good sized backyard in a nice neighborhood near where we had lived on Verna Street. Both streets go from Esplanade Avenue to the back fence of the Fair Grounds. Leda is the street where the Old Jockey Club was located but it didn't look haunted anymore because it had been turned into apartments that were fully occupied.

Since Mrs. Ford had taught me about planting and we now had such a nice yard I suggested to Alfredo that we plant something. The only seeds we had were red beans so we planted three or four. They were coming up nicely. Each one had already developed two leaves. We forgot to tell Aunt Bea about our garden so when she mowed the grass, she mowed down our garden. So that was that.

There was a nice shady area between our house and the house next door where grass wouldn't grow so Alfredo and I took it over as a good place to build an elaborate road system for our little cars. We dug a canal so we could use a cigar box top to make a bridge over it for our cars. We even had a town laid out with streets and each had an address on one of the streets. We drew a house floor plan and a driveway to our garage. I was the one who made up all this stuff. I know I was getting a bit old for this sort of play but it kept Alfredo busy and out of Aunt Bea's hair.

The neighborhood was full of boys. I don't believe I ever met a single girl around there. There must have been about twelve boys. Suited me. I liked the boy's games better anyhow. We built stilts, kites and balsa wood airplanes. We all went together to the movies on Saturday to see the serial. We played endless numbers of board games and cards on my front porch and drank gallons of Cool-Aid. In the evening we played 'I spy' under the street lights. For some reason we used the street light on Verna street as base and could hide only on that street and only within those two blocks to the right and left of the lamp post.

Two of the boys, Harold Dittman and his brother George were in our group even though they lived on Verna. They were the sons of Dr. Dittman whose home was right behind our house. He and his wife had four or five children besides Harold and George but all of them suffered from spastic paralysis. I felt so sorry for that family.

In the fall of 1935 when it became time to return to French Camp I did not want to return. The charm of it had worn off long ago. The food had always been bad and it never had improved and I was tired of the inadequate bathroom facilities. Not one thing had improved since I first went there. Also, the older I became the tighter the rules were applied. There was no more free-wheeling wandering over the area. But go I must so Alfredo and I were fitted out with whatever we needed, trunks packed and train tickets bought. On the way to board the train we stopped by the French Market where Aunt Bea bought some fruit for us to eat on the way. The big purple plums were the best ever.

I was in seventh grade. Lessons were never hard for me except math as usual. It was just that the whole boarding school experience was beginning to pall.

One of the dorm rooms right next door to the Dean of Women's room was set up as an infirmary with two hospital beds in it. I spent a lot of time in there that year. One good thing they gave me to eat when I was sick was cream of tomato soup. I really did enjoy it and still do. We had never had it at home. The only soup mother ever made was beef vegetable. The best part of being sick was not having to eat in the dining room where the only things they served that were worth eating were the cornbread muffins and the biscuits.

On the floor in the closet in the infirmary was a collection of old magazines that I especially enjoyed. They were from many years earlier with interesting old illustrations and advertisements. Some of the ads were illustrated by Maxfield Parrish. I enjoyed his work so much that I read a book about him. I looked for his work and read some of the books he had illustrated. As an adult I bought his biography that was copiously illustrated with his work. I still have it and get it out now and then and I enjoy it still.

*Friend, Soledad, my special pal,
and her sister Carmen*

*Mrs. and Mr. Ford*

*Nathalie at 13*

## *Good Bye French Camp*

When it was time to go home for Christmas my mind was made up. No more French Camp for me! I packed my trunk with all I owned. Then I went to the little boy's dorm and packed all of Alfredo's belongings. I got the trunks put on the rickety school bus and taken to the train station, bought one-way tickets, checked the trunks through to New Orleans and went home to stay.

We arrived on my thirteenth birthday, December 20, 1935, the day I received my Mickey Mouse watch. I told my mother, "I am not ever going back to French Camp. I would rather starve with you if necessary." The depression was very depressing at this time. Work was hard to find, the thirty-five dollars a month of Dad's Veteran's pension helped but didn't cover all expenses.

We were living in the ground floor apartment of a duplex at 53 Allard Boulevard. The street runs from Orleans Avenue to Dumain Street, I think. It may go all the way to City Park Avenue. I just don't remember. Dad was living with us again because the hatchery business had failed. Al Ford was living with us while taking a course in Morse code radio communication at night and working trucking cotton bales in a cotton warehouse during the day. The cotton warehouse was on the river, of course, so he went to work on public transit. Many times he walked to work and back to save the fourteen cents carfare.

I met the girl who lived in the upstairs apartment. She wanted me to go and see her Christmas tree. I went up to see it and it was beautiful. They had used the new Angel Hair made of spun glass fibers, stretched over the whole tree that made an aureole over each light. We didn't even have a tree. Aunt Bea was living a few streets over with Grandma Darcey. They were invited to come and share Christmas with us such as it was. There would have been no presents at all if Aunt Mabel had not come. When she saw how things were, she went to the drug store, the only store open at that hour, and bought a few games and toys. For all I know she may have brought the food we had that day.

While I had been in French Camp in the fall semester the Fords sent Mother to a college in Indiana to learn how to distinguish the sex of just hatched baby chicks. There was a market for that skill. The Fords were trying hard to get us back on our feet.

When school started in January Alfredo and I were enrolled in John Dibert school. The New Orleans schoolboard considered Mississippi schools inadequate so I was automatically, without even an examination, put back to do the sixth grade over again. It hurt my pride. I had always worked hard and made good grades in everything but arithmetic. It was quite a blow since I was already old in my grade because I was born in December and had to wait until I was almost seven to start first grade. So there I was, even further behind through no fault of my own.

No sooner had we started school than we had to move again. This move was to accommodate Grandma Darcey, Aunt Bea, Carlos, Alfredo, Al Ford, Dad, Mother and me. In February we rented half of a two-story double at 114 Sherwood Forest Drive. When we lived on Sherwood Forest Drive before we lived nearest to Carrollton Avenue. This time we lived nearer to City Park Avenue. Mother now had a good job at Picou's Hatchery using her newly acquired skill. The Fords opened a feed store on Metairie Road on the point right next to the railroad tracks. They were still trying to find something for Albert to do. Unfortunately, neither Dad nor Albert knew a thing about running a business. Both of them knew about the good results you could get by feeding animals properly but neither of them knew how to sell so that venture soon ended.

Alfredo and I would meet for lunch. There was a small grocery on the corner across the street from the school. We would go there and buy a French bread sandwich and a half pint of milk and go to eat it in City Park. After eating we always, at my insistence, threw our trash in the trash can, then went to play on the playground. Thanks to my Mickey Mouse watch we were never late getting back to school.

I had always wanted to take music lessons. I wanted to learn to play the violin. The music teacher in Lockport convinced Mother that it was better for me to take piano lessons first and learn to read music before attempting such a difficult instrument. I started piano lessons in Lockport but that ended when I was so sick. At French Camp I took piano lessons with Mrs. Cook for a while but there were no practice rooms so that sort of just ended. When we moved to Sherwood Forest Drive that spring Mother went to Werlein's Music Store and bought a studio piano on time. It came with about twelve lessons. The store recommended a teacher in walking distance of our house so I began lessons again. She taught in her own home that was across Carrollton on a street off of Dumain. I could keep up with the baseball game while walking to her house because every house had the game on the radio and, since all the doors and windows were open I could hear it. I was proud of taking music lessons and was thrilled to have my own piano. I wouldn't let the boys touch it because I knew they would just bang on it. I kept it closed when not in use and I kept it dusted. I did everything but practice as much as I should have. I really preferred playing outside with the boys. Mother gave up on me and returned the piano to Werlein's.

We practically lived in City Park since it was so close. Mother would get up early and before going to work we would go to the park and play softball for a while. In the evenings after supper everyone except Grandma Darcey would divide into two teams to play a game the adults made up. One team would have a few minutes head start before the other started out to hunt for them. We played all over the neighborhood. The park was out of bounds. Also, teams had to stay together. We would sneak around bushes, fences and houses and slink along in shadows trying to elude the hunters. It's a wonder someone didn't call the police or shoot us. It was great fun and a good way to get out of the warm house on a summer's evening.

      Once in a while we children were treated to a trip to Spanish Fort, the amusement park on Lake Pontchartrain. That was a magic time for us with all the rides, games of chance and good things to eat. We loved going there even though we didn't have much money to spend. It was fun to see all that was going on.

      There was a gravel road along Bayou St. John (now called Wisner Boulevard) that went straight to Spanish Fort. In a car it didn't seem very far. One day when Alfredo, Carlos and I were playing in the park I decided it would be great to walk to Spanish Fort so we started out. We walked and walked in the hot sun on that dusty road of heated gravel. Carlos got so tired I carried him piggy-back. I couldn't keep that up for long so I had Alfredo make a seat between us with hands gripped on each other's arms. That didn't work because of the difference in our height so I had to carry him on my back again. I kept thinking it was just a little further so we plodded on and on. It seemed it would be further to go back than to go on. By the time we got to what is now Robert E. Lee Boulevard we just stopped on the corner to get our bearings. Just a little farther, maybe five or six blocks we could see Spanish Fort but we didn't care anymore. A bus came along and stopped. It seems that corner was a bus stop. I told the bus driver we didn't realize we were at a bus stop. I also told him we couldn't get on the bus because we didn't have any money. He asked us what we were doing way out there in the middle of nowhere. (The area was just being developed) I told him we had walked from City Park intending to go to Spanish Fort but we were too tired to go on. He asked where we lived so I told him. He was very annoyed with us but he told us to get in. He gave us transfers and instructions on what lines to catch to get us home. I was so relieved to be rescued. We got home just before dusk as we always did when we played in the park. I swore the boys to silence on pain of death. They kept the secret for a good while until one day Mother had them in the car and was driving down Wisner. Carlos said, "Oh, this is the street…." Alfredo elbowed him in the ribs to shut him up. Mother, picking up that there was something amiss said, "Oh, that's all right I already know about it." She didn't but that opened the dam and between them they told the whole story. By that time it was too late to punish me. I suppose she thought the pickle I had been in was punishment enough.

      Even though I was embarrassed about repeating half of the sixth grade, I enjoyed learning. After my French Camp experience with diagraming sentences

English was a cinch. I loved geography, history anything that wasn't arithmetic. I was getting better at arithmetic but I never learned to like it. We were learning singing by singing the notes as 'do' 're' 'mi' etc. I never did catch on to what they were doing. If you're going to learn a song then learn the words and memorize the tune. That business of do re me seemed goofy to me but I enjoyed learning the songs.

In 1936 Mother, Dad and I moved to 3018 De Soto Street It was an upstairs furnished apartment in a nice neighborhood but with a witch for a landlady. There was a Japanese plum tree in the back yard. She didn't eat them herself. And she wouldn't let anyone else pick them. They just fell on the ground and rotted. At least all of those did that I hadn't picked when she was away. Aunt Bea and Grandma had a house together somewhere else. I think this was when Al Ford went to California. We heard from him and somehow he ended up a diesel mechanic and worked for the railroads. Finally he found what he wanted to do and he did very well. I was glad that the three of us were together again without anyone else. That house was where I first tried my hand at making biscuits. They would have been good but that ratty old stove had a ratty old oven that baked unevenly so the bottoms of my biscuits were too brown. We just cut off the tops and ate them with butter and threw the bottoms away.

In September I started seventh grade at McDonough 28. Every girl was required to take Domestic Science a fancy name for Home Economics. In the first semester we had to learn to sew an apron and a headband to wear in the second semester when we would be learning to cook. Headbands were to keep our hair out of the food. We also studied nutrition and how to balance a meal.

In addition to all the regular subjects we had music appreciation. Classical and semi-classical pieces were played and explained. At the end of the year there was a music recognition exam. The pieces we had studied were played and we had to write down the name of the piece and the composer. I really enjoyed that subject.

In October of 1936 we moved to 3047 Grand Route St. John. The street runs from Bayou St. John across Esplanade Avenue to Gentilly Road. The house was a raised double. We lived in the right half as you face the front. There were two bedrooms, living room, bath and kitchen upstairs. Downstairs was all one room. The front part was a garage and the rest was storage space with two laundry trays in the rear part. The concrete down there was finished so smoothly it was great for skating. We put up clothes lines in there so we could dry our clothes when it was raining.

There was another raised double next door to ours to the left as you face the house. On the left side of it was the family of Camille Duvieilh, his wife, son

Camille Jr., and three daughters whose names all started with an E. The eldest daughter was the eldest child, then Camille Jr., then my friend Elma who was about a year younger than me, and her six-year-old sister. Elma introduced me to Jewel Lands who lived on the corner of our block and Lopez Street. Her sister was a beautician who had a shop in the basement of their house. At thirteen I had my first permanent at Jewels' sister's shop and finally had the curls I had always wanted. Jewel, Elma and I were all in the same grade at McDonough 28. Jewel was sickly and hardly went to school. She introduced me to Florine DeBlanc who lived on the corner of Desoto and Lopez Street. She was the daughter of the owner of the DeBlanc's Drugstore on Maurepas Street near Esplanade. She went to boarding school at St. Mary of the Pines in Mississippi so we saw her only on holidays and during the summer. We went about as a group of four or three or two if Jewel was sick. Elma and I were together most of the time we were awake. We walked to school together, ate lunch together, studied after school together and played together in between.

Elma's father owned a typewriter sales and repair store in the business district in town. They had a nice four door sedan that was used only on Sunday. Mr. Duvieilh went to work on the streetcar instead of having to pay for parking a car in town. On Sunday he took the family and sometimes I was invited, for a ride around New Orleans, Algiers, up river on the west bank, down to Chalmette, out Gentilly to the Rigolets, but not all those places on the same Sunday.

On the corner of Grand Route St. John and Gentilly Road there was a neighborhood theater named the Bell that our group attended every week end. Sometimes we went during the week if something special was playing. We roller skated for miles in our neighborhood and in City Park. We loved skating in the Peristyle because it was so big and the concrete was so smooth because the Peristyle was originally designed as a venue for dancing. The longest skating trip we went on was to Halfway House, an ice cream parlor at the end of City Park Avenue across from Greenwood Cemetery. We rented bicycles at night and rode around the park singing the latest popular songs. In summer we would get up very early to be the first ones into the swimming pool in City Park. Sometimes my mother would get up early and take us swimming at Lake Pontchartrain. I loved going to the lake early in the morning while the city was quiet. It was like experiencing the world when it was new.

Our group gathered mostly at my house because we could be undisturbed. Both Jewel and Elma had little sisters who were pesty. We couldn't go very often to Florine's house because her mother worked a good bit at the drugstore. They also came over at night on the nights when the program *Inner Sanctum* came on. We sat on the sofa with the lights off. We held hands for reassurance when that creepy program came on. It started out with a door with creaking hinges opening ever so slowly. It was enough to make your hair stand on end.

That year I had the flu just before Christmas. It seems to me I often got sick and ruined my Christmas holidays. Anyway, Christmas morning was the first day I was out of bed. When I went to the tree, I found a glorious sight—a full sized two-wheeled girls' bicycle, something I had yearned for for years. I begged my mother to let me go out on the sidewalk and try it out for a very few minutes since it was such a nice sunny day. She reluctantly agreed. I mounted the bike and rode to the corner and back then put the bike away in the basement and went back upstairs. Evidently, I was not as well as I wanted to believe because I had a relapse and spent another two weeks in bed. When I finally did get better, I enjoyed my bike so much. I let the girls have turns because none of them had ever owned a bike. Maybe their parents thought they were too dangerous or maybe it was because they had more children and couldn't pay for bicycles for all of them.

The summer of 1937 I read *Gone with the Wind* by Margaret Mitchell. It took me six or seven weeks to do it because it was 1,016 pages long. I hated it when anyone interrupted me. I didn't want to put the book down. I finally finished it and was sorry when it ended.

McDonough 28 ended at the seventh grade. High school started in the ninth grade so everybody going into eighth grade in our area had to go to Edward Douglas White School between Esplanade and Governor Nichols Streets two blocks from North Claiborne. That was about twenty blocks from home. Elma and I walked except when the weather was bad. Then we took the bus. We hardly noticed the distance as we walked and talked together. This was a betwixt and between time. We were no longer in grammar school but not yet in high school. There was nothing really outstanding about the school or the curriculum. The lunches were good. Finally! I was finished with plain old arithmetic. We were being taught *business math*. They taught us some short cuts when adding a column of figures and also how to write checks and balance a checkbook. We had a required course called *Elocution* that I hated. We had to get up in front of the whole class and speak or recite something with feeling. It seemed to me just to be a good way to make a fool of myself. When I read out loud, I just naturally read with expression but when I did it for this class I was so conscious of having to do it it came out flat. Because of that class I was relieved when my mother told me she had been offered a good job in Atlanta and she and I would be leaving almost immediately.

## *On to Atlanta*

My mother was offered a better job by Puritan Mills in Atlanta in the fall of 1937. She had to report right away or at least as soon as possible. Since she would need a car in her work she had to drive there. The car she had been using was one that Dad and Albert had built from parts from the junkyard. The body they found was a Chevrolet coupe of about 1929 vintage They bought either a four or six cylinder engine bloc. I remember sitting with the bloc between my knees while I hand ground the valves so I should know how many valves I ground but I don't. The car ran fairly well and served for running around the city and the surrounding area but it was questionable for such a long trip.

Dad didn't want Mother to make the trip alone nor could I be left in the house alone while he went with her. The solution to the problem was for me to go with her and Dad to take care of moving later after she and I found a place to live in Atlanta. That, of course, necessitated my being out of school for a time.

We left New Orleans on highway 90 east through the Rigolets on a sunny October day. Just as we crossed the last Rigolets bridge we heard a strange sound, felt a small jolt and knew that something on the car had given way. A man stopped when he saw us stop. He checked the car from front to rear and told us that a leaf in the leaf spring on the right front wheel had broken. We limped on until we reached the first garage. It was just over the border in Mississippi. When we told the mechanic our problem, he went out back to look among his collection of old parts and luckily found a leaf spring that would fit. We had to wait while he jacked the car up, took the wheel off and removed the broken spring. Then he had to fit his spring on and put everything back together. It seemed to take quite a long time and all this while a storm was brewing. Finally, it was done and we could go.

As we drove along, the sky became darker and darker as we headed toward the Gulf coast. We soon found ourselves in a slashing rainstorm. We discovered that our roof leaked. By the time we arrived in Gulfport there were purply black stains on the headliner and no sign that the storm was letting up. We saw a tourist court right on the beach and promptly took shelter. Tourist courts were a new thing just developed in the last few years. I had seen them on Airline Highway at home but I had never been in one. This court was made up of about eight individual cottages and each cottage was furnished with a bedroom with a bed, bed table and lamp, radio and a sofa. It had a bathroom and a carport. Ah, that carport. That was just what we needed to get our leaky car roof out of the weather.

The next day was beautiful and sunny so we started early and headed for Mobile where we then took US 31 to Montgomery, Alabama. We spent that second night somewhere east of Montgomery in a strange little tourist court up in the hills.

Each cabin looked like a chicken coup or a large outhouse from the outside since it was covered with board and batten instead of clapboard and had a Z braced front door. The inside was pleasant with a homemade quilt on the comfortable looking bed. It was heated with an iron pot-bellied woodstove. We needed the heat because that late fall evening up in the hills was chilly.

We arrived in Atlanta early the next afternoon and started looking for somewhere to stay. We found a boarding house on Ponce de Leon Avenue where we could stay a few days while Mother settled things at the mill. My being able to stay in Atlanta turned out to be impossible because Mother was being sent on the road immediately. I could not stay in Atlanta alone so I took the evening bus back to New Orleans to stay with Dad and go back to school until Christmas. We met the dawn around Biloxi. The bus arrived in New Orleans around ten or ten-thirty. So, it was back to Edward Douglas White until Christmas holidays.

Mr. Cole, one of the salesmen or a district manager for Purina feeds, who was a business friend of Mother's, volunteered to drive us to Atlanta at Christmas. We packed up our goods and put them in storage, shipped some of the things we would need right away and accepted the offer of a ride. I begged as hard as I dared to be allowed to ask Mr. Cole to tie my beloved bicycle onto his bumper but Dad wouldn't hear of it.

When we packed the things to put in storage, I saved out a few things like our electric iron, the silverware and some vital papers and maybe a few other things I now forget. I didn't want to lose them if it turned out we should default on the storage payments. I wish I had thought to take my Grandfather Grandjean's ivory chess set because ultimately, we couldn't keep up the storage payments so we lost everything except the family pictures. They had no value to anyone but us so Aunt Mabel went to the O. K. Storage warehouse and picked them up and saved them for us.

Mother had been sharing an apartment on Highland Avenue just off of Ponce de Leon, with a young woman who worked in the office at the mill. We were jammed up with so many of us in such a small apartment. The young lady moved out after Christmas. I was entered into Bass Junior High School. We couldn't afford the rent by ourselves so we moved to a boarding house run by a Mrs. White at 831 Ponce de Leon Avenue.

While we were living in the Highland Avenue apartment, I met a girl my age who lived in another one of the apartments. Her name was Irmgard Kern and she was from Germany. They had many interesting things. One of them was a folding umbrella about four inches long. I had never even heard of such a thing. It was small enough to carry in a schoolbag or a purse. I was embarrassed for America that Germany showed such inventiveness and we didn't. She had lots of beautiful homemade sweaters. I thought her mother had made them for her but it turned out that she had made them herself. We were the same age and I didn't know how to do that. This time I was embarrassed for myself. Also, in Germany she had already studied algebra and we didn't study it here until we were in the ninth grade. At Bass I had a Miss Richards who was wonderful at explaining algebra. She went all around the problems from different angles until she finally hit on a way that cleared it up for us. Though I liked algebra better than arithmetic I never would have made it if Miss Richards had not been such a good teacher. Thank goodness, when I moved up to Girl's High School Miss Richards was promoted there also and I was lucky enough to be assigned to her class for Algebra II.

I asked Irmgard what made them decide to come to America. She said that things were getting bad in Germany. Her father had been a wine merchant but at first, I didn't know the family was Jewish and even if I had known I didn't know what Hitler was doing to the Jews. I had begun to hear about Hitler and his incursions into neighboring countries. It was obvious that a war would have to be fought to rein him in. There is no way to make peace unless both sides desire it. Hitler did not desire it. In America we did not know how horribly he was treating Jews until our forces started finding the death camps after we joined England and Russia to fight World War II.

Soon after going to work at the mill Mother had bought a better second-hand car because the old car we had arrived in was about used up and she could not work without a car. She bought a Chevrolet two-door sedan. It was probably a 1934 or 1935 model.

I had been going to Bass Junior High School since we arrived in Atlanta. I liked it a lot better than Edward Douglas White in New Orleans. The school plant itself was modern with up to date classrooms, fine cafeteria, specially fitted music rooms and science labs, and a big auditorium with a well fitted stage and a film projection room. We had movies in general science class so we could actually see a tadpole develop into a frog and, through time-lapse photography, watch s flower follow the sun. In history we had movies showing the events leading up to the American Revolution including the signing of the Declaration of Independence. Atlanta was using advanced methods of teaching. The students were divided into learning groups according to their abilities. There were the fast learners, average learners and slow learners. That way the fast learners were not held up while the slower people were taking longer to understand the work and the slow learner was not exposed to a pace he could not keep up. In history we had to pick a particular part of what we were learning and do a project to illustrate it. Two of us worked together. For example, two of the boys decided to make wooden models of the different means of transportation for the period we were studying. All of this required a lot of research. Looking at everyone's work and listening to their explanations was very interesting and kept us all involved in the subject. It seemed a better way to learn history than by being fed a lot of names and dates to remember, though I concede that a time-line of dates needs to be remembered to help keep the chronology of history straight in your mind. There were many interesting elective courses. I had chosen to study home economics and chorus as my electives. There were well equipped sewing and cooking labs. There was a complete one-bedroom furnished apartment connected to the home-economics lab so all facets of home-making could be studied. We not only learned how to cook and sew but how to make beds, plan a balanced meal, set a proper table, plan a party, etc.

The school cafeteria was a pleasant place and the food was good. On bad weather days instead of hanging around in a gloomy basement or going back to our classrooms we went to the auditorium where we were shown movie short subjects during the rest of the lunch break. Sometimes special entertainments were brought to the school. One of the entertainments I particularly remember was Tony Sarg's Puppet Theater. He had been featured at the New York's Worlds Fair and was quite famous. He presented *Treasure Island* for us. I appreciated the opportunity to go to this fine school.

Fortunately, the boarding house was in the same school district as the apartment on Highland Avenue so I could continue to go to Bass until I graduated from the ninth grade. I think Atlanta had four high schools in the whole city, two for boys and two for girls. There was one for boys who were going on to college and a trade school for boys who were not. There was Girl's High, a prep school for Agnes Scott College and a business school for girls who were going to work in an office directly from high school. I chose Girl's High because I still had dreams of going to college.

Since mother was away, I had to take care of Dad. I washed and ironed our clothes. There were no clothes washing facilities in the boarding house, at least none for the boarders. I had to wash clothes in the bathtub on a washboard and hang them on the clothesline outside to dry. I also had to keep the room clean because there was no one else to do it. A least I didn't have to cook. The food was good for what it was, plain southern cooking. To me the best part was that there was a desert every day at dinner.

Living in a boarding house was a strange experience. I had a chance to meet a lot of people, some nicer than others. However, we had to give up some privacy. It was somewhat like living in a large not always congenial family. There was always someone to talk to and there was always something going on. We had an artist who drew illustrations for advertisements, a group of fake cowboys who sang and played guitar on the local radio station. Then there was Mrs. White's two sons and a daughter-in-law who lived there. There was a traveling photographer who took school pictures. He took pictures of Dad and me and anyone else who wanted one. We also had a Greek fellow named Anastases Demetrius Ateshaglu (sp?) who was studying at Georgia Tech. His name was so long we called him 'Steve.' He was opinionated and selfish. If he was passed a dish that he liked he thought nothing of taking all of it no matter that there were other people who had not yet been served. We soon learned not to let him have a dish until every one else had a serving. He admired Hitler. Steve's code was "Might makes right." I wonder how he felt when Hitler invaded Greece. We were gone by that time. I've often wondered if he was called home to join the Greek Army. I hope so.

One thing I had always wanted was a camera. When a Kodak Brownie camera was offered as a premium at the local drug store, I was determined that it would one day be mine. The catch was I had to purchase a certain and very large amount of goods before I could get it. I was given a green card that was punched for the amount purchased. Once the card was filled out, I was to turn in the card and fifty cents and the camera would be mine. That little Bakelite camera was probably not worth much more than fifty cents. Everyone in the boarding house knew what I was trying to do so every time anyone needed anything from the drugstore, they sent me to buy it so I could get my card punched. When the day came that the camera was finally mine one would have thought I had come into possession of the crown jewels. It came with a roll of film so the first thing I did was take a picture of Mrs. White and her nephews. I saved the remaining exposures for my coming vacation back to New Orleans.

In the summer of 1938, I returned to New Orleans to visit all of my relatives. I left on the five o'clock Greyhound bus from Atlanta. I slept for most of the night, met the sunrise over the Gulf of Mexico on the Gulf coast of Mississippi and soon arrived in New Orleans I stayed awhile at Aunt Mable's house and while there I went to visit my old friends, Elma, Jewel and Florine. We went to the park and I took pictures of everyone. Then I went to Aunt Helena's house in Raceland. Shirley, Soledad, Carmen, Sylvia and Peter were still living at home so I had plenty of company. The trouble was Shirley, Soledad and Carmen all had jobs and Shirley and Soledad were dating so Carmen, Sylvia and I palled around. Pete was only three years old. I had not started dating yet.

I volunteered to help with the housework. That pleased and surprised Aunt Helena. I don't know why it should have surprised her. I had always helped the girls with their chores when I stayed there. Hadn't she ever noticed? She made ginger bread and home-made ice-cream because she knew how much I liked them. She planned a picnic with her friend Mrs. Beula Acosta. Ms. Beula took her brother Douglas Knight and her daughter Amelia to Bayou Dulac where we met them.

Aunt Helena brought Sylvia, Peter, Alfredo and me. I had never been there before. That was the day that Peter got out of the shallow water into the deep water and nearly drowned. Alfredo, who was nearest to Peter tried to help him and got into trouble himself. Mr. Douglas dove in and saved both of them. That near drowning experience caused Peter such a fear of water he had a hard time later on passing the swimming requirement at West Point.

Since the older girls were all working during the day, I spent a lot of time with Sylvia and Peter. One day Peter and I were lying on our stomachs on the floor paging through a Life Magazine. We turned a page and found pictures of paintings by Peter Paul Reubens. There were naked people in the picture. Peter said, "I don't know why they show pictures of naked people. They look much better with their clothes on."

Sylvia and I spent more time together than we ever had before. To my surprise I found that she was an interesting person. Before this she had just been the pesky little sister. Sylvia, her friend Sister (Hilda) Guidroz and I formed a secret club that met in the shelter over the cane hoist at the dummy railroad track in the cane field. We even had a secret code. I was doing all of this to amuse the girls because, at fifteen, I was getting too old for that sort of play. I had to do something to pass the time until the older girls came home from work.

Soon it was time to return to Atlanta. Mother happened to be home that weekend. There was still some summer left so when she returned to the road, I went with her. She had to go to Waycross, Georgia where she had to call on a feed dealer. Waycross is just a small town with nothing special to recommend it. On the way there we had driven through Brunswick, Georgia which is a lovely old town. While there we drove across to Sea Island to see how the rich people lived. We saw the Cloisters Hotel where only the rich can afford to stay. I never dreamed then that in the future I would stay there not once but twice.

After she finished her work around Waycross, we went back to Atlanta to get her next assignment. Whatever it was she went on alone and I stayed with Dad. Dad and I went to the movies at the Highland theater almost every Sunday. I think admission was fifteen cents. After the movie we went next door to a delicatessen to eat supper because no supper was served at the boarding house on Sunday night. We always ordered a ham and Swiss cheese sandwich on rye bread. On Sundays when money was scarce, we left out the movie and ate at the Toddle House that was across the street and down a block from the house. They made the best chocolate pies. They also had an honor system way to pay for what you bought. The waiter would give you a tab with the amount of your purchase stamped on it. As you walked out you dropped the tab and the change into a container by the door. No one checked to see if you put in the right amount but I think almost everybody complied or they would have gone out of business.

Another amusement that was popular in Atlanta at that time was roller skating at the very fine rinks scattered around the city. We would get up a group from the people at the boarding house including Tom White. Dad would drive Mrs. White's car. She bought a car but didn't know how to drive. Dad was teaching her but until she felt confident, he drove for her. Dad was a very good skater and I was getting pretty good myself. I could do figures and skate backwards. I had been roller skating since I was five so I had plenty of experience. During these outings I was learning to dance on skates with a partner. Atlanta was such an insular town there really wasn't much to do besides going to movies and skating. It was so different from wide open New Orleans. They were still angry about General Sherman's burning of Atlanta during the Civil War. I felt that they didn't know that the Civil War was over and had been since 1863. By 1939 when we were there that was 76 years for heaven's sake. It was time for them to get over it. Dad always described Atlanta as so dull that they took up the sidewalks at nine p.m. on Saturday night and didn't put them back until Monday morning. Mother loved Atlanta, perhaps because for her it was coming home to us, but Dad and I didn't love it or even like it and never would.

I had made some friends at Bass Junior High so I had someone to walk to school with and someone to eat lunch with. My best friends were, Anne Ittner, Josie Gillentine, Mary and her sister Tommie Callaway, Ann Adams and Betty Brinson. We visited after school, especially to go skating up and down the hills of Atlanta. Anne Ittner lived further up the hill toward Decatur from me and a block or so off of Ponce de Leon. Since it was all uphill from my house it was a struggle to get there on skates. I usually walked the skates on the grass verge between the sidewalk and the street. But on the way home all I had to do was coast down the hill. That part was great.

Josie lived just outside of Decatur. Her house was on a large lot and best of all they had a pony to ride. After taking turns riding the pony Josie liked to play Monopoly. She played the complete game figuring percentages on property sales and mortgages. We spent hours at it. I've always thought of the game as Monotony especially when one goes into such extremes as doing all of that arithmetic. I hated being unable to invite them to my home but there was no way I could invite them to visit in a boarding house or stay for lunch. It made me ashamed to be living in a boarding house though, otherwise, I thought that living in a boarding house was somewhat of an adventure. It certainly was not the worst place I ever lived in.

I graduated from Bass Jr. High in June of 1939. I was looking forward to being a high school student; really grown up almost, but that was months away. During that summer I traveled all over Georgia and Tennessee with Mother. I was thrilled to be able to do that and I think she was delighted to have company. It gets very lonely on the road.

Mother had just bought a 1939 Pontiac. It was our first new car we ever owned. When Mother drove it on her job, she had trouble with it. It would be going along nicely and then stop for no apparent reason. She brought it back to the dealer and they checked it out but could find nothing wrong with it. It happened again and they checked it again. This time they took out the whole fuel system but could not find the problem. The mechanic advised her to blow in the gas tank to get the fuel to move. He thought it might be an airlock causing the problem. That worked a few times when she tried it. We were in Tennessee when it stopped again so Mother got out and gave it a mighty blow forgetting that she had just recently stopped to fill the tank. The pressure forced the gasoline back out of the tank and all over her. I had been learning to drive so I begged her to let me drive to the next town. Her eyes were streaming and her clothes were all soggy with gas sending fumes to her nose. She insisted on driving herself. When we arrived at the hotel, she checked us in and immediately asked for a doctor. The doctor told her to wash off well and put olive oil all over where the gas had touched her skin. Instead of smelling like a gas station she now smelled like a salad. Her clothes had to go to the cleaners.

While we were in Tennessee we went to Clarksville. She had some business to do there and since that was where Mr. Cole, the friend who had driven us to Atlanta, and his family lived we went to visit. Mr. Cole was not there but Mrs. Cole was very nice and made us feel welcome. They had several sons. The eldest was a bit younger than me. We played baseball and did a lot of sweating so they wanted me to go swimming with them in the creek behind their house. Luckily, I had my swim suit in the car. The creek was actually deep enough really to be able to swim. Best of all they had rigged a rope in a tree that hung over the water. We would take hold of the rope, run with it and when it was over the middle of the water, we would let go making a big splash. It was just like pictures we've all seen of the old swimming hole. They also had a skiff that we had fun diving off of or turning over and dumping everyone. We worked up quite an appetite for the delicious big dinner Mrs. Cole invited Mother and me to stay to share with them. All in all, it was a memorable day.

As soon as we were back in Atlanta, she returned to the car dealer and this time they took the whole fuel system apart again and tested each piece. The trouble turned out to be in the carburetor. When it was cast a bubble had formed in the metal and then burst leaving a tiny hole. That tiny bit of air being sucked into the carburetor was causing an airlock. Once the carburetor was replaced, we never ever had to do much to the engine more than routine maintenance. Even when the odometer passed 100,000 miles the engine was so quiet we had to rev it to be sure it was running. The body was going to pieces but the engine was still good when we traded it in.

I thought that traveling and staying in hotels would be glamorous as it seemed in the movies but it isn't. No matter how nice the accommodations are the room is impersonal. In all those strange towns we were strangers. Since we were two women alone there weren't many places we could go unescorted except to a restaurant or to the movies. Most of the time we had seen the movie feature already in Atlanta and one can eat just so many meals. That meant staying in the room and reading. Much as I love to read even that gets tiresome. I was not sorry when the trip was over. I was ready for the big adventure of becoming a high school student.

*1939-Pontiac first new car we ever owned.*

*Nathalie high school*

## *High School and Beyond*

The house at 831 Ponce de Leon was sold to a dental fraternity so the whole boarding house had to move in September just before school started. Mrs. White rented the house at 867 Ponce de Leon on the corner of Bonaventure. Moving was just a matter of carrying everything about half a block up the street and getting resettled.

Strange that this city that had no tradition of French culture should have so many streets with French names and no idea in the world of how to pronounce them. It hurt my French trained ears to listen to them butcher the pronunciations.

Atlanta is divided into four sections, North East, North West, South East and South West. Girl's High was in the south east part of the city. I think where we lived was in the north west section so the school was a long distance away. We had school busses to pick us up in the morning but in the afternoon, we had to go home by streetcar. There was a streetcar siding on the school grounds. They took us to the center of town where we then transferred to the one that took us closest to our home. I often used the time between streetcars to go to the main library in town to do research for homework assignments.

I also often went to Woolworth's soda fountain to get a cherry coke between streetcars. Sometimes my friends and I would stay downtown window shopping but not very often because time was precious.

Girl's High was enormous. It was set on large grounds near Grant Park. When seen from directly in front I judged the building to be about a block and a half long. It was three stories tall with classrooms on each side of a wide hall that ran from one end of the building to the other on the second and third floors. There was a bank of lockers by each homeroom in an alcove between classrooms. The offices, cafeteria and physical education rooms were in the basement. Probably the auditorium was down there too. There was a furnished one-bedroom apartment next to the home economics lab on the second floor.

Each freshman was assigned a senior sister who was supposed to assist the freshman to adjust to being in high school. There was also a bit of hazing too. There was Kids Day. All freshmen had to come to school dressed like a little girl with a big bow in her hair. She was given a big candy-cane she had to carry around all day. After school the senior sister took her kid sister still carrying the candy cane to the movies in town where she had to crawl up the steps to the balcony. It was fun and not too embarrassing since so many of us were going through the same thing at the same time.

Girl's High was divided the same way as was Bass Jr. High. I must have barely made it into the fast group by the skin of my teeth because I found the work very hard. I had never found schoolwork hard before. I felt I had to run to stay even. We had to have a book report in every subject except home economics. Can you imagine having a book report in Algebra? I had to read about Euclid for that but that was easier than doing the actual algebra. Thanks to Miss Richards again, I made it through algebra II. I was taking English literature, French, ancient history, algebra, biology, home economics and music. The music class was stringed instruments. I was going to learn something about playing a violin at last. The only trouble was that instead of concentrating on learning the violin we were required to learn all the stringed instruments, violin, viola, cello and bass. The hardest part of learning to play the stringed instruments is bowing. If you pull the bow across the strings with too little pressure on the bow it bounces and if you press too hard it screeches. None of these instruments have frets either. You have to find the note by ear. Nothing worthwhile is ever easy.

In English we were studying Shakespeare. It was *As You Like It* this time. We had done *Julius Caesar* in junior high. We took turns to read it aloud. Here I was back to reading with expression. We had to learn certain passages by heart. That was the easy part. Our French teacher was a French lady. Once we had been through a lesson in English, she gave instructions about what she wanted done in French and we had to answer in French. It was a really good way to hear the proper pronunciation and learn the words. Ancient history for the western world always starts in Greece. It should start at the very least in Egypt I would think but it doesn't. Anyway, it was Greece we were studying so for my project in ancient history I had a contest to see who could bring in the longest list of examples of the use of Greek architectural elements that the class could find used in the buildings in downtown Atlanta. I had to make a survey of downtown Atlanta buildings so I could judge the lists when they were turned in. Though school was hard I found it interesting and I enjoyed learning. I was looking forward to going to this wonderful school for my sophomore year but it was not to be.

There was big excitement in Atlanta in December of 1939. The premier of the movie *Gone with the Wind* was to take place at the Fox theater. In mid-December the movie stars started arriving. Once all of them had come in they were to parade through downtown Atlanta. We were let out of school so we could go to the parade. Most of the movie stars who were in the picture came and so did some who were not. They were all in convertibles sitting on top of the back seat so we could see them. Clark Gable came with his wife Carole Lombard, Vivien Leigh with her sweetheart Laurence Olivier, Olivia de Haviland, Leslie Howard, Ann Rutherford. The parade was delayed so we were standing out in the cold a long time and then the parade was long. By the time it was over my feet were cold and had little feeling in them. They felt like blocks when I tried to walk afterwards, but it was worth it. The night of the premier Dad and I were in the crowd to see the movie stars. They were in closed limousines to go to the theater. Some sat forward and waved to the crowd. The one who made a big hit doing that was Claudette Colbert one of those who was there but was not even in the movie. I went to see the movie some weeks later in the same theater where it premiered. The movie was four hours long so after about two hours the house lights came on and there was a long intermission before the last half of the movie started. Even as long as the movie was it did not cover everything in the book. If it had the movie would have been so long, we would have had to spend the night in the theater. The movie was good but I liked the book better.

My mother was selling Manamar chicken feed to dealers in carload lots. The feed was fortified with dried kelp so it had additional minerals in it and had proved to be excellent nutrition for animals. She had been given a large territory to cover. She had Florida, Georgia, Alabama, Tennessee and South Carolina. She did a phenomenal job. Every month she was the top salesman. The men resented it that a woman outshone them. They made it impossible for her to remain in the job by threatening to quit en masse. Though Mr. Card hated losing her he could not afford to lose his whole crew so he had to terminate mother. So, in June 1940 we left Atlanta and returned to New Orleans with no job and no prospects.

I was torn with regret about Girl's High yet thrilled to be going home. We packed all we had with us, set Tepete, the canary, in his cage on top of all the stuff and took off the night before we were supposed to leave because we were so excited to be going home, we couldn't sleep. Somewhere along the way—north Alabama I think—I told mother and Dad a joke I had heard recently. Dad was driving. He was laughing so much he had tears in his eyes. He couldn't see where he was going and had to pull off of the highway to recuperate. Every time the car stopped the canary started singing. It got so that when we saw a red light we turned to the canary and said, "Come on Tepete make the light change." As soon as we stopped, he sang and the light changed. Of course, we knew the light was about to change anyway.

When we arrived in New Orleans, we checked with our friends Mr. and Mrs. Edward Ward who had a big house at 2708 Coliseum Street that was divided into apartments. Mr. Ward was a purser on a ship but when he was home, he did maintenance on the house. It was in tip-top shape. Mrs. Ward was a very nice person who was a stickler for cleanliness. She kept everything spick and span. They lived in the back apartment on the second floor. When they rented you a furnished apartment it was not only furnished with furniture but there was bread in the pantry, butter and eggs in the refrigerator, sheets, pillows and blankets on the beds, soap and toilet paper in the bathroom and dish soap and dish towels in the kitchen. They said they had an empty apartment on the third floor that had just become available and they hadn't had time to clean it. We took it. Mrs. Ward came up and gave us all the extras they always provided and saw that the new stove they had just put in for the former tenants was very dirty. She was so ashamed. I told her it was ok I'd take over the job of cleaning it. I did. I don't know how anyone can get a stove that dirty in six weeks but the former tenants had managed it. There was so much burned on grease that I had to use a paring knife to scrape off enough of it so that the cleaner I was using could reach through to do some good. I worked on it until it finally looked almost as good as new but it took me several days.

The trouble with that third-floor apartment was that it was so hot. It was, after all, formed from the attic of the house and was not designed to catch any cross ventilation. There wasn't that much air to catch to tell the truth. Not only that but it was on the third floor! That made for two long flights of stairs. The house had fourteen-foot ceilings which makes twenty-eight feet of stairs. That may not sound like much but it is a lot when you have to go up and down them a couple of times a day. It was rough climbing all those stairs. The thought of that climb made us very careful to do all that we had to do downstairs before we went up and once we were up it took an important mission to make us go down.

Aunt Inez and her husband, Carter Cook owned ten acres of ground along the Galveston highway with a partially built house on it in Arcadia, Texas. Cookie who was a master pipe fitter for Allis Chalmers Company was working on the building of the Dow Chemical Plant in Freeport, Texas. They were living in a trailer near the job. They offered us the use of the house. They were glad to have someone to stay there and take care of it. We had no other choice since neither Mother nor Dad had found work in New Orleans. We moved to Arcadia, Texas in August 1940.

It was horribly hot that year. There had been no rain so the ground was baked dry. There were cracks in the yard that were wide enough for a person to put their arm in as far as their biceps. The only thing that made living there bearable was the breeze that came from the Gulf of Mexico. It was cooling as long as you were in the shade.

The house Cookie had built was about thirty-eight feet long and about thirty-five feet wide. It was divided lengthwise by a wall from front to rear. The side facing the Gulf was finished up to a point but was not divided into rooms. That side contained the bedroom, eating area and kitchen. On the other side there was a bed in a cleared area but the rest of that side was full of building materials. When Cookie built the foundation, he put lag bolts in the concrete then bolted the sills to the foundation. The area was subject to hurricanes and he was taking care to make the building as strong as possible. That was a big plus but a big minus was that there was no inside plumbing. All water had to be hauled from a hard water well at the back of the property. No matter what brand of soap a person used it was impossible to make any suds. If you washed your hair in that stuff your hair would stick out in every direction. We gathered rain water and used it to wash our hair.

Mother got a job with Uncle Johnny's Feeds in Houston. We were beginning to get ahead a little since we didn't have any rent to pay. Mother was home every night which made Dad and me happy.

One day we were adopted by a dog. He came in off the highway and decided to stay with us. He was of indeterminate breed but he was an allover strawberry blond color. Since we didn't have a dog, we let him stay. I named him Shadrack Meshach Abednego after the three children in the fiery furnace in the Bible. We called him Shag for short and he was shaggy. There was no gate in the three-wire barbed wire fence but he never went off of the property. He would sit in the middle of the driveway on the fence line and look out but he never went any further. One day Mother made a huge batch of pancakes. We couldn't eat them all. We offered one to Shag. He came and took it las though he really wanted it. We watched to see what he would do. He went into the yard and dug a hole for it then covered it up. When he returned, we offered him another pancake which he took and planted that one too.

Soon it was time for school to start so I was enrolled in the local school. It took me only one day to realize that it was a terrible school! I don't want to seem to brag but I felt I knew more than the teachers there did. I could not waste my time going to such an inadequate school so I begged Mother and Dad to check to see if it was possible for me to go to school in Alvin, Texas which was in the next county. We went to talk to the principal who informed us that we would have to pay a nominal sum of about seven dollars a month, in order to enroll me there. Mother agreed so I was enrolled. I was relieved. The county line was two or three miles back up the road from our house so I had to be driven up the highway to catch the bus to school and had to be picked up there after school every day.

Alvin, the town where the better school was located, was a small, seemingly well to do town. The citizens spent a lot of their time and money on having a fine school with a good football program and a really fine band. The town itself had two or three main streets with a post office, a few stores, a small hospital, a movie theater, a funeral home, and the office of the county newspaper. That was the down town part of town. There were some quite nice homes in the residential areas. There were several places to eat. There was a café in town and there were some hamburger places around the edges.

The school covered quite a lot of ground. The administration building was two stories tall and though it housed offices most of the second floor was devoted to a large auditorium with an excellently appointed stage. An electric organ had recently been installed. The basement contained the cafeteria. To the right as one faced this building was the Junior High School building with the Grammar School some way behind it. On the other side of the administration building was the High School campus. The two-story high school building was flanked by the home economics cottage. Behind that was the Shop building and beyond the Shop was the Band building. Directly behind the high school building were three tennis courts and beyond them was the gymnasium. Running behind the whole school was the football field and the stands. Though the school plant was impressive the curriculum was limited. They had no French program, only Spanish so I lost that credit in the transfer. The school accepted all of my other credits. I took English, Geometry, Texas History, Chemistry, Home Economics and Journalism. In every state where I attended school, I had to study the state history so I had already had Louisiana, Mississippi and Georgia history. Now it was Texas I was studying. It's a good thing that I like history so much. I'm not much for the sciences but I found Chemistry very interesting. The periodic table was a revelation to me. Some of the experiments were fun so it wasn't too bad until the seemingly easy teacher who never gave homework assignments in the book gave us an exam on the whole book at the end of the year. It was a good thing for me that he graded that exam on the curve. English was easy for me. We had some lessons in composition that I enjoyed. Strangely enough I found plane Geometry easy. It was so logical and you could look at the page and see the drawn example of what the theorem was saying. In journalism I automatically became a reporter for the school newspaper that was published as a page in the County News. I wrote features. I also worked on parts of the annual. My job was to draw illustrations for the different sections of it. I helped out with other jobs on the annual wherever needed. In Home Economics the first assignment was in sewing. We had to make a pair of pajamas for ourselves. When we all finished our project, we put on our pajamas, lined up in front of the Home Ec. Cottage and had our picture taken. The picture was published in the annual that year. We took cooking in the second semester. There was a cooking course that was offered to boys. They were taught camp cooking for the most part. Girls were also welcome to take shop.

  About a week or two after school started, we heard a hurricane warning on the radio. People were advised to take shelter in the school in Alvin. Mother wanted to go. but since Cookie had built the house so strongly Dad and I opted to stay. We didn't know about boarding up the windows then. Anyway it was already raining heavily. The wind was picking up. I went outside and tried to lean on the wind but it was not yet strong enough to hold me up. Dad went and turned the car around pointing to the road in the event we had to evacuate and brought the dog in. Soon the wind was blowing harder. Cookie had put in windows that had one big pane instead of installing windows divided into smaller panes with wood. Dad and I started going around the house checking. When we came to the window in the bedroom, we saw it had a long diagonal crack in it. Just as Dad got there the window exploded and cut the skin right off of the first joint of his second finger. I saw him turn white. Mother got busy and bandaged his hand. I found some of the pieces of the window pane embedded in my leg. I just picked them out. None of them caused enough damage for a bandage. That decided us to vacate. I packed a suitcase with sheets and towels while Dad went to turn the lights on on the car so Mother and I could find it. He could hardly find it himself. The water in the yard was knee high. When he passed the shelter of the house the wind snatched off his glasses and threw them into the water. He said he never thought he would be so glad finally to put his hand on a car tail light. After putting on the car lights he came back to get us. He carried the suitcase and guided Mother to the car. I had Shad on a leash but he was almost having to swim. We all made it to the car. We found a lot of use for the towels I had packed. I think I used two trying to dry Shad. He decided the place for him in these dire circumstances was on my lap. A fellow passing by saw our lights on so he stopped his car to see if he could help. He got in the car out of the wind. Dad tried to start the car but the wind had blown the rain into the engine so none of the spark plugs were able to fire. There was nothing to do but to sit out the rest of the storm in the car; me with a wet dog still on my lap. During the night the wind pressed on the car so hard I thought it was going to turn us over but it didn't. We all finally fell asleep. When we woke up in the morning, we found all the water gone. The fellow who had stopped to help got in his car that was facing away from the wind. It started right up so he left. We unfolded ourselves out of the car and went back into the house. Later, Dad went looking for his glasses. He found them in the middle of the driveway. There was a toe print almost touching the glasses on one side and a heel print on the other side almost touching them but the glasses were fine. All they needed was to be washed. That was some sort of miracle. We found out later that it was a good thing that we didn't drive during the storm because all the sun shelters for cattle made of corrugated iron in the pastures below Houston had been torn apart and blown across the highway. Some were embedded in the advertising signboards. They would have sliced into the car and possibly killed us. We also found out that the hurricane had taken the roof off of the movie theater in Alvin.

After our living in Arcadia a while, Cookie found a clerical job for Dad at the Dow Chemical site in Freeport. Dad lived on the site in a men's boarding house.

Mother and I couldn't stay out in Arcadia by ourselves so we moved into Alvin into an apartment in the home of Mrs. Edwards. She was British from the

Isle of Wight. Her maiden name was Edwards and she married an American naval captain named Edwards so she didn't even have to change her name. She was a widow when we knew her. She had divided her house into two apartments. After we lived there a while, we became quite friendly with Mrs. Edwards. The house was only about a block from school which made it easier for me since I was so involved in so many things and sometimes had to stay at school to finish different projects. Dad had to live in Freeport because Mother was using her car in her work so he couldn't use it to drive back and forth every day. We were glad to be in a place that was closer so Dad could come home on week-ends sometimes when he could catch a ride.

He finally bought an old Pierce Arrow and moved in with us. I think it was a 1933 or 1934 model. I'm just guessing. It was a luxury car in its day. It had a twelve-cylinder engine so the hood looked very long when you were sitting in the front seat. It was in good condition inside and out. There were spare tires in each fender well with rear view mirrors standing on top of the tire covers. It could comfortably seat seven people because there were two jump seats in the rear compartment. There were pull down silk shades in all of the back windows except the windows in the doors. There were crystal bud vases on each side of the back seat. When I sat back there while Dad was driving and Mother was in the passenger seat, I felt like I needed a telephone to talk to them. The metal used to make the body was at least an eighth to three sixteenths of an inch thick. Dad used the car to take about seven or eight people to work at Dow every day. He said he had no trouble edging into traffic coming home because the car was so big and so heavy the lighter, newer cars always gave way and let him in.

Mother planned to go to New Orleans to find work and Dad was still in Freeport. I did not want to change schools in my senior year so the principal suggested we talk to Mrs. Helen Herring who was recently divorced to see if she could rent me a room so I could finish the school year in Alvin. We went to see her and she agreed to the arrangement. I would be company for her and I could baby-sit her two children, Elaine and Nancy. Elaine was seven or eight years old and Nancy was just over a year old. It was great for me. I took Tepete and moved in. I had a room of my own in a nice brick home with indoor plumbing. After the no plumbing situation in Arcadia I had learned to value things like that. Helen was very pleasant and I enjoyed the children. Her cooking skills were minimal but though it wasn't gourmet, we had enough to eat. I helped with the dishes.

I noticed while proof-reading this autobiography that my parents were always "going to New Orleans to find work." I suppose when things are not right where you are it is normal to go home where things are familiar to try to get your life back together.

I used to take Elaine and her friend to the movies on Saturday afternoon. It was like having a little sister. The owners of the movie house had a new roof put on immediately after the storm and repaired the soggy inside with new seats and rugs. On the end of every other row in the movie theater there was a two-person seat. I suppose it was for sweethearts to cuddle in. I sat there with a little girl under each arm. If the movie became too scary or exciting, they could hide their faces in my side until things improved.

The classes at school seemed easy to me after the tough classes I had in Atlanta. Now I had time to devote to extracurricular activities so I joined the Press Club, the Debate Club (because of a good-looking male teacher) and tried out for every stage production that came along. I entered the state essay contest and won locally and at regional but lost at the state contest in Austin. The next year, 1941-42 I was elected editor of the annual. That year the debate team won locally and at regional but lost at state. Every club in the school was invited to present a one-act play at Stunt Night. The Press Club wanted to participate but no one could think of what to do. I suggested we do the skit *Toot Toot the Stranger* that my cousin Juliet learned at camp. She and some of her family presented it at one of our family drama nights in Raceland the summer before our move to Texas. I had the lead role of the queen. My robe of state was an old lace curtain and my scepter was a large peppermint stick. WE WON! We were asked to present our skit at the anti-aircraft base near Arcadia which we did. I was also in the senior play that last year. By the way, the good-looking male teacher got married during the first semester and transferred to a school in Houston. The new debate teacher was fresh out of college and her name was Miss Bunny. She was ok but, well, just not the same. So, I was stuck in debate that I was not crazy about. Every time I had to get up and argue my side of the question, I was so scared I had trouble breathing much less thinking. Just think, all that suffering for nothing.

I was happy in that nice school except for the fact that I was older than most of the students in my classes due to having been put back to do the sixth grade over when I transferred from French Camp to New Orleans and due also to my losing credits when I transferred from Atlanta to Texas. A girl being older than her classmates makes dating difficult. There were some students taking extra classes who had already graduated. I dated one of them named Steve Koenig. He played the violin beautifully. War was in the air. We knew we would have to be involved sooner or later. Steve joined the Marines so he wasn't there to take me to the senior prom.

I had my first paying job while I lived with Helen. I started working at the County Newspaper after school or whenever the publisher needed me. I think I made about four dollars a month. I was assigned to cover all the unexciting things like obituaries, birth announcements, weddings, etc.

At Thanksgiving that year Helen had her mother keep the girls so we could join my mother in New Orleans. Dad drove Helen's car. I was thrilled to be with my parents again. We stayed in the boarding house where Mother and Aunt Mable were living at 4515 Prytania Street. We shared a very nice dinner at the boarding house. Helen received a guided tour of New Orleans by people who knew the city thoroughly. Dad had to get back to work and I had to get back to school so we were back in Texas by Sunday night.

One Sunday a few weeks later Helen decided it was time for her to get out of the house for a while so she took us all for a ride around the countryside. Just as we got back on the Houston-Galveston highway returning to Alvin we heard on the radio that Japan had bombed Pearl Harbor on that morning, December 7, 1941. We hurried home and sat by the big radio in the living room and listened to the news. Roosevelt declared war on Japan and Germany so we were in it at last. Eligible men were conscripted into the Army. Many of the fellows joined the Navy or the Marines instead. The whole nation joined in the war effort. People planted Victory gardens, children gathered scrap metal, especially aluminum and we all submitted to rationing. Now that the war had started, rationing began. There was a shortage of many things. Of course, most of the gasoline was being used in Army vehicles and airplanes. Tires. sugar, coffee, meat and shoes were rationed. You had to have a stamp to get the rationed items. The government would declare the time when a stamp number was valid and it could be used only then and not before. Rationing caused a lot of civilian hardship but at least we were safe at home and not being shot at so we didn't complain much.

At Christmas I left Tepete in Helen's care and went to be with Mother and Dad in New Orleans and stayed at the boarding house with them. I don't remember much about it except that my parents gave me a beautiful gold ring with a green stone. I had never thought of wanting a ring but I loved it. When I returned to Alvin Helen was devastated to have to tell me that Tepete had died. She swore that she had fed him and kept his water filled. I told her I was sorry too but he had lived a long time for a canary and had probably died of natural causes.

Just before the end of school the seniors were given aptitude tests. I was surprised when I ended up in top ten percentile of the students in Texas in math! I was in the top ten percentile in the other subjects, too.

Since Steve was in California in the Marines, I went to the Senior Prom stag and so did other girls whose boyfriends were already gone. Some of the fellows who were too young to enlist were at the prom so some of us stags and some of the fellows and their dates decided the prom was a drag so we piled into cars and went to Houston. There wasn't much going on there either so we decided to get hamburgers at one of the drive-in places. After that, in all our prom finery, we went to the park. We went to the swings where the boys pushed the girls. Our dresses billowed in the wind. I remember it as a very nice time. Our evening was a lot more fun than the prom had been.

Mother had a job with Uncle Johnnie's Feeds in Houston doing what she had been doing in Atlanta, selling chicken feed to dealers. I suppose they needed salesladies since the men were being drafted. Things were looking up financially with Dad and Mother both working. The depression was ending. It was about time! We had been struggling financially for about twelve years.

I graduated in May 1942. Mrs. Edwards and Mother were there to cheer for me. Dad couldn't make it because of work. We celebrated by going to the drug store and having ice-cream sodas. I had been elected to the Quill and Scroll Society, an honorary journalism society, a year before and in 1942 I was elected to the Honor Society, an academic achievement society. Since I had finished high school in the upper third of my class, I should have been given a scholarship to a college. When I asked the principal about it he said I wasn't eligible because I had gone to their school for only two years. Such crazy rules! I didn't see why that should make any difference. I had earned it! But we didn't contest it. Neither my parents nor I knew that other scholarships were available and could have been applied for.

Now that the family was back together it was my turn to leave. Since I knew there was no chance for me to go to college, I had to find some way to prepare to earn my own living. I had an offer from dad's sister, Caroline Greandjean Moreno, Aunt Carrie to me, to stay with her and go to a business school in New Orleans. Within a few days of graduation, I was on the way to New Orleans to take up her offer. She had investigated and found one that was being run by a maiden lady of good family named Miss Ellis. The school was called the Twentieth Century Business School and was held in the Queen and Crescent Building in the business district. I had taken and passed typing in Alvin. Since I couldn't go to college, I guess this was the next best thing. My interests were all in the humanities but without a degree you can't earn a living in any of those subjects. I took typing again and shorthand. I was doing fairly well with shorthand and my typing was good so Miss Ellis recommended me to a lawyer to fill in while his secretary was out sick. She did that for each of us as we became more competent to give us on-the-job training and also so we could earn a bit of extra money. I can type at the rate of fifty words a minute but I never became proficient in short hand and, thank goodness I never needed it in any of the jobs I ever had.

Miss Ellis was a society maiden lady evidently struggling through the depression like the rest of us. I felt honored when she invited me to tea at her home on Jackson Avenue just off of St. Charles Avenue one Saturday afternoon. It was a lovely big house full of antiques where she lived with some of her family. I was surprised to find that they had no screens on the windows and so they still had to use mosquito bars on the beds. I thought that by 1942 everyone in the city would have screen doors and windows.

Aunt Carrie and Uncle Albert owned the house at 8132 Hickory Street on the corner of Dublin. All their children were married and gone from home. Their second son Bert had been drafted and was serving in North Africa so his wife Jennie was staying with them. Aunt Carrie and I got along quite well. She enjoyed showing me family pictures and telling me family stories and I enjoyed seeing the pictures and hearing the stories. She and Jennie and I enjoyed playing Liverpool Rummy also known as Contract Rummy. We would sit on the front screened porch after supper and after the supper dishes were done and play. We played that the first person who said, "I'll buy that" and grabbed it got the down card. That caused a lot of fingernail gouges and a lot of hilarity.

The back porch was screened too. We ate super out there and it was more pleasant than eating in the house on those hot summer nights.

On Sunday evenings Aunt Carrie always had what she called, "open house." Whoever was visiting and was still there at suppertime was invited to stay and eat with us. The big dining room table was always set with extra covers to accommodate these extras. She usually baked a cake on Saturday for these Sunday suppers. Sometimes she would let me decorate one of them.

Aunt Carrie had a rule that whoever was living at her house had to go to church on Sunday no matter what religion he might be. She insisted that I had to go to the nearby Presbyterian Church. I had just about given up religion by then but I went reluctantly the first two Sundays I was there but my heart wasn't in it. It was no use to try to buck her and cause a lot of trouble by refusing to go. On Sunday I would get all dressed up as though I was going to church but instead, I went to Audubon Park, sat on a bench and read a book until it was time to return. I don't think she ever knew the difference.

In October Cookie caused Dad to get fired. He was jealous because Dad had found a better job without Cookie's help. Cookie liked to have people beholden to him so he trumped up some excuse or other to get Dad fired. Uncle Johnnie's Feeds had to let Mother go because of gas rationing. She was not in an essential war industry so she couldn't get enough gas ration stamps for all of the traveling her job required. Both of them went back to New Orleans. They stayed at the same boarding house on Prytania as before. I left Aunt Carrie's house and joined them there.

Mother was taking a course in tool making. Dad worked at Todd shipyards doing electrical inspections on Liberty Ships. Every shipyard in the nation was building Liberty Ships as fast as they could to replace all the shipping that was being sunk by German U-boats. I was still going to business school. While we were living in the big upstairs room Deda came to stay with us. She had married Phonzo Gilbert and was about to have her first child. I don't know why she was having it here because they lived in Port St. Joe, Florida. Maybe she wanted it to be born near her mother. Whatever. Anyway, it was nice to have her. I remember all of us were in the waiting room at the hospital. There was Phonzo, Aunt Helena, Mother and me. It was my first experience at a birth. It seemed to take forever. I suppose that is how it is when you are waiting anxiously for news. As soon as the doctor came out and told us it was a girl and both mother and baby were doing fine, Phonzo went off to the florists looking for jonquils, Deda's favorite flower. Jonquils were out of season so it took him a long time to find them but he came back with a bouquet of them for her.

Mother heard that the Army Air Corps was looking for teachers for the technical school in Gulfport, Mississippi. She told Dad about it and wanted to go and apply but he was reluctant because he knew that neither of them had had much schooling and might not qualify. She convinced him that by now their life experiences had taught them enough to at least apply. She knew that he knew electrical systems inside out, upside down and backwards. All they could do was say no. They went to the interview, took the tests and both were accepted. Dad was to teach electrical systems and Mother was to teach basic tools in Ground School in Gulfport. Since Aunt Mabel and Alma were staying at the same boarding house where Mother and Dad had been, I stayed with them and continued with school.

There was a fellow named Bill Posey who lived in the boarding house. He worked at the Southern Regional Laboratory on the lakefront testing cotton fibers. He had been friendly with Mother and Dad and had often joined us in card games. He and I dated a few times. He thought he was in love with me but I was not in love with him and I told him so. Nevertheless, if I stayed home with a cold, he sent me flowers and candy, or books or anything he could think of to do for me. It was embarrassing since I could not return his love.

I felt like I was spinning my wheels. Everyone was either in the armed services or was busy doing war work of one kind or another. By February of 1943 I decided to give up school and join Mother and Dad in Gulfport. I packed my suitcases and took the train. Bill Posey came with me to the station and gave me a big Valentine box of candy. On the train I was seated with a lieutenant who was returning from furlough so we started talking and sharing the candy. Mother and Dad were living at 3318 West Beach apartment 6 at a place called Moody's Court. The apartment was over the court's office. It had a screened porch facing the Gulf with a nice view out over the water.

I thought I would be able to get a job at Gulfport Air Depot where my parents worked but the government had a rule that only two members of the same family could work at the same facility so that killed that idea. I kept house while my parents worked and started looking for work in and around Gulfport but there was nothing to be had. The wives of the military already had filled all the civilian jobs.

My parents liked to entertain boys they met on the field. They would invite them to the house for dinner so the fellows could enjoy a home cooked meal. The boys would bring things like onions from the mess hall that were hard to get at the civilian stores. I, of course, met these fellows and became friendly with some of them. One fellow I went out with was Chick Henn. He was from Washington D. C. I found him more interesting than any fellow I had known up to that time. He had a Harley-Davidson motorcycle that we used to ride up and down the coast road finding places to go and things to do. It was fun that lasted until he was shipped away. Then I met and really liked a young man from Chicago. He was a sweet gentle fellow and I went out with him often. We might even have been really in love but when he told me he was married I knew we had to end it.

When my Hidalgo cousins, who were working in Mobile, suggested that I try for a job there I jumped at the chance. They were living in a garage apartment on W. E. Cochran's farm in Whistler, Alabama. Dorothy was teaching in Whistler and was living with them. I joined them at the end of March and went to work at the Army Air Force, Air Service Command Air Depot at Brookley Field in April 1943. I was given a civil-service job designation number 232, clerk-typist. Shirley, Carmen and I were working at Brookley Field. Sylvia was living in town and working for the Corps of Engineers and Soledad with her baby, Diane, was living at her sister-in-law's house while her husband was in the Seabees somewhere in the Pacific.

In May Shirley, Carmen, Sylvia and I moved to 1559 Fernway in Mobile. It was a short street a block from and parallel to Government Street. I think the street at the nearest corner was Springhill but I am not sure. Fernway was a pretty little street. There was a little park down the middle of it with a fountain. Dorothy moved to Whistler. We rented two big bedrooms in a private home. We had the use of the kitchen for eating our breakfast and preparing our lunches to take to work. We ate our main meal out, usually at Morrison's Cafeteria, the same Morrison's I had admired when I was four years old. Whenever they had red beans on the menu, I had the hardest time getting them to put the rice on the plate first and then to pour the beans over it. Evidently, they had never seen beans served that way before. Mobile and New Orleans are not that far apart. One would think that the custom of eating beans over rice would have spread at least that far.

Shirley, Carmen and I worked in warehousing. The areas were divided into classes of materials handled. Shirley and I were in office supplies. I don't remember what class Carmen worked in but her work was very similar to ours. We received invoices from our troops, checked our inventory and sent them as much as we could from the current supply. The troops were fighting in North Africa at that time. Soon after I went to work, they initiated a new system of keeping track of inventory and I had to help install it. This work was all done by hand in 1943 long before IBM and electronics. When new stock came in, we entered the amount on the card for that product. Each time we sent any of it out we subtracted that amount from the total. When we took inventory, we made corrections on the card if necessary. If the people using the system did a careful job the inventory and the card record should have been the same. There were three shifts, so there were bound to be errors because not everyone is as conscientious one as another.

The shifts were: Day shift 7 to 3—Night 3 to 11- Graveyard 11 to 7. At most government instillations women were not allowed to work the Graveyard shift. Personally, I preferred the Night shift because we could sleep late, shop, eat dinner at noon in a nice restaurant or even go to a movie.

I forgot to mention our transportation. It is important because Brookley Field is a long way from the part of town where we were living. This all happened before I joined my cousins. Shirley and Carmen went to the bank and asked for a loan to buy a car. The bank refused them because they were women. Women didn't buy cars, men did. They needed the transportation so they went back to the bank and asked for a student loan. The bank granted that so they used the money to buy a car that they therefore named Professor. Professor was second, third, or even fourth hand and getting to the end of its life so it was sometimes reluctant to start. When that happened everyone but the driver got out of the car and pushed it into a start. Anyone who bought a car during that time had to buy second-hand. There were no new cars built during the war.

After I had been there a while, I was sent to a school on the field to learn Military Correspondence. As it is in so much of the service there is a right way to do things, a wrong way and the Army way. There is no explanation to why the correspondence has to be so different. It just is.

Work was not difficult. The best part was having my own money to spend even though, with rationing, there was a limit on what one could buy and a limit on what was being manufactured.

We all went to USO (United Service Organization) dances. It was the patriotic thing to do. It was good for the service men and for we girls because, with the shortage of civilian men, where else was a girl to get a dance partner? My cousins went to the Presbyterian church on Government Street and I joined them when they went to the entertainments there. We danced with a lot of soldiers and sailors and met a cross section of American men in the process. It was a revelation to me to realize how limited my knowledge of men was. There was one fellow from New York who, while dancing, told me that, "The girls down here ain't got no class." And I thought, "This fellow ain't got no manners." I wouldn't have tried to get his approval by changing anything about myself to try to please such as he. He was the worst I met so that was not so bad. Once I met a man who had been studying to be a priest. He was fascinating to me. We danced one dance then spent the rest of the evening talking about everything. It was stimulating since he was so well educated. One extreme to the other!

At one of the dances at the Armory I met a fellow who had been an Arthur Murry Dance School instructor. Dancing with him was wonderful. I felt like I was floating. I found myself doing steps I never knew I could do. We must have covered every inch of floor in that huge room. I don't think I ever knew his name and I never saw him again but I have him to thank for the most memorable evening of dancing of my life.

Every now and then we went to visit our parents. It was hard for me to coordinate my visits with my parents because they would be on one shift and I was on another. They were still entertaining fellows from their classes with home cooked meals so I met some of them on my visits. Of all the fellows I met at home I liked Alfred Groh best. He was from Wilkes-Barre, Pennsylvania and had been to college. We had great conversations. The trouble with getting to meet these fellows was that as soon as they finished the Ground School courses, they were shipped out. Alfred was good about writing. His letters were full of his current experiences (as much as the censors let get through), his dreams, his philosophies. They were never about love. Love was not a part of our relationship. He had a knack for writing in a way that made even the most insignificant thing interesting. I destroyed his letters when I got married but I wish I had kept them. Years later I met a couple in the Navy who were from Wilkes-Barre. I said that I knew one person who was from there. When they asked who it was, I told them it was Alfred Groh. They said they knew him and that he was teaching English and Composition at the college there.

I started talking to my cousins about moving to California and finding jobs there. Carmen and Sylvia thought it was a good idea. Dorothy was all for it. She had lived in California and taught there and loved the idea of going back. In preparation for leaving Dorothy sold her car for five hundred dollars, five one hundred-dollar bills. None of us had ever seen so much cash at one time so she passed it around for us to feel. I was impressed but it actually felt the same as five one-dollar bills. Just as we were about to buy our train tickets, I got a phone call from Dad saying Mother was sick and would I please come home. Shirley and I stayed in Mobile.

I put in for a transfer to Gulfport Air Depot. It took a long time for the transfer to come through but finally I was transferred to Gulfport Field, Army Air Forces Air Service Command, 38th Sub-Depot Supply. It was possible for me to work there because Mother had to resign. I was sent to work in the airplane parts section doing the same sort of clerical work I had done at Brookley Field.

The government had built housing for the civilian workers right across the street from the main gate to the air base. It was called Hardy Court and was where we lived in apartment number 55. It wasn't too bad considering that it was really temporary housing. At least it wasn't barracks. There was even a central recreation building where we could hold dances, play cards or whatever. Mother was elected mayor of the community.

When I arrived home, I found Mother in bed with both legs covered in small weeping blisters. It was some sort of allergy but the doctors could not find anything to do for it. Every time she went to New Orleans to see the doctor her legs would improve. As soon as she came home her legs got worse. We found out later that her allergy had something to do with the sandy soil around Gulfport, especially on the field where the ground was bare and was stirred up all the time by marching men and moving vehicles.

I don't think I was at Gulfport field more than a month to six weeks before we received the news that the ground school part of the base was going to be closed down. I had a hard time convincing civil-service to release me so I could move with my parents wherever they would go. The facility was moving to a place in Texas that had the same sort of soil as Gulfport so the base commander told us. He didn't recommend our going there. The reason he knew so much about the problem Mother was having was because his wife suffered from the same thing.

What do we do now? Head back to New Orleans of course. We always gravitated back to New Orleans. I suggested that we go to Dallas. We had always liked Texas. Mother went to the base commander and asked for gas coupons enough to get to Dallas where both Mother and Dad proposed to go to work for North American Aircraft in Fort Worth. That company was building Mustang fighter planes. He approved the idea and gave them the gas ration required. We headed home and stayed a few days with Aunt Helena before going on to Dallas. We stayed in a motel in Dallas until we found a unit in government temporary housing at 2803 La Salle Place. Unlike Hardy Court that had been bran new when we moved in, this place had been occupied before (by pigs I think) so we had a big job of scrubbing the place down. I was working on the floor of the shower when I began to feel really ill. Mother thought I was just goofing off but I had a fever and broke out in a rash. They called a doctor who came to the house and said I had caught German measles. He said that since I wasn't married nor pregnant that it was better to have this disease now because it often causes defects in unborn babies if you get it while you're pregnant.

Mother and Dad went to work at North American Aircraft but the same rule of two applied. I could not work there. I kept house and looked for work elsewhere. I'll have to admit that I did not look very hard. I was very lonely since I did not know a soul in the whole of Dallas. After I finished the housework, I looked for work. I answered adds but found nothing. One day while I was in town, I remembered that the Women's Army Corps was offering the chance to go to college as an inducement for women to join so I thought I'd look into it. I went to the recruiting station and found it was true. As I talked to them, I was convinced that this was the thing for me to do so I signed up. The next day I told my parents that I had joined the WAC. Dad was pleased but Mother cried most of the day. She had heard the rumor that the Women's Army Corps was formed to provide whores for the soldiers. That was a fifth-column bit of mis-information initiated by Hitler to slow down or to a stop the forming of the WAC. Why would the government spend all of that precious military money on the WAC to provide whores for soldiers? Every army since the beginning of time had done a good job of finding their own whores. After I had about a week to think about what I had done I started second-guessing myself. Maybe I wouldn't pass the physical. I started hoping I wouldn't pass the physical but, somehow, during the process of actually taking the physical my pride took over and I hoped to pass it. I did. On June 6, 1942 we heard that the Allied troops had made a landing in Normandy. We kept the radio on to catch all of the latest news. When the mail came that afternoon, I received my orders. I was to report to Fort Oglethorpe, Georgia for basic training. The packet included my train ticket and meal ticket. I don't remember how much time I was given to report but it was probably "as soon as possible."

Mother and Dad took me to the train where the last words I heard after "good-bye good luck" was "write often."

## *So Now I was a Soldier*

The train was so crowded there was standing room only. My train voucher had specified that I was supposed to travel in a Pullman car and have a berth to sleep in. Well, it was a nice thought but there was no berth available on this train. There may not even have been a Pullman car. Even if there was it was probably as full as possible. There were even people sitting in the seats in the small bathroom lobby. I kept walking (squeezing) down the aisle until I came to a spot large enough to set the one suitcase I was allowed to take to basic, on the floor. After standing for a good while I gave up and sat on the suitcase. Luckily, the spot I found to put my suitcase was right by a WAC lieutenant sitting on the aisle seat with a private soldier sitting at the window. She saw my predicament and said, "This soldier and I will take turns sitting on your suitcase so you can have some chance to sit on the seat." And that is what we did all the way to Memphis where the lieutenant and I changed trains to go to Chattanooga. That train was so empty everyone on the train had a whole seat to himself.

During the war the trains must have pulled out all the rolling stock they could find. Judging from some of the cars I rode in from Mobile to New Orleans they may even have taken cars out of museums. Some of the cars looked like they were from the 1800s with their swinging lamps, mahogany trim and straw seats; the kind of stuff you see in movies. The cars in the Chattanooga train were somewhat newer than that but not a whole lot.

When we arrived in Chattanooga there were girls gathered there from other trains who were waiting for transportation to Fort Oglethorpe. A string of Army troop transport trucks arrived. We were told to get aboard so, there we were a bunch of civilian girls in high heels and stockings, trying to climb aboard the back of these trucks. The driver was nice enough to hand up our suitcases or we never would have made it.

We were delivered to a place called "Receiving." We were marched to the clinic where we were given thorough physical and dental exams. Anyone found with hair or body lice was isolated and went through a decontamination process. Once the Army was satisfied with our physical condition, we were given extensive intelligence and aptitude tests.

In receiving we were given bedding and immediately we were taught how to make a bed "the Army way." We were introduced to barracks life, eating in a mess hall, pulling k.p. (kitchen police, translated as "whatever the cook tells you to do.") and doing things the Army way no matter if you learned a better and more efficient way to do the same thing. The Army is not receptive to new ways of doing things. If it was a good enough for Caesar it's good enough for them.

The next day we were issued our uniforms. We were dressed from underwear straight through to overcoats. As we went down the line, we held out our arms and they piled everything on them. We were issued summer shirts, skirts, tie, jersey dress for a dress uniform all in lovely khaki color, an exercise dress with matching bloomers in green and white striped seersucker; winter shirts, skirts, tie, jacket and socks in lovely olive drab as was the overcoat. Even the laundry bag they gave us was olive drab. We were issued two pairs of shoes. One pair was brown oxfords with an inch and a half heel and one was brown high-top shoes with a half inch heel. They were careful to fit the shoes properly. We also were issued a brown leather shoulder purse, khaki banana shaped hat and an olive drab hat that looked like a pot, and gloves and, finally and just in time before we fell over, we were issued two duffel bags to put most of the stuff in. Back at the barracks we were shown how to stow all this stuff. The closet and the footlocker had to be set up just so, the Army way, of course. We were to wear our uniforms from that day on. We were told to pack all our civilian clothes in our suitcase to be sent home. We kept out our own underwear and stockings because that rayon stuff that was issued was awful and would never do. The Army took care of shipping our suitcases home.

As soon as we were free from the sergeant, we started taking a good look at the things we had been issued. The rayon underwear had legs that went half way down our thighs. The underwear for winter were the style we called "snuggies" in civilian life. The legs came down to our knees. If we stretched the legs they came down over our calves and looked like the pants worn in the boxing ring in the early years. Naturally we all made fists and made believe we were boxing as we went up and down the aisle in the middle of the room. Then we tried the rayon stockings. Once we had them on, sat down and then stood up the knees bagged. Rayon once stretched does not spring back into shape. How would that look after a day's work? Rayon in non-absorbent also. What a goofy material to have used for underwear and especially goofy for stockings.

We were not allowed off of the post or even out of the receiving area even though we now looked like official soldiers. We had to stay in receiving until a group finished basic training to make room for us to move up.

When we were not occupied by jobs like k.p., policing the area (picking up trash, cigarette buts and other debris), or latrine duty (cleaning face bowls and toilets), we were allowed free time. We used it to get acquainted with each other or write letters. I wrote home as often as I could.

I met two girls from Louisiana. One was from Baton Rouge. Her name was Jeanette Hodson who said she had joined the Army to research her doctoral thesis on propaganda. The other girl was from New Orleans. Jeanette and I found her to be a hollow shell. She was the kind of girl whose whole interest was as shallow as a saucer, a nothing person. Come to think of it, I never saw her in basic. She must have washed out on the intelligence tests. Wouldn't surprise me.

Our group was very lucky when we finally did go up to Basic because we were assigned to the North Post, Company 5, 22nd Regiment. The North Post was the original cavalry post with large permanent buildings set around a large grass parade ground. There were lawns, trees and sidewalks that gave a settled neighborhood appearance to the place. The South Post, on the other hand, was new and raw looking with scraped earth and temporary barracks. I'm glad we didn't go there. All of the buildings on the North Post were three story doubles over a basement and big enough to hold two companies, one on each side. The first floor had the office, the officer's quarters and the day room. The day room was a sort of living room area with sofas, chairs, and writing desks. The second and third floors were large barracks rooms with big windows. The mess hall and the latrines were in the basement. We had washing machines and ironing facilities in the latrine area. The toilets were in stalls and so were a few showers but most of us used the big shower room in the middle that had six shower heads, three on each side. We had mostly lost our modesty from so much close association, at least in front of other women.

When we arrived in Basic, we were given a short welcoming speech by the company officer, Lieutenant Gaines. Sergeant Griffin called our names from an alphabetized list as we lined up. She marched us into the barracks room on the second floor. Starting on the right side of the room she assigned bunks as we followed along until every bunk was filled. Then she took the rest of the girls to the third floor and did the same thing until everyone had been given a bunk. Since my name started with a G, I was on the second floor and luckily, I got a bottom bunk. It is a lot easier to make a bed on the bottom bunk than it is on the top and one flight of steps to climb when you're in a hurry beats having to climb two.

Our furnishings were a bed, a closet for hanging clothes with a shelf for hats and a foot locker for folded clothes. Our clothes had to be hung from left to right with summer shirts first, then summer skirts, then winter shirts, both summer and winter shirts with the fronts facing left, summer skirts, winter skirts, exercise dress, dress uniform dress, overcoat. The tray of the foot locker had those ridiculous rayon underwear folded and rolled and set in a row on the left. I really don't remember how the rest of the tray was set up because once it was done the way they wanted it I let it stay that way so it was always perfect for inspection. I never used any of it. The bottom of the footlocker was private so it was never inspected. That was where I kept my own underwear, nylons and all my other personal things.

After our first busy day in Basic we had to fall out for retreat. The word retreat used in that sense does not mean retreating from anything. It just means that you have to be present at the end of the day at the ceremony for the taking down of the flag. Our company was standing at attention concentrating on the ceremony when a nearby cannon went off. The whole company nearest the cannon fell back. None of us knew that a cannon was a part of the retreat ceremony. After a chewing out by Lieutenant Gaines no one ever moved out of formation again when the cannon went off.

Saturday morning was inspection day. The area around our bed had to have been scrubbed with a brush and G.I. soap then rinsed with a mop. Beds had to be made Army style; if we happened to live by a window, we were responsible for any dust on the window sill. The closet and footlocker had to be arranged the way we had been taught. Shoes had to be polished and one pair had to be turned up on the bed with laces tied and sole polished. The call came from the sergeant, "Attention!" so we stood at the foot of our bed at attention as the officer walked from one person to another. She stopped at each of us and asked us our name and serial number. I answered that question so often it is etched in my brain all these years later. Well, maybe my name has changed but I will never forget that my serial number is A819036. If all went well with the white glove inspection, we would have Saturday afternoon off. If not, we faced punishment detail.

Every day started at six a.m. We had to hurry to dress and fall out for the flag raising ceremony, roll call while in formation then back inside for breakfast, make our bed and clean up our area, then fall out and march to class. We had several classes during the morning covering such subjects as personal hygiene, map reading, venereal disease and what to do about it if you think you have one, and many others I can't remember. We took P. E. just before lunch which meant we had to run up to change into our seersucker dress and matching bloomers, do an hour of P. E. then hurry to change back into our uniform to go to lunch. We had a bit of time after lunch for mail call in the day room then back to classes. Sometimes we had to march to the clinic for shots. The doctors lined up in two lines facing each other. We bared our arms. As we passed between the line of doctors, they gave us shots, mostly by sort of tossing the syringes like darts. I think we must have been immunized against every disease known to mankind at that time.

In the afternoon we were often taken to the theater where we were shown a segment of the series *Why We Fight*. That was to sharpen our anger at the enemy and hone our desire to further the Allied Cause. We were already trying to further the Allied cause by being in the army. There wasn't much more we could do. We finished our day about four in the afternoon so that gave us time to write letters or do our washing or just sit around and visit if we had nothing else to do. At six in the evening we had to fall out for retreat and flag lowering before going in to the dining room for dinner. After dinner we had free time until nine o'clock lights out.

After two weeks of basic training we were allowed to go off the post. My friends Jeanette Hodson, Virginia Boles, Juanita Martinez and Jeanette Henschel and I chose to go to Chattanooga to get back in touch with civilization. We went to a fine restaurant where we ate off of china, instead of metal trays; ate with silver flatware, instead of stainless steel; where we were served, instead of having to stand in line and the table was covered with a starched white tablecloth. We had cloth napkins instead of paper ones. I don't remember what we ate. The food was not as important as the accoutrements. It was almost a revelation to us that such luxury still existed in the world since it had seemed such a long time since we had enjoyed such comforts.

After we ate, we rode the funicular railway up the side of Lookout Mountain and visited whatever there was to see up there before returning to base. It was refreshing to be free of army routine for a while.

I found it strange that the line-up of the marching order of a platoon had the tallest people in the first rank. The rest were in descending height with the shortest girls in the rear rank. Poor things, they almost had to run to keep up, I suppose if the shortest were in the front the rest of us would be stepping on their heels. Maybe the army knows what they are doing after all. I was in the fourth of fifth rank from the front. The girl right in front of me, Vera Baker, walked with a hitch in her left shoulder. Her shoulder would go up and down instead of staying level. She didn't always keep in step either so for me to keep in step while watching that shoulder go up and down on the off beat made it hard for me to stay in step but I was determined to learn to ignore her. Somehow or other our platoon consistently won the blue ribbon at Saturday's parade. We were chosen to give a marching exhibition at a baseball game in Chattanooga. We were being taught some very fancy marching maneuvers that confused some of the girls so they were excused from the drills. I was very happy when Vera Baker was one of them. I don't remember many of the commands but one of them was "double to the rear by the right flank march." We had to turn completely around twice while marching then turn at a right angle and continue to march forward without losing a step. Another command was "To the four winds march." In that maneuver the right rank turns right, the left rank turns left, the right center rank turns to the rear and the left middle column keeps going forward. That was the easy part. Getting back together again depended on everyone responding immediately to the order to reassemble. We practiced the commands over and over until we had the whole thing down pat. At the seventh inning stretch we made an excellent showing. We did the WAC proud.

Part of our training was map and compass reading. We were taken to

Chickamauga Battlefield Park where we were supposed to find our way from one monument to another by using a map to set our route by coordinating the compass with the map we were holding. I found my way but not by compass reading. I just followed the group ahead of me. I didn't learn to coordinate a compass with a map until I became a Girl Scout leader when it was taught in leadership training. That happened about 1959-60.

We had to learn how to use a gas mask. The officers marched us to a big tent where two companies were taking the training. We were told to make a circle facing the center with our backs near the tent walls. The instructor stood in the center and showed us how to place the mask over our faces and blow the air out to seal it. We did that a few times before all masks were ordered stowed in the carrying case. Then an instructor opened a can of tear gas. We put the masks on as fast as we could but not fast enough because we emptied the tent in a hurry with our skin tingling and our eyes streaming tears.

In six weeks, basic training was over. It was a sad time because we had become a cohesive unit and hated to part with each other. We were sent to a staging area to await our assignments. When I joined the WAC in Dallas, I was allowed to pick my first duty station. I had chosen to serve at Love Field in Dallas so I knew where I was going, I just didn't know when. Staging was chock full because other companies besides ours had finished training at the same time. Now we were waiting for paper work. Our orders had to be typed along with transportation vouchers that had to be made up. We had too much time on our hands. Isn't it strange that we grumble about work we have to do and we grumble when we have nothing to do? It seemed to us as though we would stay in the staging area forever. In about ten days our orders finally came through. Quite a few of us were put on the train to Memphis. Vera Baker and I were the only ones from my company in Basic who were assigned to Love Field. In Memphis our train was shunted onto a siding to wait for an engine to take us on to Texas or to let a troop train go by. I don't know which. While we were stopped, I slipped off of the train and sent my parents a telegram telling them I was on the way to Love Field. They met the train in Dallas where we had a brief hugging session before my being loaded onto an Army truck and taken to the field.

The WAC area for Love Field was just outside and across the street from the gate of the main installation. We had our own mess hall with women cooks. The food there was much better than the main mess hall on the field. When a person in the service arrives at a new place, he has to sign on to the installation by going to the personnel office, the health center, the warehouse to be issued bedding, etc. That endeavor took up almost a whole day, mostly in waiting to be served. After that I was assigned my job in the Army Air Corps, Air Transport Command, job designation, clerk-typist.

I was assigned to the Ground Training School, film department. I was in charge of the film library. My job was to check training films into and out of the library, order new films, splice damaged ones, clean films that got fingerprints and dust on them as they were used. I was trained as a sixteen-millimeter film projectionist. There were certain films that pilots had to see periodically such as survival in the arctic, survival in the jungle. There were others about airplanes. It was technical information not very interesting to me. I did enjoy the survival films though, at least the first five or six times I showed them. There were also films showing the air approach to different airfields especially if there were special conditions the pilot had to be aware of. The approach to Reykjavik, I think it is in Iceland, is between two mountains with a lot of turbulence. The plane that took the pictures of the approach evidently was being affected by the turbulence and juttered up and down. I thought there was something wrong with the sprockets so I ordered another copy of the film only to find it did the same thing.

I found some of the films interesting at first but after showing them a few times not so much. Once while I was showing a film, I fell asleep. When the lights came on, I found that the film had broken and was piled up on the floor. I had to hand roll it onto the reel then take it back to the library, splice and clean it. I tried to be careful not to let that happen again and it didn't.

Every week I received a large can of film that had a feature film, a cartoon, a newsreel and a documentary of a different hometown somewhere in the United States. The films purpose was as a morale builder. Love Field was a staging area for troops going to North Africa. When North Africa was secured it became a staging area for the Italian campaign. Conversely, our planes were used to evacuate the wounded. There was a large hospital at Love Field where I showed the film each week to the convalescent wounded.

During my first weeks in Dallas I was in the latrine ironing my clothes when I met a girl someone told me was from France. Her name was Madeleine Brabant Floyd. She told me that she was from Memphis, Tennessee but she was born in Lille, France where she grew up. Her father owned cotton mills in France. He came to America to buy cotton in Memphis where he met his wife. They lived in France where they raised a family of four children. Madeleine was the second child. They returned to Memphis when Hitler invaded France. That was why Madeleine had a southern accent mixed in with her French accented English. Madeleine married a man whose last name was Floyd in Memphis. They were married only six weeks when he was sent overseas. He was in the air force, either a pilot or some other member of an airplane crew when he was shot down over Lille and was killed. That was why she had joined the army. She introduced me to a girl she met in her barracks named Zue Vance from Fort Worth, Texas.

I was on station two weeks before I could get leave to go home. Home was at 3221 Grafton Street, Oak Cliff, Texas. Oak Cliff was a fairly new subdivision of Dallas and was across the Trinity River from Dallas proper. Dad and Mother had taken the plunge and bought the house after I was in the service so I had never seen it. They came to the field to pick me up. After that I learned how to get there on public transit. I took a bus to the center of town then transferred to the Oak Cliff streetcar. That was a long, long trip to the end of the line. After that I had to walk two blocks up hill to get home carrying a small suitcase. They had bought a two-bedroom one bath frame cottage, with a living room with a fireplace, dining room ell and a kitchen. There was a large yard. The back gate led to an alley where the garbage was picked up.

It was great being home, eating good food, drinking good coffee and getting a chance to catch up on all the family news. Sometimes I brought some of my friends home and sometimes Mother and Dad met us in town to go out to eat or to a movie. Madeleine particularly enjoyed talking French with Mother and Dad.

Special Service branch of the Army was in charge of morale. They brought musical artists and movie stars to the field for us to enjoy. I especially remember hearing and enjoying Yasha Heifitz, the violinist. I had gone to the movies to see *Frenchman's Creek.* Yasha Heifitz played between showings. The theme music of *Frenchman's Creek* was "La Mer" by Claude Debussy. Heifitz played that and "The Maid with the Flaxen Hair" by Debussy also. He played anything we asked him to. I loved the movie and I was enthralled by Heifitz.

Special Service also put on theatricals using talent found on the base. One time I was in a musical that I barely remember. It was something about the Floradora girls only the roles were reversed. Boys played girls and girls played boys. Another time my theatrical bent led me to try out for a one act play called *Untitled*. It was about a soldier who had died and the people who had known him. Each person had to tell about the man from their viewpoint. I was given the part of his sweetheart. It always scared me to get up and act in front of people but I kept doing it. I must be a masochist!

By being in the Army I had a chance to go to theatrical offerings I never would have been able to afford. The U.S.O provided tickets to all the things that came to Dallas. I had the chance to see many ballet companies, several operas and some solo singers. It was a cultural education for me.

I think it was in February or March of 1945 that I had a three-day pass so I decided to visit my cousin Shirley Hidalgo who had recently married Jerry Robichaux and was living in San Antonio, Texas where Jerry was stationed at

Hondo Field. In order to have enough time to make the visit worth the trip I had the three days start on Monday but I left on the train Friday right after work. I was worried every time I saw an M.P. because I was away from the base without a pass on the weekend and could have been arrested for being AWOL. I arrived in San Antonio without incident and had a nice visit. Shirley asked me to stay an extra day, the day I should have been traveling back, because someone she wanted me to see was coming in. The only reason I took the chance was because she said Jerry would fly me back so I could arrive in time. It was Sylvia who arrived in San Antonio and I was glad I stayed. We had a nice visit. Jerry's job was piloting a plane that was set up with several desks with Norden bombsights installed so navigators could learn how to use them. He rounded up some navigation students for a night flight specially to take me home. When we arrived at the field and Jerry went to file his flight plan, he was told that he had orders to report to New Mexico where he was to be taught to fly B-29s. The flight officer didn't want to sanction the flight to Dallas. Jerry somehow convinced him that these fellows needed night training and the flight had already been made up so he okayed it. We drove to the hangar and boarded the plane. I had to wear a parachute. I was in my regular uniform skirt. It wasn't easy pulling up those straps over a skirt but I managed it. While I was putting it on, I was praying I would not have to use it. I had a chance to sit in one of the desks and look through the bombsight. I had no idea what to look for and couldn't see much at night anyway. I had on earphones so I could hear the radio talk between Jerry and the checkpoints along the way. We landed at Love Field in the teeth of a "blue-norther." A jeep came out to meet us. We were freezing. Especially Jerry who was in his shirt sleeves. Both of us were trying to get warm wrapped in my raincoat. Jerry had to file a flight plan back to Hondo. Operations didn't want to let him fly in such bad weather but he told them he had to get back because he had orders to transfer to New Mexico immediately. Reluctantly they let him file his flight plan so he took off for home. I reported to the WAC charge of quarters as fast as possible and all was well.

    In May I was eligible for a furlough. Since I was able to be home a good part of the time, I thought I would visit relatives and friends in Louisiana for my vacation. My plans were nearly wrecked because I had been having a lot of dental work done and where a wisdom tooth had been removed, I developed a dry socket. No blood clot filled the place where the tooth had been, leaving the nerves exposed and causing an unbelievable amount of pain. The dentist gave me some pain medicine that turned out to be codeine. I didn't know that codeine made me sick so I went home and started taking it. I kept running to the bathroom to throw up. I decided to quit taking the medicine and was well again. I went back to the dentist on the field and told him I couldn't take codeine so he packed the socket with something that helped with the pain so I could finally go on my furlough after losing the first week being sick.

Dad took me to the train station where we stood on the platform talking while waiting for the train to board. While we were standing there a Marine was standing near us trying to catch my eye but I wasn't interested. He was brown as a nut with jug ears, a big nose and green eyes. There were always soldiers, sailors and marines trying to flirt. When the train was ready Dad and I boarded and found all the window seats taken. I picked an aisle seat where Dad stowed my make up kit and other stuff on the shelf, gave me a kiss and left. I brought a magazine to read so I opened it and started reading. I noticed that the marine sat right across the aisle from me. When the porter came by, I asked him if he would let me know when a whole seat became empty. This was the 5 p.m. train from Dallas to New Orleans and we were in a coach. As usual no Pullman cars were available so we would have to sit up all night. I thought I could at least lie down, stretch out and get a bit of sleep if I had a whole seat to myself.

After we passed a few stations the porter came to tell me that the last seat at the back was empty so I reached to take down my make up kit and other things to transfer them to the back seat. When I got there the marine was already sitting in it. I stood there and said, "Oh, the porter said the seat was empty." I turned to return to my former seat. He said, "Please sit down and talk to me. I am just back from the Pacific and I have never met any of the girls in the service." When I turned to go, I saw that everyone in the coach was looking over the back of their seats waiting to see what would happen because they all had seen him slip behind me to go to that back seat. I felt embarrassed being the center of so much curiosity so I after stowing my stuff I sat down. We introduced ourselves to each other so that is how I met Bill Nelson. We spent the whole night talking. At first, we were trying to find out if we had any mutual friends. Then we talked about places in New Orleans and our memories of them. I suppose we must have talked about the war and our service experiences. Finally, as we approached the outskirts of the city, he asked if he could see me while I was there. I said I supposed it would be all right if he first came to meet the people I was staying with. He agreed. I was going to stay first with Aunt Carrie. I thought she would be a good judge of character and would know if it was ok for me to go out with him.

When we stepped off of the train in New Orleans, we were puzzled by all of the noise. Horns and steam whistles were blowing, bells were ringing. Bill's aunt, uncle and brother were waiting for him on the platform. They told us that the noise was to celebrate the end of the war in Europe—V.E. Day, April 28, 1945. Bill introduced me to Uncle Gus and Aunt Lucy Lyncker and his brother Jack. I could tell that they were very nice people.

The first date we had was to attend a fraternity dance. When Bill called to ask me to go, I told him I did not have a formal with me. He said that Sidney Lemarie would get his sister to lend me one. When Aunt Carrie learned that he knew the Lemarie family and was accepted into their home she was satisfied that he must be a nice fellow. Somehow our family and the Lemarie family were related. When he came to deliver the dress, I introduced Bill to Aunt Carrie and Uncle Albert. They liked him right away so all was well.

He asked me what I had planned to do while in New Orleans. I told him I wanted to go horseback riding. He took me to a stable out by Lake Pontchartrain. He didn't tell me that he had never been horseback riding before. He had to have his horse led away from the stable by one of the stable hands and after the stable hand left, he still had trouble making the horse move. We had fun anyway. After the ride, we had a picnic in City Park eating the lovely lunch that Bill's Aunt Lucy had packed for us. We ate the lunch then rented a rowboat and took a ride around the lagoons. That evening we were invited to dinner by Aunt Lucy. His family was very welcoming and kind. Now our relationship was sanctioned by both sides. The next day I introduced him to Aunt Bea and Aunt Mabel. We covered a lot of ground in a short time. We went to some nightclubs, ate lunch at Commander's Palace, walked to Audubon Park and sat on the low branch of a big oak tree and talked all afternoon. We talked so long we had to take a taxi to his aunt's house where I had been invited to dinner. We wouldn't have made it in time if we had tried to use the streetcar. I knew by then that he was the man for me to marry but, of course, I would not do anything so precipitous; besides that, he hadn't asked me. I wonder if he knew then?

In between dates with Bill, I visited my cousin Louise Moreno Johnston and met her two little daughters, Judy and Lillian Lea and had a chance to visit with her brother's wives Jennie and Bootsie and their children. George, Bert and Louise had bought houses next door to each other on Turnbull Drive in the Gilmore subdivision just off of Airline Highway in Metairie. The men were at work. One evening George invited several of us to go sailing on Lake Pontchartrain. He had a small open cockpit sailboat with a removable centerboard. I think the boat was designated as in the Lightning Class. He kept it at the yacht harbor. The night was lovely. I was sitting on the deck just in front of the jib enjoying the breeze and the wave action when, all of a sudden, all of the city lights went out. They were practicing a blackout procedure. It was strange to be out on the water and not to be able to see anything on land. It was just a black shoreline.

The next day I informed Bill that I was going to go to Raceland to see the rest of my family and then go home. We agreed to write each other to keep in touch. By a stroke of luck my cousin Deda was in Raceland with her daughter

Diane who was about two years old. I hadn't seen Deda since we lived in Mobile. We had a great visit even though Diane dug in my suitcase and exposed a roll of film I had already shot.

Not long after I returned to duty, orders came to the field from Air Transport Command Headquarters in Washington D. C. for the need of a particular job description. I was one of six girls on the field who qualified. One was one of two sisters who didn't want to be separated, one was pregnant and was going to be discharged. I don't know what reason the others had but I was selected to go. I had to leave work to go to the barracks to pack. Then I had to check out of all the places I had checked into when I arrived. Every time one changes stations one has to turn in his bedding. He is then issued new bedding at the new station. I had to call my parents to tell them I was leaving immediately and couldn't see them before I left. Then I had to report to Eastern Airlines to catch a flight to Washington. A civilian had to be "bumped" to make space for me. It was the first time I had flown in a civilian passenger plane. I enjoyed the comfort and the amenities of the trip very much. It was dusk when we passed near the capitol building just before landing at the National Airport in Washington. No one was there to meet me so I had to take a taxi to the W.A.C. area that turned out to be about two blocks away. It was walking distance from the airport but not with two stuffed duffle bags to carry. I reported to the C.Q. who assigned me a bed for the night.

The next day I reported to the W.A.C. officer but she didn't know who requested my services. We never did find out. Imagine! Some pour civilian had been bumped from the plane for nothing. After sitting around for two or three days I was assigned to a job in the Weights and Balance Office. That was where the course in military correspondence I had taken at Brookley Field several years before came in handy. Weights and Balance was concerned with how to load a plane without overbalancing it either front to back or from side to side. As soon as the engineering study was done the Weights and Balance office closed and I was transferred to the Weather Office. I worked there just in time to assist in the shutting down of many of the weather stations and weather ships that were serving the European Theater of operations.

While I was in the Weights and Balance Office, Captain Richards, my immediate boss, thought I should be put up for promotion. I was a private first class at the time. I told him I had been in the service long enough to have been a sergeant. My promotion to corporal had been messed up by my being transferred to Washington. He put me up for buck sergeant and I got it. That meant a little more money. I had been making about fifty dollars a month. After the promotion I was probably making fifty-five. In the air corps the enlisted grades don't mean that you handle troops. It just means a difference in pay.

There was an area on the W.A.C. post that was a café of sorts. They sold beer, hamburgers, sodas and a few other things. The food in the mess hall on the field was not very good so I ended up eating somewhere else as much as possible. The place was called "The Continental Room." I ate in the Continental Room often but I ran out of money before the month was over so I decided to try being a waitress to supplement my meagre income. Male soldiers were allowed to come onto the W.A.C. base to go to the Continental Room where they could buy beer. It embarrassed me to take tips for services I would have been glad to provide. Besides, taking tips made me feel like a servant. Some of the girls who worked there had an easy joking way with the fellows. I was so out of place I couldn't think of a thing to say to them. I worked for about a week but soon came to the conclusion that sort of work was not for me.

The bed I had been assigned the first night I arrived was in the 7th wing at Gravely Point. That was the name of the W.A.C. area for the Air Transport Command in Washington. It was actually in Virginia not very far from the Pentagon. The women in the 7th wing were a great bunch. We were all very friendly except for a very few. At one time the commanding officer of the W.A.C. told us that we had her permission to turn one of the cadre rooms into a day room and whoever did the best job would win a prize. The cadre rooms were set aside for non-commissioned officers but they were not being used that way anymore. Our group, encouraged by Maggie Rose, took her up on the offer so we started in on the project. First, we painted the walls pink. Then Maggie and I painted two figures on one wall. We copied a decal of a Swedish peasant boy and girl. Maggie did the boy and I did the girl. As we got into it, we were determined to win the prize. One girl who was good at sewing made a cover for the army cot then made pillows to match for a sofa. Another girl said she knew where she could get a wine barrel. We had someone cut it to make into a chair. The fellow I was dating, George Anderson, was in charge of interior maintenance of Air Force One and knew how to upholster so I asked him to upholster the back and the cover of the barrel to make a seat. When the day of inspection came, we won the prize! It was a floor lamp, just what we needed to complete our parlor. The seat to the barrel chair was removable so we stored our snacks in it, crackers, cheese, peanut butter and such like. It was nice to have some place besides the latrine to write letters or to read after lights out.

I don't remember how I met George Anderson. Maybe I met him when we were both on k.p. He was a nice undemanding fellow so we had some pleasant times. The hangar for the President's plane was just across the road from the side of the WAC area so I used to go over there to visit with George and watch him work on our barrel chair. One night he offered me a chance to visit Air Force One so I went aboard. It was beautifully fitted out. At that time the interior was decorated in shades of blue. There was a big desk where the President could do his paperwork. There was a booth to eat in and places to sleep for himself and his staff. I was careful not to touch anything. I'll bet the F.B.I. would not have approved of having casual visitors on the President's plane.

George was helping Captain Tom Roberts repair his motor launch. Captain Roberts' boat had been moored next to a boat that caught fire and had damaged the side of his boat. When I first saw the boat, it was under reconstruction and the temporary repairs weren't very attractive but he was using it anyway to cruise up and down the Potomac every Sunday. Once they had it looking fairly decent Captain Roberts invited us to join them on their Potomac cruise. His wife, Irene, packed a picnic lunch that we all enjoyed. She and I talked about all sorts of things while the men talked boats. She told me she was British born in India. I knew by her speech that she was British. She said that she had studied to be a nurse because there was such a pressing need during the war but that she hated it and often had to run to the bathroom and throw up because of the sights she had seen. She gave it up once she had married Tom. They invited George and me to dinner several times. Home cooking beats mess hall food any day of the week.

Since our air base was open all of the time for incoming and outgoing air traffic the mess hall had to be open twenty-four hours a day. George had made friends with the cooks so after he and I had gone to the movies he took me to the mess hall where he picked out a couple of steaks and cooked them just the way we wanted them. They were cooked much better than when the cooks did them. The food provided to the mess halls was always the best to be had. It was just that the cooks were not top-quality cooks. They could ruin anything.

George built a sailboat for himself out of an airplane wing tank. He kept the boat in a boathouse within walking distance of Gravelly Point. He invited me to go sailing with him after dinner one night. I'm always game for an adventure so I agreed. I had been sailing once before and then only as a passenger so I didn't know much about handling a sailboat. The night was beautiful and the breeze was adequate so we were sailing along enjoying the ride. George was handling the tiller so he gave me the job of handling the mainsail. The wind picked up all of a sudden. We could see that a storm was coming. We were trying to hurry back to the boathouse. I could see that the wind was pulling the boom over the side. I thought that was bad so I was hauling it back in. We started skudding fast before the wind. George shouted, "Let it go, let it go!" By the time I understood what he was saying and let go we were near the landing. George turned the boat but we were going too fast. The boat turned on its side and dumped us in the river. We were near shore where it was shallow, about four feet deep. We stood up, righted the boat and found ourselves soaked to the skin. It was pitch dark in the boathouse so we went into separate corners and took off our soggy clothes. We wrung out as much water as we could and had to put the wet clothes back on to get home. Yuk! Walking the few blocks we had to walk with soggy pants rubbing my thighs was very uncomfortable and made the trip back to the barracks seem longer than the trip out but there was no help for it. I took a warm shower and went to bed. I learned a sailing lesson that night. DON'T PULL THE BOOM IN WHEN THE WIND IS BLOWING HARD.

Several girls in the 7th wing and I became fast friends. We went out to eat, to the movies or other entertainments in Washington. My best friend, Mary Jane Stamper from Youngstown, Ohio and I decided to take horseback riding lessons. Every Saturday we went to the stable near Rock Creek Park. She was short, about five feet, two and had never ridden before so they assigned her a docile but rather portly horse. I had ridden before but I was by no means to be thought of as an experienced rider. They assigned me a retired racehorse who was narrow. I was five feet six so it was easy for me to hug the horse with my knees because my legs are long and the horse was narrow but poor Mary Jane's legs stuck almost straight out on her big horse. We walked our horses on a short path from the stable to the beginning of the bridle path in Rock Creek Park where we took our lessons. The path passed at the bottom of a ten-foot cliff. On my second lesson we were passing the cliff. On top of the cliff some boys were getting their jollies rolling down clods of mud to startle the horses. Mine jumped off of all four feet and landed to the right of me. I went up and straight down and landed on my bottom in the relatively soft dust. The horse had stopped so I got up and walked over to him and was climbing back on. The teacher was riding back to tell me to get right back on or I might not have the courage to get back on later. He needn't have bothered to tell me that. He didn't know me or he wouldn't have come back. I am not easily discouraged when I make up my mind to do something and I was determined to take the lessons. We were riding an English saddle. It is almost as flat as a tortilla with practically no pommel and a very low cantle. Your knees have to be bent so you can hold on by hugging the horse with your thighs. First, we learned to ride a trot. You have to catch the rhythm of the horse's movement. The idea is to rise in the stirrups touching your bottom to the saddle on every other beat. It is the hardest to learn and the least fun to ride. He told us to lean over and place our hand on the horse's withers to feel the difference in his movement between a canter and a gallop. After a few weeks we were taught to pull up on the reins suddenly to make the horse stand on his hind legs. I loved every minute of it. I had always wanted to learn to ride and though I wasn't in Washington long enough to become proficient I satisfied my life's longing to ride a horse. Later on, I had the opportunity to use what I knew a few times.

Sometimes George and I would go to Washington to a nightclub. One night we were at the Willard Hotel dancing. When we returned to the table, he ordered a drink and asked if I wanted one. I didn't know what to order. I had seen that Old Fashions were not much liquid to drink so I ordered that. It tasted good so after another dance or two I ordered another one. We danced and drank and were having a good time. I ended up drinking four Old Fashions in too short a time so I was reeling. George very kindly took me back to the base in a cab, walked me in to report to the C.Q. who happened to be a friend of mine. She saw to it that I got safely to bed. I was learning about my capacity for alcohol (not much and not too fast no matter how good it tastes).

Another place we liked to go was the Trade Winds. It was on the first floor of the building and had many support posts. Every post was decorated with coconut palm leaves. Coconuts were cut open and fitted with electric lights. The whole place had a tropical island atmosphere. We went there mostly to dance. I never ordered anything stronger than a gin fizz after my embarrassing Old Fashion experience.

After Bill had been home about a month, he had been sent to Fort Lauderdale, Florida. There were houses being built nearby. I don't know whether they were being built on the post or outside. Anyway, he made some extra money working on them. He and I had continued to correspond. I was also writing to Alfred Groh. He had served as a waist gunner on B-17s in the Italian campaign and was lucky still to be alive. He said they had been flying in planes that had been shot up badly and were holding together with hope while just across the fence there were brand new B-17s. It seems he was resentful that the army took chances with their lives sending them up in beat up old planes when they had good ones sitting there doing nothing. He told me all of this after he had been released from the service. None of that would have passed the censors if he had tried to tell me all of it while he was still in Europe. He was taking a journalism course at Columbia University in New York. I received a letter from him asking me if I could get a three-day pass to come to visit him. I got one as soon as I could and took the train to New York. He had reserved a room for me at the King's Crown (?) Hotel on 116th Street near Columbia University. He couldn't come to meet me at the station because of his schedule so I was on my own in unknown territory. I tried to catch a taxi. Every time I thought I had one and turned to pick up my suitcase someone else got in and rode off. I finally held my suitcase and shoved my way into the next taxi that pulled up. I was surprised at how unmannered the people were and how rickety the New York cabs were. I was used to the Yellow Cab Company in New Orleans who used leather upholstered limousines for cabs and had cab drivers who manhandled your luggage for you. The cabs in New York looked like tin cans on spools and the drivers, if not downright surly, were not helpful.

It was night by the time Alfred came to pick me up so we started walking and talking, holding hands as we went along. We walked over to Grant's Tomb on the Hudson River, then down the whole length of Central Park to 42nd Street. He hired a hansom cab to drive through Central Park. You can't see much of the park at night. When our ride was over, we walked to Times Square and from there to Mama Leonie's, an Italian Restaurant. The place was decorated like a village in Italy. There were strip gardens and statuary everywhere. It was overdone in my opinion. Ah, but the food! First, they brought a board with bread, olives, cheeses and other things I can't remember. By the time I ate some of that I was pretty well filled. Yet there was more. We had to have spaghetti and meat balls and a salad. By the time we finished eating it was three a.m. I was surprised at the crowds still up and about at that hour. There were so many people on the sidewalk we had to walk along the edge of the street to make any headway. I wondered if it was like that every night?

We rode the subway back. Noisy things, subways. It is impossible to talk over the noise so everyone either reads something or stares into space. They go fast since there are no cross streets to slow them down. They stop every now and then at transfer stations but the rest of the time they really travel. They are efficient at moving people from here to there quickly but I would hate to have to ride them every day.

The next day Alfred had several morning classes but in the afternoon, we went to Greenwich Village to another Italian restaurant. It was in the basement of a building so we had to go down some steps to get to the door. I don't remember the whole sequence of the visit but we managed to hit all the spots that count like the Automat and Scharff's; places one sees in the movies. We even went up in the Empire State Building but we didn't go to the observation deck because it was November and the clouds were low and nothing could be seen. We did go to the 84th floor. There are express elevators that took us to the 26th floor that go so fast our stomachs stayed downstairs and didn't catch up until we changed to a local elevator on the 26th floor. Since it was no use to go to the observation deck, we went to the 84th floor and saw where an airplane had slammed into the building a few weeks before our visit. In our office in Washington we had a radio on all the time so we heard the news report about the plane hitting the Empire State building almost as soon as it happened. I think it might have been a fighter pilot practicing who got lost in the clouds. I don't really remember the details but I know it was a single engine plane that hit. The area was cleaned up and the side of the building was repaired by the time we went to look at it but the scar of the sliding engine was still on the bronze elevator door.

Of all the places a person wants to see when in New York he wants to see the Stature of Liberty. The government had closed access to it during the war to prevent sabotage and though the war in Europe was over the war in the Pacific with Japan was still active. The only way to get a closer look at it was to take the Staten Island ferry that passes near to it, so we did. We went into a café on Staten Island and had a cup of coffee then took the ferry back to Manhattan. I didn't see much of Staten Island but I think it is probably a bedroom community to New York.

I had such a wonderful time visiting with Alfred I thought I was half in love with him. But I loved Bill. Confusion. Alfred had not done much to indicate he was in love with me so I don't know why I was so uncertain. I kept writing to Bill and getting letters from him. Alfred's letters became fewer and fewer. I excused him because he was carrying a heavy schedule of classes. He was supposed to visit me in Washington but he never did come. I took that as a good sign of a lack of interest.

I was due another furlough so I decided to go home for Christmas. I asked Bill to come to visit at our house for Christmas but he said that after being away for three years he thought he should spend Christmas at home. I asked him to come for the New Year instead. He said he could manage that.

Bill had been discharged from the Marines in October and had returned to New Orleans where he was enrolled in Loyola University. He had completed two years before the war so he wanted to finish his B.A. degree. His tuition was being paid by the government with a small stipend for incidentals. Bill had served for three years in the Third Marine artillery battalion headquarters in the Pacific Theater in a clerical position. One of his jobs on the islands was to send up a balloon with a small candle lit lamp then follow it with a theodolite to get windage for setting the cannons. He also served as assistant at Mass for the priest, sort of a grown up alter boy. Thank goodness he was not in the Marine infantry. They are the ones who land on the beaches first and did all the fighting to establish a foothold. The artillery was brought ashore after the infantry established the beachhead. The G. I. (G. I = government issue—at first the words were used for any clothing or equipment commonly issued to a soldier. Then it became used as a name for the men who served), Bill of Rights passed by Congress was one of the best pieces of legislation that body ever thought up. Having so many men and women use the college privilege provided the country with a huge number of educated people and was the best way to integrate the military back into civilian life.

But I digress. Anyway, Bill came for the New Year celebration that turned out to be not very celebratory. Dallas is in a mostly dry county. There are no night clubs, no place to buy a cocktail. It is a B.Y.O.B. (Bring Your Own Bottle) situation. You can have whiskey with you when you go into a place then buy set-ups. They just don't know how to celebrate in Dallas. Aside from that draw back we had a nice visit. Mother and Dad got to know him better. We found things to do. We all played cards. We decided we all liked each other.

Too soon duty called. Bill had to register for the spring semester and I had to get back to Washington.

The war with Japan ended in August 1945 so things were winding down. There wasn't much work to do anymore. There is nothing so boring as going to work and finding nothing to do. We all began to long for a return to civilian life. When I returned from my furlough there were rumors that our W.A.C group were to be moved to Fort Meyers near the Pentagon. There were other rumors that the army was starting to demobilize the troops on a point system that no one seemed to understand. Those who had been in longest would be expected to get out first. It was an unsettling time.

One evening I was called to the gate because a man wanted to see me. I thought it was Alfred who had come at last but it was Colonel Stanley Hidalgo, my cousin, who was back from the European Theater. He had been serving as an aide to General Patton. I was glad to see him. I ran back to the barracks to put on my dress uniform so I could go off the post with him. He and his wife, Millie, had rented an apartment in Washington so I went with him to visit. After that I had dinner with them and babysat for them several times when they had somewhere important to go.

Alfred's letters became scarcer and scarcer so I finally quit writing. If he wanted to correspond the ball was in his court. I never heard from him again.

Early in 1946 Merit Flights were inaugurated. They were supposed to be a reward for anyone who had earned a Good Conduct medal. They were really intended to give flying hours to idle flyers to keep up their qualifications. The war was over and demobilization was in progress so we were reaping some of the rewards. Some of my friends and I were on the second such flight to West Palm Beach. Florida and sunshine sounded great in March because it was cold and gloomy in Washington. We flew down there in a C-54. It was equipped and fitted out to carry parachutists. The seats ran along the length of the side of the plane facing the central aisle and were hollowed out to accommodate a parachute pack. The pack filled the hollow seat so the parachutist's legs were then level with the edge. We had to fill the hollow with our folded overcoats to make the seats level enough to be comfortable. We hit some rough air on the way. Some of the fellows and girls got motion sickness but I didn't. In fact, I got up to go to the back of the plane to get a cup of coffee and some doughnuts. As I was walking down the aisle the plane suddenly dropped out from under me as we hit an air pocket, then came back up and met me as I was falling down. I managed to keep my balance. I went on and got my coffee and doughnuts. There was a storm ahead so, rather than go through it and suffer all the turbulence the pilot chose to climb over it. He climbed to twelve thousand feet. The plane was unpressurized with no provision for extra oxygen so we became cold and sleepy. The crew chief gave us blankets to spread in the aisle for us to lie down on. We covered with our coats and slept for the rest of the flight.

We stayed at an air base in West Palm Beach. The next day we were taken by bus to spend the day on the beach. One evening we all went skating at a local roller rink. We flew down on a Friday and returned on Sunday so it was not a long vacation, but the visit in the sun made a nice break for us.

I was back from Palm Beach a day or two when I received orders to pack up and report to Fort Sam Houston in San Antonio, Texas for separation. When what I had been wishing to have happen actually happened, I was reluctant to leave all of my friends. I left Washington on the Baltimore and Ohio train and this time I really did have a berth in a Pullman car. In St. Louis I changed to the Katy line. There were quite a few soldiers on the same train who were going to Fort Sam Houston for separation, too. They asked me if I knew how to play gin rummy. I told them that I had played a lot of rummy games but I never had played gin so I said, "No, teach me." We used my suitcase placed on our legs for a table and started playing. We were not gambling. I won so often they accused me of lying. I told them I had played cards all of my life starting at four years old so I knew how to play cards but that was the first time I had ever played Gin. We talked and laughed and ate together and had so much fun we were almost sorry to have the trip end.

The armed services thought that they had to teach us how to be civilians again so it took several days to go through the discharge process. We had to have thorough physical and dental exams and had to get our legal papers in order. The fellows I had met on the train and I got together to go off the base to eat and to visit San Antonio. At separation each former soldier was given a badge to wear to show he had served. For some reason it was called "The Ruptured Duck." Back on the base we finally came to the important part, our separation-pay. With my money, train ticket and meal ticket, but without all of my uniforms except the one I wore home, I found myself on the train to Dallas, back where the whole adventure started. I still didn't know anyone my age who lived there. I felt like a fish out of water.

*Nathalie, US Army Air corps, Air Transport Command*

*Bill*
*Rose Garden in City Park*

## *Back to Civilian Life*

Mother and I went shopping for some new civilian clothes. I had worn a collar and tie for so long that I felt uncomfortable in clothes that showed my collar bones. The two-hundred dollars that I received on separation from the service was not going to last very long so I knew I would have to go out and look for a job soon.

Bill had asked me to let him know as soon as I got home from the separation center. We didn't have a phone at home yet so I had to go to the drugstore to use the public phone there. We must have talked two hours or more. I found out later that call had cost thirty-seven dollars! That was a huge amount for a long-distance call at that time. He wanted me to go to New Orleans for Easter. He took the drugstore phone number and made arrangements for me to be waiting at the drugstore for his call at a certain time. In between the phone calls he wrote a lot of letters. I knew he wanted to ask me to marry him. I decided I would have to go to New Orleans to tell him in person that I could not marry him because of our difference in religion since he was Catholic and I was Presbyterian, sort of.

So once again I was on a train. I arrived on the Saturday before Easter and was staying at Aunt Lucy's where Bill was living. Bill and I were in the sitting room at the back of the house talking while waiting for dinner to be ready. My mind tried to get me to tell him I couldn't marry him but my tongue wasn't paying attention. Within three hours of my arrival we were engaged. Oh, Lord! What had I gotten myself into? I was in such an emotional whirl that I had to run to the bathroom and throw up most of my dinner. That night we were going to the Blue Room with Bill's friends Henry Bryer and his wife Cookie Glass. On our way to the Blue Room I stopped at the desk in the hotel and sent Mother and Dad a telegram to let them know that I was engaged.

During the next week we shopped for an engagement ring. We went out nearly every night during spring break. Sometimes it was just to the home of one of Bill's friends. I found out that my cousin, Shirley was at the Baptist Hospital having just delivered her first baby, so one of our outings was to visit her and go around to the nursery to admire the new baby. We went everywhere together. After about ten days I felt that I should not keep staying at their house. They had no guest room and Uncle Gus and Aunt Lucy had given up their room to accommodate me. I got in touch with Mrs. Ward to see if she had any place for me to stay. Fortunately for me she had an apartment that was rented to a teacher but the teacher was on a trip so she let me stay there.

During the day while Bill was in school, I visited with my relatives who still lived in town. I took Carlos to Pontchartrain Beach where we rode everything and played almost every game on the boardwalk. I think we rode the Zephyr (roller coaster) at least three times.

I went to Raceland to visit the Hidalgos. Shirley was home from the hospital with the baby, Michelle, by then and staying at her mother's house. One of the first things she said to me was, "You should marry that fellow." I told her that was just what I was planning to do. I had begun to get used to the idea of being engaged by then.

I went back to the apartment at Mrs. Ward's and called Bill to let him know I was going home the next evening. We picked the Court of Two Sisters as the place to spend our last evening together for a while. We planned to be married on the 12th of September 1946 between the end of summer school and the beginning of fall semester. We would both be going to college after we were married. I was going to go to Newcomb. We enjoyed our dinner and hated having to say good-bye and lingered so long over it that I nearly missed my train. I caught on to the last car as it was pulling out of the station. Bill ran alongside and handed up my suitcase. I arrived home on Mother's Day.

Back in Dallas I found a job with Dunn & Bradstreet. I needed to save some money to pay for a very small wedding. Aunt Lucy enthusiastically started buying us linens and things we would need to set up housekeeping.

My job with Dunn & Bradstreet was classified as statistical clerk. I had to record the number of investigative reports brought in by each investigator, the number of reports written up by each typist and the ratings given. There were other statistics I had to keep records of, I just can't remember them. Each week I had to compile a report that was sent to the main office in New York.

Dallas brags that it might get hot there but it is a dry heat, therefore more bearable. Well, it was hot that summer. It was 106 degrees. We worked in an air-conditioned building that was kept so cold that we had to wear a sweater in the office. At the end of the day when we opened the door to leave work it was like walking into a wall when that 106 degrees hit us. That was the hottest, driest, longest summer I ever had to live through. Our house was not air-conditioned. Dad bought a big box fan he placed on the floor. In front of it he stood the kitchen chairs and hung wet towels on them to get some moisture in that dreadful dry air. I sat at the table in front of this arrangement to write letters to Bill. My arm slipped in puddles of sweat. He wanted a letter every day but I couldn't manage that. I probably wrote just about every other day though.

I started to plan my wedding. I found out that Dallas has different traditions about wedding planning from New Orleans. I asked Shirley to be my matron of honor and Bill asked his friend, Dan Murphy, to be his best man. Uncle Gus, Aunt Lucy and Bill's brother Jack came to Dallas and stayed at the Adolphus Hotel. Uncle Gus invited all of us to join them for dinner at the hotel which we all did. We could not marry in front of the alter in the Sacred Heart Cathedral because it was a mixed marriage. We had to have the wedding in the priest's parlor. So, instead of a bridal veil and white dress I wore a blue light wool suit with wolf fur cuffs. The fur on each cuff was as big as a muff. I could not find anyone to make a tiered wedding cake so I had to settle for a huge round one. They have no wedding photographers. After the wedding we took some snapshots then went to a professional fashion photographer for wedding portraits. We had a wedding brunch at the Adolphus for the wedding party but we couldn't stay for all of it because we had to catch our flight to New Orleans.

It is almost unbelievable in this day of jet planes and rockets but our plane left Dallas at one twenty in the afternoon and didn't arrive in New Orleans until around seven o'clock after having stopped at Shreveport and Alexandria. It was a propeller driven two engine plane that could carry about twelve to fourteen people.

The limo from the airport took us to the Roosevelt Hotel so we went to the Fountain Lounge and had dinner. We danced while waiting to be served. One of the pieces we danced to was the "Anniversary Waltz." That sort of became "our song" for a while. After dinner we took a taxi to the furnished apartment Bill had rented at 3232 St. Roch Avenue where we started our new life.

*Nathalie in City Park*

*Nathalie and Bill on their wedding day*

*Bills first day at work*

# First Year

It was very difficult to find housing after the war. The only place Bill could find that we could afford was a furnished apartment that was part of a double house. It was very inconveniently located way out in Gentilly. Since we were going to schools located in the Uptown section of New Orleans it gave us a long bus ride twice a day to get to and from school. The house had been built during the war when some materials were not available. The most glaring example of that was the faucets that were bare of chromium. The house looked like a single cottage but was divided into two unequal sized apartments. The owners of the house occupied the larger apartment while the smaller one was ours. We had a living room, kitchen, bedroom with a closet and a bathroom. The furniture was fake rock maple. In the living room we had a sofa, a chair and a lamp. In the bedroom there was a bed, dresser, table and lamp. The kitchen had a dinette set, an apartment sized stove, and a former electric refrigerator that had been converted to an ice box. There was an extra-large oblong sink with cabinets under and over the sink with a few kitchen utensils, pots and dishes provided. Bill brought along his father's Morris chair to add to our furniture collection. It was the same chair he was sitting in when we became engaged.

Bill very gallantly carried me across our new threshold even though he weighed only about 134 pounds and I weighed 124, and so we were launched into our new life laughing.

Bill's clothes were already in the apartment but I had to empty my suitcase and put mine away. He took his shower while I was doing that. I was sitting on the foot of the bed sorting things when all of sudden the bed collapsed. Bill was putting on his pajamas when he heard the crash. He rushed out to see what happened. I was sitting there stunned but unhurt. We started laughing and got busy putting the bed back together.

I don't remember the exact progression of our days. We had a lot to do to get ourselves ready for the fall semester and not many days to do it in. Aunt Lucy and her maid, Augusta Graves, had cleaned the apartment before Bill moved in. I think he had lived there a few days before I came. Aunt Lucy had provided sheets, extra pots, mop, broom, dustpan and other housekeeping essentials. Our wedding gifts had to be unwrapped and acknowledged. We received most of the pieces of the eight place settings of our chosen silver pattern and then finished the set with the money gifts we received.

The day of college registration arrived so we rode public transit making our three or four transfers to get there. That was a trip we had to make both ways every day thereafter and not often together since our class schedules seldom matched.

The hour spent on traveling back and forth gave me time to do my homework. I was running just to stay even with learning to keep house and learning to cook plus studying. I was surprised to find my friends Madeleine Floyd and Zue Vance registering at Newcomb also. There were several of us that were older than the usual college students who were starting school at the same time. We tended to stay together in our off time.

I found out that Zue learned in the spring that she needed another math credit to be able to qualify for college entrance. She bought the book (I don't know which math subject she needed) and over the summer she taught herself the math, passed the exam in it and so was able to enter Newcomb that fall. That takes brilliance and a lot of determination.

After the school day I had to do our washing in the sink. Since the sink was so big it was easy enough to wash most things in it but the sheets were a problem. After washing them Bill and I would go outside and, with him on one end and me on the other, would twist in opposite directions to wring them out. He helped me to hang the wash. They never dried over night so we had to leave the clothes on the line until we returned from school and hope it didn't rain before one of us got home to take them down.

We ate dinner at Aunt Lucy's on most Sundays. That gave me a break from having to cook. I know Bill enjoyed those Sundays because he ate food he was familiar with. Aunt Lucy and Bill's mother, Barbara, were sisters whose maiden name was Schmitz. Very German. I was learning to like most of the German dishes but my tradition was French so I had learned to cook Cajun and Creole dishes. Thank goodness Bill was a person who ate and enjoyed almost anything put in front of him. He had to put up with my inexperienced cooking. I became a good cook because I enjoy good food but I never loved doing it. I did it because I had to. I remember my first bout with making a roux. I was trying to make grillades. I had to throw away two attempts before I finally made a passable roux. Once I got passed that the rest was easy.

During our Thanksgiving time off Bill and I sat on the floor of the apartment cleaning the baseboards with soapsuds and old toothbrushes. I don't think they had been cleaned since the house was built. Maybe sitting on that cold floor is what caused us to come down with such severe colds. We were sick for a couple of weeks. I don't think we ever finished the job.

We had Thanksgiving dinner at Aunt Lucy's. I surely am glad that my cooking was not tested by having to cook it.

Mother and Dad sent us a box full of all of their Christmas ornaments. I don't remember if we had a tree or just shared Aunt Lucy's tree. If I know me, we probably had our own tree.

In February I realized I was pregnant. I had morning sickness all day every day. Finally, I had to give up school.

During Mardi Gras season that year Aunt Lucy was going to a ball, riding with one of the Lacourage neighbor's daughters who was driving when the car was hit in the rear side door right where Aunt Lucy was sitting. She was taken to the hospital where they found she had a broken pelvis. She had to stay in the hospital three or four months. Bill and I had to move to her house to take care of Uncle Gus and Jack. So now my amateur cooking was going to be tried sorely. I could hardly stand the smell of the food I was cooking.

Dr. Bloch gave me phenobarbital to try to control the vomiting but it made me so sleepy I could hardly function. It didn't do much good with the throwing up either.

Bill was getting near the end of his studying for his Bachelor of Economics degree. When he and I were both going to college we received two checks from the government so we had some money to live on. Once I dropped out that cut out one of the checks so it was getting critical that he finish his degree work and graduate so he could get a job. My "morning sickness" was finally over after four months so I was able to go to his graduation on May 30, 1947 and a joyful time that was.

Now, to find a job. Bill hardly knew where to start. He spent all of June looking. Uncle Gus was a purchasing agent for his company and he belonged to the Purchasing Agents Association so he knew people all over the city. He suggested that Bill go to the purchasing agent for New Orleans Public Service and ask if there was anything available for a person with his qualifications. The man checked with the personnel department and told Bill to go for an interview. They had an opening in the Treasury Department. Bill applied for it and got it. He came home and said, "Hooray, I got the job. Now I'm looking forward to retirement."

While we were staying at Aunt Lucy's, Mother and Dad sold the house in Dallas and came to New Orleans. They stayed in our apartment until they bought a double house on Abundance Street with the intention of raising it and starting a washateria under it. They couldn't get the place rezoned from residential to commercial so the business could not be started.

The double houses in that area were built end on to the street. Each two doubles faced each other across a green space. Our building was the second from the corner and separated from the one facing Elysian Fields Avenue with a tall wooden fence. The property facing Elysian Fields was zoned commercial.

We gave up our apartment and moved into the other half of their house at 2164-66 Abundance Street on June first. As happens every time we move, we had a lot of cleaning to do. Every room had to be scrubbed down. I even found food stains on the inside walls of the bedroom closet! After the rooms were clean, we had the walls repapered and the trim painted.

We had two bedrooms and no furniture, or very little and with not much money to buy any. Bill had his Morris chair and I used a canvas beach chair in the living room. We made bookshelves out of bricks stacked up with planks across them on one wall. So that was our living room furniture.

We had to have a bed so that was the first thing we bought. Aunt Mable's husband Dick Wood—Uncle Dick to me, said he knew a fellow who had a mattress factory. We had his friend make us a box spring and mattress double bed sized. It came with six legs to screw into the box spring so that was our bed. I made curtains for our bedroom windows.

Once Bill got a job we could buy a few things. Kirchman's Furniture store was offering a complete kitchen for under one hundred dollars so I bought it. It included an apartment stove, a cheap wooden table and four chairs and an ice box. Refrigerators were not in full supply yet since it was barely two years since the end of the war. Mother had one that she bought second hand and also a secondhand washing machine.

After Bill started working, I bought a chest of drawers so we would have a place for our folded clothes. We fixed up the other bedroom as a nursery. We had a nursery patterned wallpaper hung in there and I bought some frilly curtains from Sears for the two windows. Next, we bought a crib, a baby sized wardrobe and a bathinet. I replaced the knobs of the wardrobe with children's blocks. Bill's cousin Ulloa gave us the highchair she had used for her son Tommy. Everything was ready. All we needed now was a baby.

In the alley behind the house where we liked to sit there was usually a breeze. Mother and I sat there and sewed and embroidered baby clothes all of that summer. Aunt Lucy sewed and embroidered baby clothes all that summer, too. We probably had enough clothes for two babies.

The baby was due in October. I was hoping it would be born on Dad's birthday, the 15th but Barbara didn't arrive until the 16th. She was born at Touro Hospital in New Orleans.

Touro was not air conditioned and October was still hot. There was a big oscillating fan on the wall but all it did was stir up the hot air. I was in a double room with a woman who talked on the phone all the time and had visitors who came and stayed until the nurse had to tell them that visiting hours were over. She was a pain in the neck. I was glad when she left.

In those days a woman was kept in bed for ten days after giving birth even if she suffered no complications. I went home after several days in the hospital and had to stay in bed. My mother did a good job of taking care of me but she hadn't handled a baby since I was born. She was afraid of handling Barbara, especially when giving her a bath. Soapy babies are slippery. It must have taken her two hours to give Barbara her first bath. The time became shorter as she became more proficient. I was anxious to get up and take care of my own baby but Bill and Mother insisted that I follow the doctor's orders. Aunt Helena stopped by one day while Mother was struggling with Barbara's bath. She said, "Gertrude, don't be silly." Aunt Helena put a towel on her lap, put Barbara on the towel soaped her up, rinsed her, dried her. The whole process took about three minutes. As soon as the ten days were up, I was finally able to start learning how to take care of my own baby.

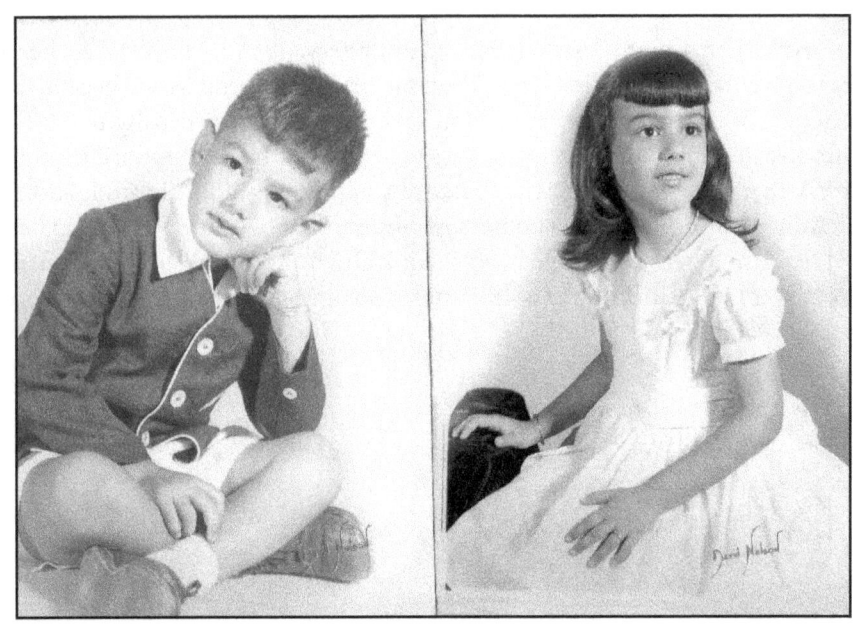

*Clark and Barbara Nelson*

*Shelby Nelson*

*Shelby Nelson age 12*

## *The Rest of the Years*

It was never my intention to go through all the years of our marriage one by one. A few facts should cover it such as our addresses and when we moved, the births of the other children and a few highlights. After I gave my children the original draft of this story to read, they seemed to think I should have written more. I never had any intention of going through the years one by one. Their childhoods are theirs to write. I will expand on some of the events of our lives that caused major changes. I hope that will satisfy some of their concerns.

Barbara Marguerite Nelson was born October 16, 1947 at Touro Hospital in New Orleans while we were living at 2166 Abundance Street in New Orleans.

William Clark Nelson III was born February 5, 1949 at Baptist Hospital in New Orleans. We always called him Clark. We were still living on Abundance Street.

The last three were born at Mercy Hospital in New Orleans.

Shelby George Henry was born August 20, 1954 while we were living at 4432 Eden Street in New Orleans.

Christine Marie was born June 6, 1957. We always called her Tina. We were living at 63 Thornton Drive in Chalmette, Louisiana.

Nathalie Elizabeth was born November 6, 1965. In the family she was and is known as Tootie. The name comes from our calling her Sweet Patootie when she was a baby. We shortened it to Tootie and the name stuck. We were living at 357 Walter Road in River Ridge in Jefferson Parish, Louisiana.

We lived, as I said, first at 3232 St. Rock Street. That place no longer exists having been torn down to make way for I-10 east. We then moved to the double, 2166 Abundance Street. We bought a house at 1021 Joan Avenue in Metairie, Louisiana in the Gilmore Subdivision. Access to that subdivision is through Turnbull Drive that runs off of Airline Highway. We moved into the house March 18, 1950.

Clark was born February 5, 1949 while we lived on Abundance street. His formula amount had to be doubled within a week after we came home from the hospital. He was a big baby and was always hungry. He was a good baby as long as his stomach was full. I would sit and rock him as I had rocked Barbara. He stayed awake and enjoyed it. As soon as I put him in the bed he went to sleep. His arrival meant that he needed to be in the crib so we bought a youth bed for Barbara. She found it easy to get out of it so it took us a while to teach her that when she was put to bed, she was supposed to stay in it and go to sleep.

We put our name on a long list to buy a Jeep station wagon. We waited and waited. With two children and their gear to transport we finally gave up waiting.

Christine Nelson

Tina Nelson

Nathalie Elizabeth Nelson
at age 6

Nathalie Elizabeth Nelson

While we were still living on Abundance Street we bought a second hand car. It was a pre-war Pontiac that had been used during the war as a taxi so it wasn't in great shape but it did give us some freedom.

    Bill felt as though there was no future in the job he had at Public Service so he applied for a commission in the Marine Corps. They replied that at 27 years old he was over the age for a 2nd Lieutenant so he could not get a commission in the Marines. He then applied for and received a commission in the Navy as a lieutenant, junior grade. They jumped him over the whole grade of ensign. This was during the Korean War. He was sent to Supply Corps School in Bayonne, New Jersey. When he finished the course, he was assigned as Supply Officer aboard the heavy cruiser Des Moines. We sold the house on Joan Avenue and moved to Norfolk, Virginia in July 1951. We never could have made it to Virginia in the Pontiac. We probably wouldn't have made it over the border to Mississippi in it. The day we went to trade it in it quit running near the second hand lot so we coasted onto their driveway and stopped in their parking lot. They accepted it as a down payment on a newer Studebaker. We ended up loving that car. We drove the Studebaker and arrived in Norfolk on July fourth, of all times. We considered ourselves lucky to find a room to rent for the night. When we started hunting a place to live, Norfolk was so jammed full of Navy people we couldn't find anything. We did find Pete Viscardi, a friend of Bill's from New Orleans. He and his wife invited us to stay with them until we could find something. After a few days we finally leased an apartment at 415 Mayflower Apartments in Virginia Beach. The rent was high. It was way over our housing allotment. The Navy allowed $89.00 for rent and that place cost $400.00 a month. I had only $8.00 leeway in my budget. In September when Bill went to sea with the Sixth Fleet to serve in the Mediterranean for six months, I started looking for a job. A beach community in winter really didn't offer many opportunities. I couldn't find anything that paid enough to cover day care for two children and have enough left over to make it worthwhile. My mind was going round and round in circles trying to figure a way out of my dilemma. I was telling my mother my problem when she suggested that I move to Houston. She would rent a house big enough for all of us. She would take care of the children so I could go to work. That sounded good but how was I to move? I had absolutely no money to pay for a cross country move and the Navy pays for moves if you have orders to move from one station to another. They don't pay for voluntary moves. I went to the Red Cross but they couldn't help me. Mother solved the problem by going to talk to Mr. Harris at Allied Van Lines. He said to tell me to come on to Houston. He would send movers to pick up my furniture and goods and I could pay him back when I got a job. I was flabbergasted that a complete stranger would take such a chance. Mother had rented a big house at 812 Donovan Street so everything was ready for us. An added attraction of going to Houston was that my cousin Sylvia was living there in a subdivision near where we would be.

We left Virginia Beach on October 14, 1951. I had packed the clothes we would need for the trip in suitcases and put them on the floor in front of the back seat. I put a sheet on the crib mattress and set it on top of the back seat and over the suitcases making a nice flat place for the children to sit. They could look out of the window, play, look at books or sleep. That arrangement would never be allowed now with all the safety rules but it worked great. I also took my silver with me. Before I left Virginia, I sent my parents a telegram to let them know we were on our way.

The first night we made it to Tuscaloosa. I pulled up at a gas station to use their pay telephone to call Uncle Cyrus. I was so tired from all of that mountain driving my legs were trembling. He told me how to get to his house so we spent the night with them. I sent a telegram to let my parents know we were safe with Uncle Cyrus. We left late from Tuscaloosa. I think it was ten a.m. by the time we were on the road. We ate lunch in Meridian, Mississippi. I was so pleased when a lady stopped at our table and said. "If my grandchildren behaved as well as your children do, I would take them out more." We arrived at the outskirts of New Orleans just in time to get caught up in heavy evening traffic and arrived at Aunt Lucy's in time for dinner. The next day we celebrated Barbara's fourth birthday. I called Aunt Bea and Aunt Mabel to see how they were doing. Aunt Bea wanted to go to Houston with me to visit with her grandson. The next day I went around to pick up Aunt Bea and we were off on the last leg of our journey. I sent a telegram to let my parents know we were on the road again. A day or two later the people at Western Union got in touch with Mother and said they had been keeping up with my progress from Norfolk and they wanted to know if I had reached Houston safely. When she told them we were there and safe they were relieved that the end of the story turned out ok.

The house that Mother rented was at 812 Donovan Street, the first street just outside the northern border of Houston off of North Shepherd (Ave.? Street?) I think that N. Shepherd was the road to Dallas before the Interstate System was built. There was a huge room that had been built onto the side of the house that had been used as a child care center by the people who owned the house. We put the children in that big room with a bed on each side. There was plenty of room left over for them to play and any mess they made was out of sight of the rest of the house. The house was on an acre of ground with a thick lawn of St. Augustine grass. One of my first expenses was a rebuilt gasoline powered lawn mower that I bought from Sears. Dad and I had to spell each other in order to cut all of that grass. What we really needed was a lawn tractor but that was way out of my price range. There was a garage with a set up for a washing machine in it. There were two other buildings that were chicken houses. We had no use for them. At the back of the property there was a pine grove and in there was a pipe frame with swings. The only trouble with all that land was that the children couldn't play outside much because of the chiggers and red ants. It was a good thing they had so much play room inside. One-time, Clark fell sitting right on a large red ant nest. I quickly took off all of his clothes, put him in the bathtub and washed off all of the ants. He was covered with ant bites. I called Dr. Bickle, the pediatrician Dr. Shafer in New Orleans had recommended, to ask what more needed to be done. She said I had done all that needed to be done and Clark was in no danger from the ant bites unless he showed an allergic reaction. He didn't so all was well.

As soon as we were settled, I went to a job finding agency so I could get to work. They sent me to Rice Institute where there was an opening in the registrar's office. After an extensive interview they hired me. I had to pay the job agency from my first pay check. After that I payed off Allied Van Lines in several installments until that debt was clear. Dad was working somewhere I think but I can't remember where, so we had enough income with his salary and my salary and Navy allotment check to cover rent and current expenses.

Rice Institute was exactly south of where I lived so all I had to do was to drive down Shepherd almost all the way to work. I found that Texas drivers are wild. They drive as though they were on horseback on the open range. I was lucky not to get in a wreck with one of them. I did come close once on a rainy slippery day. I stopped in time but I ended up crosswise on the road.

Bill was disappointed that I had left Virginia. He had no idea how lonely a beach community can be in winter or how desperate I was with so little money and no buffer amount. His ship returned to Norfolk and stayed there a while before going down to the Virgin Islands where the Navy used one of the unoccupied islands for target practice with the big guns. We had kept in close touch by writing very often. Once he was stateside, he called whenever he could.

Bill wanted to make the Navy his career. After my short experience with the Navy I was not so sure. If a superior officer gives a party and invites you, you have to go so you have to find and pay babysitters. Then when you're at the party you can't leave until the senior officer departs. If he is a party guy you might be there until sometime in the morning. All that protocol stuff does not appeal to me. Also, I didn't care for all of the moving around you have to do. I had enough of the nomadic life in my own life already. I told him if he really wanted to stay in the Navy, we could look at the United States map and take diagonals from Maine to the California border with Mexico, and the Canada, Washington state border to the Georgia, Florida border. Wherever the two lines crossed he could buy me a house. We would stay in that one place and he could fly home whenever he was back in the States. He was not thrilled with that arrangement so he decided to get out of the Navy and be a civilian again.

He was released from active duty in July 1952. He joined us in Houston where he searched for work but couldn't find anything. Public Service was holding a job open for him but he had to report within six weeks of leaving the service or risk losing it. He returned to New Orleans and lived with Aunt Lucy and Uncle Gus until we could join him. I had a commitment to stay at Rice University at least a year so I couldn't leave until October.

At Rice we were working on redoing the college handbook. There is nothing duller than a college handbook to have to read over and over to revise, send to the printer then proof read the galleys, send in corrections then proof read again to be sure the corrections were actually made. I was so glad when the final version went to the printer. Besides handling the regular correspondence of the office, filing and trying to clean up about fifty years of old files, I made stencils of the final exams for several of the professors. The hardest one to do was for the math professor. There is no key on the typewriter for the math symbols. I had to draw them onto the stencil by hand. If I messed them up I had to redo the whole thing and try again.

Jack had finished high school at St. Aloysius and had worked for a while at a print shop. He was engaged to Joyce Dirblun and the wedding was set for September 27, 1952. Joyce asked that Barbara act as a junior bridesmaid for her so on one of Bill's visits to Houston he had to take Barbara back to New Orleans for a dress fitting. Neither Barbara nor I remember if she just stayed in New Orleans until we came or whether she returned to Houston. It would make sense that she stayed because it takes more than one fitting for a fancy dress.

I had to have clothes for Jack's wedding so I went to Sakowitz in Houston and told them what I needed. I tried on several dresses until I found one I liked. I stayed in the dressing room wearing the dress while the salespeople then selected hats, purses, gloves, jewelry and shoes to coordinate a costume. I selected from these choices so when I left there I was completely outfitted. It was the most wonderful shopping experience of my life.

Bill was anxious for us to join him so he rented half of a dinky shotgun double house at 4432 Eden Street where we moved in September of 1952. I had obtained leave from Rice to move a month early so we moved to Eden Street and were settled in time for me to attend Jack's wedding. I think that Eden runs from Broad Street to Jefferson Davis Parkway. The house had a living room, our bedroom, a bathroom off of a small hall, children's room using bunk beds because there was no room for two separate beds, kitchen, outside wash shed. All of the rooms were one behind the other so to get from one room to another you had to pass through each bedroom since there were no other halls except the short one by the bathroom. Everybody in New Orleans knows what a "shotgun" house is but everyone in America does not, that is why I explained it. We were so crowded in there I hardly had room to clean under my bed with a dustmop. There was no room to get the handle of the mop down far enough to reach under my bed.

I could tell that Bill was not happy in his job after his stint in the Navy where he had heavy responsibilities as Supply Officer aboard ship. Among other responsibilities, he had to handle and account for over a million dollars in Uncle Sam's money. After that experience the make-work job in the Treasurer's Office was unfulfilling. It is terrible to spend your life doing work you hate. I knew that before the war he had wanted to be doctor but that takes so long and he had no pre-med courses so it was too late to try for that. I asked him if he enjoyed the law courses he had to study to earn his economics degree. He said he did. I suggested that he study law at night school. He registered at Loyola Law School. Now he could see a light at the end of the tunnel and he was much happier.

Having him gone every night put a heavier burden on me but I felt it was worth it. I had to raise the children, take care of any emergency, pay the bills. When he wasn't at school, he and the other law students were studying together. It was a struggle for both of us but I didn't mind because it was to better our lives. I found out much later when Tony Ochapinti (sp.?), one of the law students, told me that if it wasn't for Bill insisting that everyone in the study group keep their nose to the grindstone, he, Tony, never would have made it through law school. Tony was an interesting fellow. He already had an engineering degree. He had an old Cadillac that might have been the first airconditioned car in New Orleans. He had put a window air-conditioning unit in the trunk. Then he installed two plastic vents from the trunk over the back of the back seat to send the air into the body of the car. I don't know why he needed another degree

In the fall of 1952 Barbara started kindergarten at Wilson School while we were living on Eden Street. She seemed to enjoy it and got along with the children well. It was too far to walk and she would have had to cross Broad Street which was too dangerous for a kindergartner. That meant that I had to drive her there and pick her up every day. The next year Clark was in kindergarten and Barbara was in first grade. There were so many students in the schools that they had to "platoon." That meant that children went to school for a half day. Clark's class had to platoon. That also meant that instead of two trips to take the children to school and pick them up, I now had to make three trips.

Soon Bill was transferred to the enlarged law section at Public Service under Floyd Lewis. Bill was on his way. This act made Bill happy since he could see some hope for advancement within the company.

I became pregnant so we had to start looking for larger living quarters. I tried to rent something larger in the city but all of the landlords quailed when they found out we would have three children. The only solution was to buy a house. There was nothing for sale in the city that we could afford. Uncle Gus was checking various sites and found some well-built houses in our price range in Chalmette. We checked them out and chose a lot and the style of house we wanted. Uncle Gus loaned us the money for the down payment. We ordered the house in April of 1954. We were hoping to get in before the baby was born who was due in August. It was not to be. The baby, Shelby, was born August 20, 1954. So, with a baby bed in my bedroom we were even more crowded. Now I had to take a baby with me every time I either took the children to school or went to pick them up. On top of that Barbara was going to dance school so I had to drive her there and pick her up. I bought a car bed. One end of it stood on the back seat while the other end hooked onto the back of the passenger seat. The baby was too young to sit up so that was a good solution.

We finally moved into our house at 63 Thornton Drive in Chalmette on March 18, 1955. Barbara and Clark went to school at C. F. Rowley Elementary in the middle of our subdivision. Bill needed the car to go to work and then to school. I put Shelby in the Taylor Tot walker. Barbara and Clark walked until Clark got tired and rode behind Shelby to go to register the children at the school. It was very cold that morning so we were all bundled up. On the way home it was even colder since Shelby and I were headed straight into the north wind.

For some strange reason every house I have ever owned faced west.

The house was yellow brick veneer built on a slab. We went often to watch the progress of the building. When the slab was poured and curing, I walked around on it and thought, "It is a very small area. How am I going to fit all of us in here? I am the one who is going to have to find a way to live in that small space." Yet magically, when the walls were up the house somehow looked bigger. None of the three bedrooms were large. In fact, the boy's room was so small it barely held the bunk beds and a chest of drawers. We joked and said, "This room is so small you have to go out into the hall to change your mind." There was a large living room with a dining L, a long narrow kitchen and 2 bathrooms. The laundry area was in the kitchen on the carport wall. We had two entrances, one in the living room and one door in the kitchen that led to the carport. The yard was fairly large and was of leveled sand but was bare of grass. One of the first things we did was have a back fence installed. It was made of redwood boards woven around the posts, I think we had put in St. Augustine plugs to make the front lawn. When the St. Augustine sent runners into my garden or over the sidewalk, I pulled them up root and all and planted them in the backyard. Of course, once you have a lawn you need a lawnmower. I had bought a lawnmower from Sears when we lived on Donovan Street in Houston. I think it was a rebuilt second hand machine when I bought it so I probably had to buy a new one by the time we were in Chalmette. We planted a celeste fig tree in the backyard and a Chinese elm in front of the front door to give us shade from the merciless summer sun some day when it grew larger. Bill put up a swing set for the children. As always, our yard became Mecca for all the children in the neighborhood. That was fine with me because then I knew where my children were and what they were doing. We ended up living there for eight years.

I was pregnant again. Christine Marie, always called Tina. was born June 6, 1957. As it turned out that was also the day that Bill graduated from Law School. Needless to say, neither one of us made it to the ceremony. I was so proud of Bill for sticking to it for those four years of night school. It had been hard for both of us but it was worth it. As Bill said, "Now when someone asks me what I do I can proudly say, "I'm a lawyer." I was also proud of Bill for staying in the Navy Reserve and keeping his Navy Commission up to date by doing correspondence courses and going on two-week training duty every year. He was promoted steadily and reached the grade of Lieutenant Commander. When he retired from work, he received a Navy retirement pay as well as his retirement income from Public Service.

One morning while Bill was dressing for work, we received a telephone call from one of the Lacourrage girls telling us that Aunt Lucy called their house for help because she was having a heart attack. They called her doctor and an ambulance and she was going to Baptist Hospital. Bill finished dressing in a hurry and went to the hospital. She was in the hospital for a while then came home but she was limited in what she could do. Uncle Gus died sitting in a chair in the living room early in 1961 and Aunt Lucy died in the fall of that same year. Both are buried in Metairie Cemetery. They had no children so their estate was divided between Bill and Jack. I think the only specific bequest in their will was some money for Augusta Graves who had worked for them for many years.

What was the best way to divide all the silver objects, the fine china, towels, sheets, furniture? We put all the silver objects on the dining room table and Bill and Jack drew straws. Jack won first choice so he picked what he wanted, Bill chose something then the boys turned the choosing over to Joyce and me. When it came to the silver flatware Joyce said she didn't want it but she did want the china so I gladly took the silver service and she took all of the china set. We did the same with everything we wanted. None of us wanted the furniture. It was old fashioned mostly from the 1920s and none of it was valuable. We sold it to a second hand furniture dealer. Once the house was empty, we put it up for sale. They lived on Iberville Street right behind Beauregard school and one house over from the cross-street N. St. Patrick and one block from Canal Street. It was a very convenient location. The house was solidly built and in top condition because both Aunt Lucy and Uncle Gus immediately repaired anything that needed repairing. The kitchen had been completely remodeled in 1951. The house was on the market about two weeks when it was sold for about forty thousand, I think, so each family received twenty thousand from the sale. Not a bad price for the time. Uncle Gus bought the house for $8,000 in 1939 or 1940.

New Orleans Public Service was part of the Middle South holding company. There were several companies included in it; Mississippi Power and Light, Alabama Power and Light, Arkansas Power and Light and Louisiana Power and Light, and New Orleans Public Service. There was a meeting called of the staffs of these companies. Arkansas sent all of their staff to the meeting in the company plane. The plane crashed so they lost all their company officers at once. They checked through the Middle South group to replenish their staff and chose Floyd Lewis, Bill's boss, for their new president. Floyd had to report immediately so he had to go to Arkansas alone while his wife Jimmie stayed behind so she could take care of selling the house. Floyd and Jimmie had been asking us to come to see their new house ever since it was built in 1954 but it is a long way from Chalmette to River Ridge and with Bill in night school we never did have a chance to get there. When Floyd left for Arkansas, Bill was made head of the Law Department at Public Service.

When it became evident that Moher and Dad would have to live with us we knew we had to start looking for a bigger house, something we could all afford. We were in River Ridge looking at a house on Robin Lane. Since we were so close, we decided to pay a visit to Jimmie finally to see the house they had built and to see Jimmie before she left. We knew the house was for sale but we had no idea of buying it.

When we saw the house, I fell in love with it. It was a split-level floor plan. The bottom was covered in brick and the top was finished in cedar shake on the outside. The lots in that area were sixty feet wide and one hundred something deep. The Lewises had bought two lots so the frontage was one hundred twenty feet wide. The lot ended up measuring about three quarters of an acre. There was a circular driveway in front of the house and a straight driveway into a carport on the side. The Lewises had six children so inside it had five bedrooms and two full baths. As we entered the front door there was a large foyer on the ground floor. Immediately to the left was a big room that was supposed to have been a hobby-workroom according to the printed house plan but they had made it into a bedroom for their niece who was going to college here. There was a large den, a powder room and the laundry room. also, on the ground floor. Five steps up to the second level from the foyer was a big living room and five steps up from the den was the kitchen. The dining room formed an L with the living room. Incongruously there was a door to the back of the house in the dining room that I considered ugly and a waste of space in a room that was already rather small for a big family. So.to sum up, on the second level there was a living room, dining room and kitchen. Eight or so steps up from the kitchen the third level contained four bedrooms and two full baths. Jimmie said the plan they used to build the house had left out steps to get to the bedroom level. When they realized that during building the only place to fit steps in was in the kitchen.

  The house was perfect for us but we didn't think we could afford it. They were anxious to sell and we were anxious to buy. We owned a lot across the lake where we were intending to build a house. We even had an architect friend draw a plan. But with Bill having to represent the company at the New Orleans Council meetings that sometimes lasted into the night we had decided not to build over there but to stay on the south side of the lake. I didn't want Bill to have to drive that causeway when he was tired. Floyd accepted the lot as a down payment on the house. They owned a horse but there was no place for it at their house in Arkansas so they left the horse and the saddle and all of its tack to us. My children were thrilled. We all moved in on January 28, 1963. The mover said we had as much stuff in the attic in Chalmette as we did in the living area. By the time he had loaded my parent's things and came to get mine he had to order another truck. We arrived after dark on that cold night. The door to the side driveway was on the north side of the house and had to be open so they could unload so there was a cold wind blowing through the house. They put the furniture in place but they put all of the boxes in the den in a pile that almost reached the ceiling. They left a path around the pile so we could get to the powder room and so we could get to the carport. It took us about four months to get all of the boxes emptied and the stuff in them put in place. The heating system got a good testing after the movers left. It worked fine and warmed the house so we could change into our night clothes without freezing.

  One of the first things we did was to plant a fig tree. Then Bill decided we needed a pecan tree. We obtained a catalog from Bass Pecan Company in Mississippi and started finding out about the different varieties of trees available. We liked so many of them we ended up with three different varieties of pecan trees planted on the place. The best ones for eating and cooking were the Delicious and the Stuart. I didn't think much of the long thin paper shelled one, the Mahan. We had one Delicious, two Stuarts and one Mahan.

  Ever since we had moved into 357 Walter Road the children and I had done all the yard maintenance. That yard was so big it took almost all day on Saturday to mow it. I bought a self-propelled lawnmower which helped make it a bit easier. We had kept the concrete benches that Aunt Lucy had in her backyard. I had placed one under each of two trees. Clark and I would take turns mowing around a section while the other rested on the bench. The boys and I did the weeding of the several gardens. I think I did most of it, really. The boys didn't know a good plant from a weed and often pulled up my plants. Bill decided we needed a riding lawnmower so on the recommendation of a fellow at work and without consulting me he bought one. It was not what we needed for that big place. It was really too light for the job. It wasn't any faster than doing it by hand and soon became rickety. Then he came across an electric lawnmower advertisement and bought that. It was very good and we used it for years. When it wore out, I said I wanted a John Deer lawn mower and since I was the one who had to use it and he had tried all these other ones I finally got what I wanted. It was easy to get the boys to cut the grass because it was fun to drive. After Bill retired, I would drive the lawn mower and he used the hand mower to do the edges. Finally, we became too old for that kind of work and had to hire it done. No one ever did the job as well as we had done it and it cost us four hundred dollars a month to get an unsatisfactory job.

  Mother was still working as manager of a dress shop on Mirabeau Street in New Orleans when we moved into the house in River Ridge. It was a long drive every day so we kept encouraging her to retire. When she finally did retire and was home all of the time, I realized that no matter how much we loved each other and cooperated with each other a home had to have one person running it. I decided to go to work. I found a job at the Federal Land Bank typing up loans. I decided that since we really didn't need the money I was earning, I would save my salary for college tuition for my children. The bank had a standard test they gave to incoming office personnel. Later, after I had been there about two or three weeks the lady who gave the test told me that I had passed it 100% and was the only one in all the years that they had given the test who ever did. The work was boring because each loan on a piece of property included a detailed description of the land and improvements. If you ever buy a piece of property read the detailed description and you will understand why I was almost glad when I found I was pregnant again. Jokingly I told Bill. "If you didn't want me to go to work why didn't you just say so." It was the same old story every time I was pregnant, I had morning sickness all day every day. I had to quit work. So much for that experiment. What was I doing pregnant at forty-three years old?

  Nathalie Elizabeth was born November 6, 1965. I had disposed of all the baby accoutrements except the clothes Aunt Lucy, Mother and I had made and bought for Barbara. Thinking back, I believe we still had the Taylor Tot walker.

Everything else, bed, high chair etc. had to be bought new.

The only thing of significance that happened in 1966 that I can think of was that Grandma Darcey (Oceana Marie Pierce) died July 26, 1966 in Raceland, Louisiana. She was ninety-six years, seven months and six days old. She was buried with Grandpa Darcy in St. John's Episcopal Cemetery in Thibodaux, Louisiana.

However, 1968 is another matter. First of all, Clark surprised us by joining the Army to become a parachutist and was called to take basic training even before he could go to his high school graduating ceremony. He was sent to Fort Bliss near El Paso, Texas for basic training in May 1968 and finished in July 1968. Shelby, Tina, Nathalie, Bill and I decided to go to the ceremony at the end of basic to pick Clark up. From there we stopped in San Antonio to visit the Hemisfair. Shelby came down with the twenty-four-hour flu that day so I sat on a bench in the German exhibit in air-conditioning with Shelby's head in my lap while Bill took Nathalie and went with Clark and Tina so they could enjoy the rides. Bill never did like to go on boardwalk rides himself. After some time at home Clark was given orders to report to Redstone Arsenal in Alabama to train as a missile technician in August 1968. He kept complaining that he had joined the army to become a paratrooper and had volunteered to go to Viet Nam so they finally sent him in January of 1969 to Fort Gordon, Georgia for advanced infantry training and in April to Fort Benning, Georgia for Pathfinder training since the fighting in Viet Nam was mostly in the jungle where paratroopers could not operate. He did get paratrooper training. After his first jump he called me on the phone bursting with excitement and said that the experience was so wonderful that everyone should have a chance to do it. I told him he could have my turn. In July he was sent to Viet Nam. He wrote fairly regularly so when I didn't get a letter for quite a while, I became worried. When he could write again, he told me that he had been shooting a mini-gun from a helicopter and the gun jammed. He tried to force the bullet into the hot barrel of the gun and it backfired and injured his right thumb. He could not hold a pen with his bandaged hand. Because he was injured while on duty in a war zone the army wanted to give him a purple heart. He absolutely refused. He said he didn't want to have to tell his children if he ever had any that he received a purple heart for being stupid.

When he came home for a one-month furlough in 1970 he talked and talked about his experiences. Some days he would start talking to me at breakfast and would still be going strong when the children came home from school. He told me that at one time they were on a mountain he called Nuey Bah Din (phonetic spelling). The Viet Cong surrounded the bottom of the mountain so they couldn't get off and had to be resupplied with everything they needed by helicopter. He had to help unload the helicopters as they hung close to the side of the mountain. There were people of the press embedded with his group and one of them was giving them trouble with his bellyaching. When the next helicopter was unloaded, Clark picked the fellow up and threw him into it and told the pilot to evacuate him so they could have some peace.

On June 27, 1968 I was taking a bath when the phone rang. Bill answered it and I could hear him saying "Oh, no." and other such phrases and I thought Dad had died. I called out, "What happened?" That's when he told me that his brother Jack (Joseph Jacob Nelson) had been killed in a car accident. He was only thirty-seven years old. He worked for Frito-Lay Company. The company had transferred him to Houma, Louisiana. I think he was the district manager but I am not sure. There are two important factors that contributed to his death. One of them is the lateness of the hour. The accident happened at 10:30 p.m. The other factor was that he had recently bought an air-conditioned Chevrolet station wagon. He was returning late from a company meeting in Baton Rouge. In late June it is very hot in Louisiana so we have to suppose he was driving with the air-conditioner on. That model Chevrolet had a leak in the floor of the back deck that allowed discharge from the exhaust to enter the body of the car. We think carbon monoxide put him to sleep. There was a trailer truck loaded with cattle coming in the opposite direction. Jack's car was crossing the center line. The cattle truck driver pulled onto the shoulder as far as he could when Jack's car hit him. The car was totaled and Jack suffered fractures of his face and head exposing his brain plus he had bone fractures all down his left side. One hopes that the carbon monoxide had already killed him so he didn't have to suffer the trauma of that terrible crash. The accident happened about two miles north of Thibodaux on highway 1. He was taken to St. Joseph's Hospital in Thibodaux where he was pronounced dead. The Chevrolet company accepted responsibility and settled the claim with a large sum of money. His body was brought to New Orleans. Bill ordered the funeral home to seal the coffin. He wanted Joyce and their children to remember him the way he looked when they last saw him, not the way he looked after the accident.

Joyce moved back to New Orleans, bought a house in River Ridge and went back to work for the telephone company. Her mother was dead and her father was alone. He sold his house on Nashville Avenue in the city and moved in with her. He took care of the house and the children so she could work.

Dad became increasingly disabled. He had trouble walking, especially climbing the steps, and he was falling down often. His speech was becoming almost unintelligible. Mother bought him a wheelchair and they moved to the ground floor bedroom. He could propel himself so the chair helped him to be more independent. He was in and out of the Veteran's Hospital and was sent from there to a nursing home in Slidell. Mother moved to Slidell to an apartment building owned by a friend of theirs so she could be sure Dad was well taken care of. Cookie had died so Aunt Inez went to live with Mother. The person in charge of the apartment building left soon afterwards so Mother's friend asked her to be the manager. That was a break because free use of the apartment was part of the deal. When Dad's veteran's eligibility ran out, we had to take him home. Mother rented a hospital bed to make it easier for her to take care of him. Within four days of his being home he died in September, 1968. He was buried in Hope Mausoleum in New Orleans.

One day not long after Dad died, Mother read in the newspaper that the Council on Aging was being formed. She said, "If there's anything I know something about it is about being old." She went to see what it was all about and met Priscilla Engolia who was in charge of the local chapter. She volunteered and the two dynamos started getting things organized. A lot of their work was with local politicians. Mother found she was good at getting the politicos to come through on their promises. They worked together so well that when Priscilla was put in charge at the state level, she hired Mother as her assistant. So now at seventy-two Mother was embarked on a whole new career. She said, "If I had known how much fun it was in politics I would have gotten involved in it sooner."

Mother heard through the Council on Aging that the Catholic Church was just about ready to open an apartment building specifically for old people called the Christopher Inn located on Royal Street a block from Elysian Fields across the street from Washington Square. She went to see about it and rented a corner apartment on the ninth floor. She was the first resident to move in. She renewed her acquaintance with Eugene Lundsgaard her old friend from the days of their Five Hundred card games. His wife had died several years before so they decided to get married. They married in June 1969 and lived in the apartment at the Christopher Inn.

Lunds (as we had always called him) was still working in the business district so he caught the little Vieux Carré bus at the corner of Royal and Elysian Fields every day. One rainy morning he stepped out to board the bus at the same time as the bus pulled down to pick him up. The bus ran over his foot and mashed it. Instead of going to court to decide just who was at fault in the accident, Public Service offered a large sum of money to settle the claim. Lunds accepted the offer.

They used the money to build a one-bedroom apartment on the back of my house. To do that the car port had to be removed and a new carport built. The building was started In September of 1976. Our driveway and the circular driveway in front of the house was paved with clamshells. Every time a car passed over the shells they tended to move out on the edges and invaded the grass. We were always fighting to keep them within bounds. While we were in the building mood Mother decided to have everything paved. We shared half the cost.

I had always hated the ugly door in the dining room. I wanted to have a deck that was to be built right behind the dining room. I wanted that whole wall removed and a twelve-foot sliding glass door installed. While we had the builders there Bill and I decided to go ahead with the plan. He had his architect friend design a deck. When the builder saw the specifications he said, "Mrs. Nelson, when the next hurricane comes you can take shelter under the deck. It'll be the safest place in the parish." I redesigned the steps so they wrapped around the corner of the deck and had the builder add a long built-in bench down one side. Behind the bench we had him add a pipe frame so I could put hanging baskets of flowers on it. Everyone who saw the result said it was wonderful. We could sit at the dining table and look out at the parklike view of our backyard. It also made the dining room seem larger. We enjoyed sitting out there in our deck chairs even in summer because there was a swamp maple tree about five feet from the edge of the deck so there was always shade. Best of all, I finally got rid of the ugly door in the dining room and the awful concrete steps outside.

Bill had become head of the law department when Floyd had to leave. He then became a vice president of New Orleans Public Service. When Public Service and Louisiana Power and Light were melded, he became a vice president of both companies. When the two companies were to be put together Bill was given the job of figuring out how to do it. That took a lot of thought and diplomacy. The move was as smooth as possible.

Lunds loved being outside and would like to have helped us maintain the grounds but he was too old. He began losing his balance and falling forward. He died in December of 1980 within a year of the beginning of those episodes and was buried in St. Roch Cemetery in the tomb with his first wife. He didn't get to live in the new apartment very long.

In July 1982 Mother and I went to Innsbruck, Austria to the University of New Orleans' Summer School. I wrote up the whole trip when I returned and will not repeat it here. I value what I learned, not so much from the classes in summer school as what I learned about the people and customs in Austria and Italy and what I learned about myself.

In the summer of 1985 I instigated a trip to Disney World. We rented a motorhome and invited our daughter Barbara, her husband John, and her sons Corbin and Mark Goertz to join us. John researched how to get the most out of Disney World with the least time wasted standing in line. The motorhome was an old Winnebago that had seen better days. We had no trouble with the engine or the tires but some of the inside fittings needed help. So, while the men drove, Barbara and I repaired everything. It was in better shape when we turned it in than it was when we left.

I had been to Disney Land in California and enjoyed it. Disney World is about four to six times better especially with John's research information. It advised that once you enter the gates ignore everything as you pass through and start at the rear and move forward. It worked great. We rode everything we wanted to ride in the morning and encountered shorter lines. About midday we started meeting the crowds that had started at the front. The lines were longer so we talked with people around us and were old friends by the time we got to the gate of the ride. His research suggested eating lunch in the top of hotel where very few people think to go. In the afternoon we went to some of the exhibits. I enjoyed the whole day. The next day we went back to see the rest of the exhibits. The boys enjoyed the fact that we were camped at the Disney World Campground and we got to ride the little bus that was a series of open cars pulled by a sort of tractor. It doesn't go fast but it saves a lot of walking.

After Disney World we started driving down the keys. We tried shelling in the Atlantic but the beach on that side of Florida is not very nice and there are hardly any shells. John had brought a screen room that we set up in front of the motorhome every night. We hung a light in the top of it and played cards after putting the boys to bed. We used the screen room every night on that whole trip. We went down all the keys until the one just before Key West. Barbara and I wanted to go on but Bill and John said the keys were all alike and they were ready to turn around and go home. Since they were driving, we went home. All of us thoroughly enjoyed the trip in the "Bingity Bangity Winnebago." Bill and I wanted to buy an RV.

We started shopping for a motorhome and found that they cost a lot. That's when we settled for a trailer.

Bill retired on January 1, 1986. We had bought a travel trailer and a Ford van to pull it. His fellow workers at the company gave him a screened room to attach to the awning as a retirement present so we were ready to travel. We tried it out by going to camp on the beach at Destin, Florida. We were very happy with it. The only trouble is that it was a lot of work to set up at a campsite. All the jacks had to be worked manually to get the thing level. Bill was getting old to have to do all of that manual labor. Another thing about a trailer is that it takes a professional driver to back one up properly. We made a few trips with it. One long trip was to Fort Davis, Texas to visit a minister friend of ours who had been transferred there. Mother went with us. She was thrilled because she finally had a chance to travel "West of the Pecos." Another trip was to Waco, Texas to look at a piece of property. We were thinking of retiring there but the place that had caught our eye looked better far away than it did up close. The house was beautifully set on a large piece of ground but the interior was chopped up into a lot of small rooms. I didn't want to have to go into a lot of renovation. It was winter, and though the heater worked very well in the trailer, we found that our beds touched the walls so that when we turned over our arms touched the inside walls and they were cold. The very next day I went to Walmart and bought three single bed electric blankets. That solved the problem.

The next summer my cousin Louise Johnston said we could use her condo at Perdido Key, Florida. We parked the trailer in front of the condo to take care of the overflow of people who wanted to go to the beach. We were so close to Pensacola Bill and I decided to check out motorhomes. We made a deal for a thirty-five foot motorhome that had self-leveling automatic electric jacks, more interior space and more beds, and a generator. We traded in the trailer and the van. They told us to go on home and they would prepare the motorhome and deliver it to us in Louisiana. We had always kept up maintenance on the trailer and van but Barbara helped us clean up the trailer until it looked brand new. We even shined the plastic tub-shower until it seemed never to have been used. They delivered the motorhome and took the van and trailer back to Pensacola. The next time we saw the RV dealer he told us that the trailer was no sooner on the lot than it was sold. They had a harder time selling the van.

Bill and I took the motorhome on a shakedown trip up the Natchez Trace to French Camp, to visit the boarding school I had gone to so many years ago. It was a nice trip. At least Mississippi has bridges that are as wide as the road now. We didn't encounter any one lane bridges on the whole trip. The school has changed. They have taken down the Girl's Dormitory and the High School buildings and replaced them. I didn't get to go inside but they have to be better than the buildings I knew. They now have a celestial observatory up on a high hill and their own radio station that broadcasts farm news and weather to the surrounding area. I was disappointed that it didn't look the same. I don't know why I expected it to stay the same way I remembered it, nothing else has. We loved traveling in that motorhome.

I proposed to Barbara that we take her boys to the Calgary Stampede in Alberta, Canada. She readily agreed. Unfortunately, John had work that couldn't wait so he didn't get to go. We picked them up in Kentucky at John's mother's house in Louisville. His sister was interested in looking inside the motorhome so we left her visiting it while we went into the house. She came in and said, "My goodness. That's a condo on wheels, And it's so clean." I was a bit offended about the "clean" part. Did she expect us to be dirty?

When we left Kentucky we went to St. Joseph, Missouri where we were to pick up Nathalie. She was in college at Loyola in New Orleans and had an end of term exam she had to take so she was to fly to Missouri to join us. We waited and waited and waited. Somehow, she had missed her flight but we finally connected. We left the next day for Canada.

We took a side trip to Mount Rushmore. It was very impressive and I took a lot of pictures. I had a chance to use my telephoto lens to get a close up of the presidents. Going up a mountain in a motorhome is fairly easy. But going down was something else. There were some curves in the road called "pigtail" turns. We nearly burned out our brakes. The little car we towed was adding extra weight to the motorhome and making it harder on the brakes so we stopped, unhooked the car and I drove it down the mountain and back to the campground in Rapid City, South Dakota. We went to a Mexican restaurant in Rapid City that was so good I always remember it as the best Mexican restaurant I ever ate in.

We had reserved a campsite in Calgary and went to as many events of the stampede as we could. There were parades to watch and Sioux Indians to visit. We were in the stands to watch the race of the chuckwagons and all sorts of events with horses and cowboys. We tried their hot dogs. Yech! They need to study up on making hot dogs. We also tried the Grape Nuts from a Canadian grocery. Not good. Another thing they need to study up on. Before we left home I had told several people I talked to that I was going to the Calgary Stampede. Every one of them said don't miss going to Banff since you'll be so close. When we left Calgary we went to Banff and camped in their national forest. We had mule deer cropping grass right in front of the motorhome. We took the little car that we towed and rode all around. It is absolutely gorgeous. We went to Lake Louise, Jasper, Moraine Lake the Athabasca Glacier. We were at the glacier on July Fourth and it snowed! We were in the motorhome. We parked it and took a ride in a specially equipped vehicle to ride on the glacier where we then got out and walked around. When we returned the door-key didn't work. The lock was frozen! The little side vent window on the left side was slightly open so we wiggled it open large enough to push Mark in so he could open the door from the inside and let us in.

We thoroughly enjoyed the Canadian Rockies. It was so beautiful. Every turn in the road presented us with another breathtaking scene.

When we left Banff we went to Edmonton to see the shopping mall we had heard about. It is fabulous. It is as long as the Empire State building is tall. There is a huge swimming pool inside that the boys and I swam in. There was a high slide the boys were sliding down that looked like fun so I climbed up and tried it out. They didn't believe their grandmother would go down that slide but I did. It was great and I would have done it again except for the climb. If there had been an elevator, I would have done it over and over. There is so much in that mall. There's an automobile dealership, every kind of store. There is a copy of a street in Paris and of Royal Street in New Orleans. I told them that the copy of Royal street was authentic except that it was too clean. Just for decoration there was a full-sized square-rigged ship in the middle of the of the walkway. I surely am glad that we went out of our way to see it. We drove east on Yellowknife Highway in Canada to Winnipeg. Not much to look at there. We would have kept on going east in Canada but the heater quit working. When we looked in the campground book the nearest place to get it repaired was in St. Paul, Minnesota so we crossed back into the States. We visited places in the Twin Cities—Minneapolis, St. Paul—while the heater was being repaired. Since we were back in the States we just kept driving home. We dropped Barbara and the boys off in Kentucky and then drove home.

In either the fall of 1994 or the spring of 1995 we had a deluge that dropped over twenty inches of rain in twenty-four hours. There were road repairs at Hickory and Airline Highway that caused a blockage in the Soniat Canal so it could not drain properly so the water backed up in our area. Bill and I were sitting in the den looking at television when Mother called and said her toilet wouldn't flush. I went over to see about it, I noticed that the rug was soggy. I went to look out of the door and found the whole place flooded and about to come into my part of the house. Luckily Clark was spending the night. He picked up Mother and carried her upstairs. He and Bill and I were carrying everything we could pick up to the second level. When we ran out of room there, we took things to the bedroom level. The water was coming in so fast we couldn't save everything. The next day the water was out of the house but the street was still flooded. There was a dirty sludge left on the terrazzo floor and also all of the soggy stuff we hadn't been able to rescue. Our maid, Anna Mae Bazile, heard about the flood in River Ridge and knew we needed help so she hitched a ride in a dump truck to be able to get to the house. I sure was glad to see her. The next day Marge Ward, Nat's mother-in-law, came to the house to see if she could help. We started opening cabinets and finding messes in each one. She cleaned out the cabinets in the den that had all of our board games and jig saw puzzles in it. She had to use our snow shovel that Bill's mother's family had brought with them from Chicago. It was the perfect tool for that job because it was flat and wide. That made it easier to dig out all of that soggy cardboard.

The first thing we did was call USAA where we had our homeowner's insurance, to report the damage. Right away they sent out someone to assess the damage who was very thorough checking things I would never have thought about as being covered. When I was moaning about all of the genealogical research books that I had lost she said, "Research books? Go ahead and order replacements because they are covered." As soon as her report went in and was evaluated, we were sent the money. So many of our neighbor's insurance companies took over a year to get things settled.

Almost everything in Mother's apartment was ruined. The next day we emptied her apartment and set all of her stuff on the circle driveway to dry if it could. She had just bought a new mattress and box spring which was a total loss, of course. The rugs had to be torn out and disposed of. It was all so traumatic I cannot remember who we called to do the repairs but it was probably the builder who had built Mother's apartment. Since we were one of the first people to call him, we were either at or near the top of his list so the repairs started within two weeks. We had made the room off of the foyer into an office. Clark lifted up whole drawers of files and saved them. The walls in the office and the den were wood paneling and were so warped they had to be removed and replaced with sheet rock. The insulation bats in all of the walls on the ground floor were soggy and had to be thrown away and replaced.

We organized the stacks of saved furniture, books, etc. to make paths so we could access the doors. Upstairs we made paths from our beds to the bathrooms. It looked like a second hand junk shop in our living quarters. During all of this confusion and stress Shelby called from Phoenix and said he and Patty had separated. She told him to take his stuff and leave. He had lost his job sometime before that because the company moved its headquarters to Tucson. Patty had such a good job in Phoenix that she didn't want to move so he was without a job at that time. He didn't know what to do. I told him to pack up his stuff in his truck and come home. She seemed to resent this easy solution. I suppose she wanted him to suffer. She had once told Shelby that he had lived a "fairytale childhood." Whatever. In our family, as it always was in most of the south, families stuck together and helped out in time of trouble so it seemed a natural reaction to me. She was from Pennsylvania. Maybe they don't have the same family cohesion there, or maybe it was just her family that felt that way. He came home and added his junk to ours and we struggled along in our "second hand junk shop" until the rebuilding was finished.

When Mother's apartment repairs were finished and all of her dishes, pots and pans were sanitized in her new dishwasher she decided she needed an over the toilet cabinet on poles so I bought one for her but hadn't had time to install it. She couldn't live in her apartment anyway until it was furnished. She had to buy all new furniture since nothing in her apartment could be saved. I took her companion-wheel-chair and we headed to Kirchman's Furniture Store. As I wheeled her around, she told the salesperson, "I want that, and that and that." She must have used up more than three quarters of her insurance money in about forty-five minutes.

The furniture was delivered in a few days. She and Anna Mae were busy moving her back in. Bill and I had to go to the commissary that day. I told Mother

I would put up her pole cabinet over the toilet when I returned.

She decided she could put up the cabinet herself so she went up the steps to the living room where I had left it and had Anna Mae help her to get it. When she was coming down the steps, she missed the second to last step and ended up flat on her bottom on the terrazzo floor. Anna Mae called an ambulance and sent her to East Jefferson Hospital. By the time we returned from the grocery and I arrived at the hospital she had been x-rayed and the doctor found that she had a broken pelvis. She was in the hospital a long time. She absolutely refused to let them take her to physical therapy because it hurt too much so she never walked again.

When she came home, she was bedridden and needed twenty-four-hour care. I was unable to care for her because she was unable to do much for herself. I had to hire people to take care of her. The person on the day shift had to cook for her. I don't remember what the cost was exactly but it was over a thousand dollars a week. I paid for it with her money. She had some savings, but her only income was her Social Security check. Since I paid her bills for her, I had insisted that she have her Social Security check put on direct deposit in the event that she became unable to sign the check. She didn't want to do that at all. She wanted to see that check in her hand, but she could understand the sense of it so she finally agreed. Paying for twenty-four-hour nursing soon used up all of her reserve. I certainly could not afford to pay for the nurses. Regretfully, I had to put her in a nursing home. I knew she didn't want to go there but it was the only solution. The place was in Harahan but right on the border of River Ridge. I went to see about her every day. I washed her clothes and brought them back in the afternoon. I took her out to lunch or just for a ride. Her favorite ride was over to look at Lake Ponchartrain. I went over for my morning visit and I found she had been put under "hospice" care. I didn't really know what that meant. The person was putting her into a clean gown so I helped her get it on. I couldn't stay long because I had a morning doctor's appointment. I put my cheek to her cheek to say good-bye and her skin was burning up. I told her I'd be back as soon as I could. She must have died soon after I left because Bill called the doctor's office to tell me that the nursing home had called the house to tell us she was dead. She died January 17, 1997. She was exactly ninety-six and a half years old. Mother was buried in Hope Mausoleum with Dad.

I loved our home on Walter Road and was so proud of it. I never in my wildest dreams thought we would ever own such a fine place. We did own it free and clear when we sold it. I have worlds of memories connected to it. We lived there for thirty-six years until December 31, 1999. Mother and Lunds had died and all the children were gone. It was too much house and too much yard for two old people. We sold it to a young couple who needed the apartment for the wife's father to live in. They wanted us to move before Christmas 1999 but I told them

I could never make that. There is so much to do for Christmas it is not a time for packing and moving. I told them I could make it for the end of December. So it was set. For years after we moved from Walter Road, I found that many of my dreams were still set there and often included cutting the grass for some strange reason.

We had bought a townhouse that was under construction but it was not finished when we sold the house on Walter Road. We rented an apartment in a complex called The Creeks at the end of Hickory Street near Citrus. We put all our furniture, except what we needed to furnish the apartment, in storage. We went once or twice a week to watch the progress on the building of our townhouse. It didn't take us long to realize we could not get full use of all three floors without putting in an elevator. That was one of the best decisions we ever made.

We moved into 3801 North Hullen Street, Metairie, Louisiana on April 26, 2000. I loved that place, also. It was more formal than the house in River Ridge. As you enter the foyer the dining room was off the hall on the right. There was no door, just a large opening flanked by two white columns. At last, a dining room big enough for big family dinners. Further down the hall on the right there was a coat closet and then the door to the elevator. The stairs with a graceful banister rose from the left side of the foyer to the second floor. Under the stairs was the powder room. The hall ended in the living room. There were two glass double doors with fanlights, one on each side of the fireplace, opening onto a patio from the living room. We decided we didn't want to fool with burning wood in the fireplace and cleaning out ashes so we had gas logs installed instead.

There was a door from the dining room to the kitchen but the kitchen was open to the living room with a breakfast counter as the dividing line. On the second floor there were three bedrooms and two full baths. We used one bedroom for a TV room furnished with a leather sofa and two leather chairs. The closets were full of my grandchildren's toys. When they were visiting, they had all of the middle of the room to play in. The master suite was at the front with two French windows leading to a balcony. The third bedroom was a guest room. The third floor was actually the attic. There were different ways to use the space provided in the plans but we had it finished as one big room and used it for an office. Bill and I each had our own computer desk and computer, file cabinets, book cases and a tall metal cabinet with office supplies in it. I kept my slide screen, slide projector, slide canisters and all of my cameras, filters and lenses in one of the closets. I was doing family genealogy so I had over a thousand dollars worth of research books in the book shelves. Bill had law books. We had a safe built into the wall. Right in front of the safe but facing into the room Bill had his regular desk located. He did the household accounts and other business there conveniently sitting between the desk and the safe so he could access either of them easily. We had the office connected to the household air-conditioning and heating systems. When we weren't traveling, we spent most of our time up there.

Everyone who owned a townhouse in Hullen Townhomes payed a monthly fee that covered maintenance of the common areas so no more grass cutting chores for us. We had a landscape company plant and maintain the gardens.

My cousin, Shirley Hidalgo Robichaux, died June 12, 2013. She was ninety-two. Tina, Nathalie and I went to Raceland for the funeral. Even though it was a sad occasion it was wonderful getting to see all of Shirley's children and grandchildren. Out of twenty-six first cousins I am now down to three, Alfredo Huete, Charles Darcey and his sister Janet Darcey Haynes. These cousins are all on my mother's side of the family. Charles has died since I first wrote this so there are only Alfredo, Janet and me left of the group. All my cousins on my father's side are dead. Shirley's daughter Janine turned to me at Shirley's funeral and said, "You are the matriarch of the family now." I asked, "What does it take to be a matriarch?" She answered. "You have to be old." I said, "Well, if that is all it takes, I am surely qualified."

This autobiography was on my old computer. The thing just up and quit one day. It was fried. Nothing could be recovered so I lost everything I had on it. I never did trust computers as archives so I have hard copies of everything that was on it. I am reentering the information and rewriting this autobiography as I go along, in 2020. I wanted to be able to print out copies to give to my grandchildren.

We enjoyed the lovely house on North Hullen for fourteen years. Bill was suffering congestive heart failure and I was physically unable to take care of him and maintain the house and cook. He had his 92nd birthday in March and I had become 91 in the previous December. We decided to go into assisted living at a nearby facility called Sunrise. We passed up and down West Esplanade Avenue often and had watched its progress as it was being built. We moved into the facility on July 1, 2014. Bill was not well and wanted me with him at all times so I didn't get to socialize very much. We met a lot of nice people at our table as we ate in the communal dining room. The people who ran the place and the people who were called care givers all seemed friendly and helpful.

Bill declined rather rapidly. He fell a few times. One night he got up to go to the bathroom. He was fumbling around trying to turn his walker around. I heard him fall. He called out, "Nat, help me." I could not pick him up and he couldn't help me to help him. I pulled the cord to get help. Two people came right away and got him back to bed. He said, "Oh hell, I've still got to go." I waited to help him but he didn't make any effort to get up. I concluded later that was the moment he must have died. I got back in bed and went back to sleep. When I got up in the morning, he was in the same position he had been in when the care givers had put him back to bed. I got dressed for breakfast and he seemed still to be asleep. I thought to myself it was better to let him sleep. He could always get breakfast later. When I returned from breakfast he still had not moved. I began to suspect he was dead. I called the desk and asked for someone to come and check him. I think Iris, who ran the place and Janet, head of activities and also a nurse, both came and confirmed my suspicion. I had lost my dear life companion of sixty-eight years! I could hardly take it in. He died August 30, 2014 and was buried in Metairie Cemetery. I went through the funeral in a stunned condition. I was reacting automatically but I didn't feel like I was participating. It took me a long time and a few bouts with a psychiatrist to pull myself together.

Bill and I were married for sixty-eight years and we still loved each other. I feel I have lived the ideal married life everyone aspires to. How did I get so lucky? In my mind I know that nothing lasts forever but when it is so good it is difficult to give it up.

After Bill died I did mix with the other people. It was a blessing to have companionship at such a time. I enjoyed living at Sunrise except for the food. I never could understand why they had to take such good ingredients and end up with such tasteless dishes. They kept telling me it was a balanced meal. Well, if people don't eat it, no matter how balanced it is it won't do them any good. Wouldn't it be better to produce tasty food that people actually eat instead of a balanced meal that gets thrown in the garbage can?

About six weeks later the staff seated a lady, Frances Rodgers, at our table. Her husband John had just died after a very long illness. I took it upon myself to make her come out of the funk I knew she must have been in. Helping her helped me. I told her a new joke every day and let her know that I was there for her no matter what. We formed a solid friendship.

She went to the opening of a new assisted living facility in Kenner called "Inspired Living." She was impressed with it and moved there. Many months later I went there, too. I hated the name of the place. It sounds so stupid I can barely get myself to say it. Whatever the inspiration was that caused them to name it that got lost in the shuffle after it was opened. As at Sunrise, the staff and the residents were mostly very nice but the food was horrible. I was hoping the food would be better but no such luck. I suppose institution food is institution food no matter where you go. It was bad at French Camp but I had charged that to the fact that I was used to Cajun and Creole cooking and they had a different tradition in Mississippi. Surely the Army food was not very good even though the government bought all top-quality ingredients. They should have recruited top-quality cooks. You have to know how to combine ingredients to make food taste good. You do have to use quality ingredients to make a quality product and it isn't all that hard to do.

Finally, when I could stand the food no longer, I bought a house. My daughter, Barbara, and I are living together. We eat at Tina's house because she is a good cook and likes to cook. Barbara and I are both good cooks but we really don't like to cook so this arrangement works well for us. We moved to 4609 Young Street, Metairie, Louisiana March 1, 2020. We each have a bedroom and a full bath, plus a room big enough for two desks, two computers, file drawers and bookcases. There's a living room, kitchen, dining area, garage, carport and a nice fence for her dog Snickerdoodle to be able to go out in the yard. I am enjoying the dog. My family always has had dogs. So, life goes on. Nothing is ever perfect but this situation suits me.

If my children find that I did not write about their lives much they can chalk it up to the fact that I left their lives for them to write. I wrote a bit more about Clark because he died December 8, 2016 and is not here to tell his own story.

Further news of some people mentioned in the story:

**Steve Koenig**—was assigned to the Marine Band and never saw combat. I met him in the shoe department at Sears on North Shepherd in Houston when I went to buy shoes for Barbara and Clark in 1950. He was the manager of the shoe department. We exchanged news of people we knew and he told me he was married.
**Bill Posey**—Mother ran into him in her work with the Council on Aging. He had joined the Coast Guard and served in the Gulf of Mexico during World War II. He was married and had children.
**Chick Henn**—went back to Washington D.C. and married his girlfriend. They rode his motorcycle through Mexico on their honeymoon.
**George Anderson**—who was from New Jersey stayed in D.C. after the war and started a boat business. When I met him again in 1951, he was married and had two children.
**Alfred Groh**—Bill and I met a Naval officer and his wife at the Officer's Beach in Virginia Beach in 1951 who said they were from Wilkes-Barre, Pennsylvania. I said I knew a person who came from there. They asked who it was. I told them it was Alfred Groh. They told me they knew him. He was an English professor at the college there and he was not married.

*W. Clark Nelson III*

*Barbara and Clark at Jack's wedding*

# FAMILY MEMBERS

NELSON—GRANDJEAN FAMILY
William Clark Nelson, Jr. m. Nathalie Marguerite Grandjean
Children: Barbara Marguerite Nelson
         William Clark Nelson III known as Clark
         Shelby George Henry Nelson
         Christine Marie Nelson
         Nathalie Elizabeth Nelson

NELSON—SCHMITZ FAMILY
William Clark Nelson m. Barbara Mary Schmitz
Children: William Clark Nelson, Jr.—known as Bill
         Joseph Jacob Nelson—known as Jack

SCHMITZ—BECHT FAMILY
Joseph Schmitz m. Barbara Becht
Children: Barbara Mary Schmitz known as Bobbie
         Lucille Elizabeth Susan Schmitz known as Lucy
         (Lucy m. Auguste (Gus) Lyncker. They had no children of their own but they reared Joseph Jacob (Jack) Nelson after both of his parents died. Bill Nelson who was nine years older than Jack was old enough to have himself emancipated. Uncle Gus and Aunt Lucy acted as grandparents to Bill and Jack's children.

GRANDJEAN—DARCEY FAMILY
Sidney George Grandjean m. Gertrude Marguerite Darcey
Children: Shelby George Henry Grandjean
         Nathalie Marguerite Grandjean

GRANDJEAN—FREMAUX FAMILY
Georges Henri Grandjean Perrenoud Comtess (he dropped the last two names when he came to America from Switzerland) m. Francine Joséphine Frémaux
Children: Mélina Flore Grandjean
         Léon Henri Grandjean
         Caroline Reine Grandjean
         Louis Emile Grandjean
         Sidney George Grandjean

DARCEY (DARSE, D'ARCE, DARCY)—PIERCE (PEARSE) FAMILY

Pierre Joseph Darcey m. Marie Oceana Pierce
Children: Helena Veronica Darcey
    Peter Joseph Darcey, Jr.
    Jesse John Darcey
    Gertrude Marguerite Darcey
    Mabel Marie Darcey
    Inez Julia Darcey
    Cyrus Charles Darcey
    Beatrice Ann Darcey

LIST OF FIRST COUSINS
GRANDJEAN Family:
Melina m. (Harry?) Gabriel
    Edmond
    Harriet
    Melina died young and the children were raised out of state. I never knew them. I met Edmond after I graduated from high school.
Léon m. Rose Todd
    George died in infancy
    Richard
    They lived out of state. I didn't meet Richard until 1988.
Caroline m. Albert Moreno
    George
    Albert, Jr. (Bert)
    Louise
    They lived in New Orleans. They were older when I was still a child. I knew them but not well. Louise and I became close after we were both grown and married.
Louis m. Marie Blount. No children.
DARCEY family:
Helena m. Emile Hidalgo.
    Dorothy
    Everett
    Stanley
    Shirley
    Soledad
    Carmen
    Sylvia
    Peter

Peter (Darcey)– no children
Jesse m. Judith Labat
    Jesse, Jr. known as J.C.
    Alla(h?) Mae
    Betty
    Wilbur
    Juliette
Mabel m. 1. Matthew Acosta
    Beverly (adopted by 2nd husband—known as Beverly Wood)
m.2. Christopher Dickson Wood known as Dick
    Alma
Inez m. Carter Cook—no children
Cyrus m. Margaret Rydell
    Cyrus Charles, Jr. known as Charles
    Dolores
    Janet
    Warren
They lived in Tuscaloosa, Alabama so, though I met them many times over the years I didn't get to know them well.
Beatrice m. Alfredo Francisco Huete (pronounced—Wetty) from Nicaragua.
    Alfredo, Jr
    Carlos Cyril

*Nathalie middle aged*

*Nathalie—98th Birthday*

www.ingramcontent.com/pod-product-compliance
Lightning Source LLC
Chambersburg PA
CBHW031431150426
43191CB00006B/469